Historic Newspapers in the Digital Age

In recent years, cultural institutions and commercial providers have created extensive digitised newspaper collections. This book asks the timely question: what can the large-scale digitisation of newspapers tell us about the wider cultural phenomenon of mass digitisation? The unique form and materiality of newspapers, and their grounding in a particular time and place, provide challenges for researchers and digital resource creators alike. At the same time, the wider context in which digitisation of cultural heritage occurs shapes the impact of digital resources in ways which fall short of the grand ambitions of the wider theoretical discourse. Drawing on case studies from leading digitised newspaper collections, the book aims to provide a bridge between the theory and practice of how these digitised collections are being used. Beginning with an exploration of the hyperbolic nature of technological discourses, the author explores how web interfaces, funding models and the realities of contemporary user behaviour contrast with the hyperbolic discourse surrounding mass digitisation. This book will be of particular interest to those who want to investigate how user studies can inform our understanding of technological phenomena, including digital resource creators, information professionals, students and researchers in universities, libraries, museums and archives.

Paul Gooding is Research Fellow in Digital Humanities in the School of Art, Media and American Studies at the University of East Anglia.

Digital Research in the Arts and Humanities
Series Editors: Marilyn Deegan, Lorna Hughes, Andrew Prescott
and Harold Short

Digital technologies are becoming increasingly important to arts and humanities research, expanding the horizons of research methods in all aspects of data capture, investigation, analysis, modelling, presentation and dissemination. This important series will cover a wide range of disciplines with each volume focusing on a particular area, identifying the ways in which technology impacts on specific subjects. The aim is to provide an authoritative refection of the "state of the art" in the application of computing and technology. The series will be critical reading for experts in digital humanities and technology issues, and it will also be of wide interest to all scholars working in humanities and arts research.

Also in the series:

Historic Newspapers in the Digital Age

"Search all about it!"

Paul Gooding

Routledge
Taylor & Francis Group

LONDON AND NEW YORK

First published 2017
by Routledge
2 Park Square, Milton Park, Abingdon, Oxon OX14 4RN

and by Routledge
711 Third Avenue, New York, NY 10017

First issued in paperback 2018

Routledge is an imprint of the Taylor & Francis Group, an informa business

British Library Cataloguing in Publication Data
A catalogue record for this book is available from the British Library

Library of Congress Cataloging in Publication Data
Names: Gooding, Paul, 1981– author.
Title: Historic newspapers in the digital age : search all about it /
Paul Gooding.
Description: Milton Park, Abingdon, Oxon ; New York, NY :
Routledge, 2017. | Series: Digital research in the arts and humanities
| Based on the author's dissertation (doctoral)–University College
London, 2014. | Includes bibliographical references.
Identifiers: LCCN 2016029084 | ISBN 9781472463388 (hardback :
alk. paper) | ISBN 9781315586830 (ebook)
Subjects: LCSH: Newspapers–Digitization. | English newspapers–
History. | Library materials–Digitization.
Classification: LCC Z701.3.N48 G66 2017 | DDC 025.7–dc23
LC record available at https://lccn.loc.gov/2016029084

ISBN 13: 978-1-138-33018-4 (pbk)
ISBN 13: 978-1-4724-6338-8 (hbk)

Typeset in Baskerville
by Wearset Ltd, Boldon, Tyne and Wear

To my late father, Jeremy Gooding. Greetings from the digital age: I think you'd have liked it here.

Contents

Illustrations

Figures

Table

Series preface

This series explores the various ways by which engagement with digital technologies is transforming research in the arts and humanities. Digital tools and resources enable humanities scholars to explore research themes and questions which cannot be addressed using conventional methods, while digital artists are reshaping such concepts as audience, form and genre. "Digital humanities" is a convenient umbrella term for these activities, and this series exemplifies and presents the most exciting and challenging research therein. Digital humanities encompass the full spectrum of arts and humanities work, and scholars working in this area are strongly committed to interdisciplinary and collaborative methods. Consequently, the digital humanities are inextricably bound to a changing view of the importance of the arts and humanities in society and they provide a space for restating and debating the place of arts and humanities disciplines within the academy and society more widely. As digital technologies fundamentally reshape the sociology of knowledge, they challenge humanities scholars and artists to address afresh the fundamental cognitive problem of how we know what we know. Computing is the modelling of method, and this series reflects the belief that digital humanities proceed by examining, from many different perspectives, the methods used in the arts and humanities, in some cases modifying and extending them, and in others drawing on relevant fields to develop new ones. The volumes in this series describe the application of formal, computationally based methods in discrete but often interlinked areas of arts and humanities research. The distinctive issues posed by modelling and exploring the archives, books, manuscripts, material artefacts and other primary materials used by humanities scholars, together with the critical and theoretical perspectives brought to bear on digital methods by the arts and humanities, form the intellectual core of the digital humanities, and these fundamental intellectual concerns link the volumes of this series. Although generally concerned with particular subject domains, tools or methods, each title in this series is accessible to the arts and humanities community as a whole. Individual volumes not only stand alone as guides but collectively provide a survey of "the state of the art" in research on the digital arts and humanities.

Each publication is an authoritative statement of current research at the time of publication and illustrates the ways in which engagement with digital technologies is changing the methods, subjects and audiences of digital arts and humanities. While reflecting the historic emphasis of the digital humanities on methods, the series also reflects the increasing consensus that digital humanities should have a strong theoretical grounding and offers wider critical perspectives in the humanities. The claim that digital humanities are an academic discipline is frequently controversial, but the range and originality of the scholarship described in these volumes are in our view compelling testimony that digital humanities should be recognised as a major field of intellectual and scholarly endeavour. These publications originally derived from the work of the AHRC ICT Methods Network, a multidisciplinary partnership which ran from 1 April 2005 to 31 March 2008, providing a national forum for the exchange and dissemination of expertise, with funding from the UK's Arts and Humanities Research Council. The success of this network in generating strong synergies across a wide community of researchers encouraged the continuation of this series, which bears witness to the way in which digital methods, tools and approaches are increasingly featuring in every aspect of academic work in the arts and humanities.

Preface

This book is about newspapers, but it is also about the ways in which digital media impact on our intellectual, professional and social practices. Digitisation, and more generally the World Wide Web, have fundamentally changed how we access and use information in recent decades. It seems strange, considering how central the internet has become to my life, work and research, to think that I didn't even use the web until I was in my late teens. That said, I can't remember a world without personal computers. I learned to use a keyboard before I went to school, thanks to my father's obsession with his ZX Spectrum. I learned to type as a pre-schooler by playing ABC Lift Off, a rudimentary game where one had to input the correct key commands in order to ensure that a space rocket took off successfully. Since then, my interest in computers has gradually encompassed the use of the web for leisure, for school, for university and latterly as the subject of my research. Sometimes I feel like I'm living in the future, such as the day I discovered the joys of streaming music from a smartphone to a set of speakers. I wonder whether this sense of awe was felt by previous generations. Parts of this book are dedicated to understanding where this technofuturistic urge comes from. As my CD collection sits increasingly unused, it seems natural to wonder whether the same will happen to books, newspapers and museum artefacts. But it seems to me that the assumption of obsolescence, that is so closely linked to the innovation cycle, misses the specific benefits of digital and of physical media that give both relevance, even as digital media clearly changes our lives in some respects.

My professional interest in digitisation began during my time as a librarian for BBC Sport, which coincided with the famously ill-fated Digital Media Initiative. I won't go into the reasons for this here, but my experience in this project made me consider the ways in which digital technologies could provide meaningful benefits to institutions and individuals, while also underlining the challenges that still exist in achieving them. It was this that inspired me to embark upon my research and to turn my attention to the impacts of large-scale digitisation across the heritage sector and beyond. The effects of digitisation are felt widely throughout our culture, but high profile failures and the continued frustrations of users suggest that the golden future, which many have predicted, is yet to arrive. This book is my attempt to make sense of the disconnect between the reality of large-scale digitisation – where huge benefits to the research community nonetheless cannot disguise the limitations of some aspects of their impact – and the theoretical debate around the massive shift towards digital delivery of heritage materials. In a sense then, this is not a book about historic newspapers, despite the title, and despite the use of them as a lens through which to understand large-scale digitisation. Their unique form and materiality and their grounding in a particular time and place provide challenges for researchers and digital resource creators alike. But historical newspapers form just one part of the massive digitised archive, as libraries, archives and other memory institutions mine their collections to feed the networked crowd's hunger for more information. Despite the huge leaps we have seen in online access to our cultural heritage, the truth is that digitised resources have not yet fulfilled the promise, or indeed the threat, that many critics have identified. I will argue that the reason for this is that digital resources are still created in ways which stop the user from innovating in their approach to the material. Access is a recurring theme in this: one of the grand challenges for libraries in the digital age is to construct a framework for users to access not only digitised content but also related metadata and full text in an environment where different resources are usefully linked. This has not yet been achieved, and it is for this reason that we will see that the impact of large-scale digitisation has not been as extensive as some would claim. There are several hurdles to overcome first: paywalled resources which limit access to specific groups; collections with inadequate support for scholarly citations; the fragmentation of resources and the lack of interoperability; and a flawed reification of search and discovery as ends in themselves, which leads to interfaces which limit the range of interactions for users.

The aim of my work is to investigate the impact of these practices on users and institutions, navigating through the choppy waters of disruption, innovation and myth, to provide a realistic assessment of the impact of large-scale digitised collections. While I am extremely critical of the hyperbolic discourse surrounding digital media, I do not believe that theorisation should be avoided. Indeed, this book engages deeply with theories of the digital sublime, searches for corollaries between online user behaviour and the social life of cities, and looks to previous generations of critics to search for a framework to understand, and thus move beyond, the inflamed discourse of the digital age. I seek to understand how this discourse influences and interacts with empirical impact assessment to build our understanding of digital technologies. In doing so, I hope that my work can sit between theory and practice and thus inform the development of both. The book draws on evidence from my own case studies of major newspaper collections from UK national libraries, providing a bridge between the theory and practice of large-scale digitisation. It addresses the impact of these resources on institutional and professional practices in the library sector, the extent to which researcher behaviour has changed, and the ways that large-scale digitised collections feed into wider debates around social inclusion and the digital divide. I hope, then, that this book will provide a unique balance between the theory and practice of digitisation to date and thus contribute to our understanding of the following important questions: what are users actually *doing* with our digitised cultural heritage? To what extent have user behaviour and institutional practices been influenced by the digital turn? And what role do large-scale digitised collections play in addressing the digital divide in contemporary society?

Acknowledgements

This book was conceived over the course of my PhD thesis (2010–2014) and written during my first 18 months at the University of East Anglia (2014–2016). The intellectual work was largely done in my time as a PhD student at University College London (UCL), where I worked on exploring the impact of large-scale digitised newspaper collections with the support of the British Library and National Library of Wales. This work was funded by the UCL Impact Studentship scheme, which is designed to allow students to work on research problems with both academic and professional aspects. It surprised me that, for such a practical topic, so much of the existing literature around large-scale digitisation tended towards the hyperbolic, exaggerating both the positive and negative potential of digital media. Otherwise-technical papers make throw-away references to the universal library or to archetypal metaphors such as the Libraries of Babel or Alexandria. Indeed, it is possible to understand an author's position on digitisation purely by discovering their metaphorical universal library of choice. This book arose from my desire to find reasons for this inflated discourse, and it therefore brings together theories from varied fields into an explanatory framework for understanding technological discourses in Library and Information Science. It is for this reason that it attempts to span the theoretical, methodological and empirical aspects of assessing impact for large-scale digitised collections.

I am extremely grateful to my supervisors, Claire Warwick and Melissa Terras, for their support and intellectual input into my research, both during my time as a PhD student and since. At times, it's felt like their belief in the quality of my work has outshone my own, and without them I wouldn't have built the confidence to write this book or indeed to enter a career in academia. The book was written during my first academic post at the University of East Anglia. After spending nearly a decade in London, this felt like something of a homecoming to me: I did my undergraduate degree here and, where the institution aided my intellectual development as a student, it has aided my professional development over the last 18 months. My colleagues in the Department of Film, Television and Media Studies have provided a welcoming and supportive environment. I am also grateful to the staff of the (sadly) now closed Ashgate Publishing for their enthusiastic response to my book proposal and for supporting me in the creation of this manuscript.

Parts of this book have been presented to various audiences before publication. My nascent views on the challenges of balancing distant reading and close reading were first published in *Literary and Linguistic Computing* (now *Digital Scholarship in the Humanities*) and provide key arguments around the role of large-scale digitised collections in supporting diverse audiences. The theoretical work, which forms the basis of Chapter 2, has been adapted from an article that I published in Literary and Linguistic Computing in 2013 and presented in draft form at the Future Perfect of the Book symposium, organised by the School of Advanced Studies in 2011. A draft of Chapter 7 formed the basis of a paper that I presented at Digital Humanities 2013, hosted at the University of Nebraska-Lincoln; my attendance was made possible by a combination of an early career bursary from the Alliance of Digital Humanities Organizations and matched funding from the UCL Graduate School. My web log analysis of Welsh Newspapers Online, which forms a small part of the discussion here, was presented at Digital Humanities 2014, hosted at the University of Lausanne. I have found the opportunity to present my work invaluable, and the generous reviews, feedback and discussions I have had from these communities have assisted me in revising my work.

I would like to thank my partner, Sian Blake, for her love and support and for moving halfway across the country to Norfolk with me in 2014. I am also grateful to my mother for a lifetime of support, without which I certainly wouldn't have made it as far as writing this book.

Abbreviations

API	Application Programming Interfaces
ARL	Association of Research Libraries
BL	British Library
BNA	British Newspaper Archive
BNCN	British Library Nineteenth Century Newspapers
CC0	Creative Commons 0 ("No rights reserved")
DPLA	Digital Public Library of America
FE	Further Education
GA	Google Analytics
GBS	Google Book Search
HE	Higher Education
IP	Internet Protocol
JISC	Joint Information Systems Committee
LAIRAH	Log Analysis of Use of Internet Resources in the Arts and Humanities
LIS	Library and Information Science
LSDC	Large-Scale Digitised Collections
NLA	National Library of Australia
NLW	National Library of Wales
OCLC	Online Computer Library Centre
OCR	Optical Character Recognition
OPAC	Online Public Access Catalogues
PDF	Portable Document Format
TDA	Times Digital Archive
TIDSR	Toolkit for the Impact of Digitised Scholarly Resources
UCL	University College London
URL	Uniform Resource Locator
WNO	Welsh Newspapers Online

Introduction

"Search all about it!"

"Read all about it!" The cry of the young newspaper seller, on the streets of the city, has become a defining image in the history of newspapers. The phrase represents the novelty of each edition as it hits the streets: the public, hungry for information on the latest events, relied on the now increasingly outdated printed periodical for their fix of news. The twenty-first century researcher, though, experiences historical newspapers through the screen, where material objects become bits: zeroes and ones ready to be processed in enormous databases of text, metadata and image files for the benefit of an international audience of researchers. And this is done at a scale unimaginable to the original audiences of these newspapers. Millions of newspapers have been digitised in recent decades, providing a deluge of news for the contemporary researcher to make sense of. As a result, the discerning consumer of digitised news no longer *reads* all about it. Instead, we navigate newspapers at scale, filtering, searching, refining results and relying increasingly on our computers as creators of meaning and of sense, in a wealth of information beyond the abilities of humans to process effectively. We have, in short, replaced the shout of the newspaper boy with a new experiential paradigm, where the search algorithm dominates our experience of digitised newspapers. Increasingly, instead of reading historical newspapers, we now *search* all about the past.

Mass digitisation is a cultural phenomenon. It has influenced the direction of research, the cultural heritage sector and aspects of our wider culture. In recent years, libraries, museums, galleries and tech giants have responded to user demand by embarking on an unprecedented programme of digitising public domain materials and making them available online. The public domain has never been so accessible, never so immediate, and never at such scale: books, periodicals, newspapers, manuscripts, images and audio-visual materials now permeate information resources such as the modern library catalogue and specialist digital resources. Libraries take their collections beyond the confines of their physical surroundings and into online mass media platforms such as Google Books and Flickr. This changes the nature of our interaction with technology, in ways that are not yet fully understood, despite myriad publications on the topic. Digital media, and indeed large-scale digitisation, have been heavily theorised, and yet the discourse is dominated by claims of inevitable disruption. The consensus among critics is that digitisation changes everything and in major ways. In many respects, though, the reality is more prosaic. Technologies do not exist in isolation, or as irresistible disruptive forces, but they do interact with existing social, cultural and intellectual contexts, which all work together to negotiate their role in what many have called the digital age.

This book explores large-scale digitisation through the lens of historical newspapers from the nineteenth century and earlier, which have been heavily digitised in recent years. From their origins in the seventeenth century, through their rise to prominence in the eighteenth century, to their proliferation in the Victorian era, the importance of newspapers within society has made them a vital primary historical source. Globally, and in purely numerical terms, they represent a significant part of national library collections; the British Library (BL) alone estimates its newspaper holdings at around 750 million pages of printed material (Fleming and Walravens, 2011). Previously inaccessible, lacking in complete indexes, and representing a difficult archival format that could only be accessed in specialist environments, newspapers have been given a contemporary relevance across the academy and beyond by digital technologies. Even so, they represent just one segment of an enormous contemporary digitised archive: to re-appropriate Ranganathan's (1931) fifth law of librarianship, digitised collections are a growing organism. Commercial efforts such as Google Books (http://books.google.com) have fundamentally transformed the user's perception of scale in digitised collections, and in response academic and research institutions have created the enormous Hathitrust Digital Library (www.hathitrust.org), where its large-scale digitised collections number in the millions, or tens of millions, rather than the hundreds of thousands. This shift in scale, as I will argue, evokes the dream of a universal digital library containing all the world's knowledge. This utopian library may be an unrealistic dream, but nevertheless it shapes our expectations (Battles, 2004) and our resulting public discourse; the evocative power of technological scale has led to a rhetorical divide which conceals the true impact of digitised collections on contemporary library users.

There is, certainly, a consensus that digitisation will drive significant changes in research, teaching and information management (Coyle, 2006; Jeanneney, 2007; Hughes, 2012), but the reaction has not been universally positive. Many critics are concerned that mass digitisation could have a negative impact on existing knowledge structures. Some believe that web-based resources will damage our ability to read deeply within individual texts (Birkets, 1994; Carr, 2010), some fear the increased homogeneity of global culture (Jeanneney, 2007), while others go still further, arguing that tech companies are responsible for driving a cultural shift which threatens our existing intellectual paradigms (Lanier, 2011). A contrasting critical movement, though, sees mass digitisation as a disruptive force for good: scholars claim that it will slash the effort involved in undertaking academic research (Keegan, 2005), while Google dominates the public debate with an evangelistic vision of their role in democratising cultural heritage and facilitating unparalleled access to the world's knowledge (Brin, 2009). Although the critical debate tends towards the hyperbolic, and thus resembles the trajectory of previous technological discourses (Mosco, 2004), a huge audience of users is already actively engaged with digitised collections in the process of their research. The majority of these users, as I will argue, are engaged in tasks that differ very little from those undertaken by users in physical archival spaces: their behaviours can still be largely mapped closely to Unsworth's (2000) scholarly primitives, even if the scale of the information they apply these primitives to has increased massively. Even so, a growing minority of researchers are now attempting new forms of research, facilitated by the existence of massive literary datasets. The development of large-scale computational methods in sciences and the humanities has led some to advocate a naively technocentric model for research which eschews academic theory, relying instead upon data-driven models to create meaning (Anderson, 2008). We are, then, surrounded by evidence that mass digitisation is already having a massive impact on our thinking, yet we still know very little about its impact at the behavioural, institutional and social levels. We should be critical resource creators but, perhaps vexed by the encroachment of technology companies on areas which libraries have traditionally controlled, we have sought to digitise first and consider the implications later. To understand the impact that digitisation has had on our institutions, researchers and social constructs, we must adopt a critical standpoint which, even though it is necessarily informed by this inflamed rhetoric, seeks to take us beyond it.

Throughout the book, I use the term "large-scale digitised collections" to describe digital resources produced by national libraries. Karen Coyle has attempted to distinguish between large-scale and mass digitisation, commenting that "mass digitisation is more than just a large-scale project. It is the conversion of whole libraries without making a selection of individual works" (2006). Small digital collections, in general, have relied heavily upon human intervention to ensure quality and have therefore used time-intensive methods to maintain standards. These projects also use intellectually demanding methods to ensure that digitised content is presented in its most suitable form: these include harnessing the expertise of the academic community, encoding texts using the guidelines to predefined standards from groups such as the Text Encoding Initiative, or modelling complex research processes in the humanities (Crane *et al.*, 2005; Terras, 2005). The time-consuming nature of these methods renders them unsuitable for cost-effective digitisation on a bigger scale, meaning that large-scale projects rely upon scalable technologies such as page scanning and Optical Character Recognition (OCR) to produce searchable text and metadata. There has been little attempt to delineate between large-scale and mass digitised collections on the basis of their precise scale. Doing so is difficult: given the different formats, digitisation processes and audiences which resources adopt, a numerical indication is of doubtful use. Instead, we can draw on Coyle's definition to understand mass digitisation in terms of workflows. Google, for instance, has adopted a streamlined digitisation workflow which adopts a largely indiscriminate approach to selection. Their approach for Google Books has been to digitise complete libraries by the shelf, with an implicit prioritisation of text over other types of content. It is a workflow designed for efficiency: duplicate volumes are not weeded and quality and relevance are not considered, whereas other volumes are rejected due to size or vulnerability. By ignoring the difficult items in a collection, digitisation can be undertaken at a pace which renders duplication a trivial efficiency problem. The process relies on swiftly scanning or photographing text, with page turning done manually or, in some cases, by machines. OCR software is used to produce a machine-readable full text version of each book, which can then be used to support a search-based interface for users to discover content. Human intervention is kept to a minimum, with metadata either imported or automatically generated alongside key structural elements. The prioritisation of text within the workflow can have a negative effect on non-textual elements, meaning that mass digitisation can be most usefully applied to textual media.

The large-scale digitised collections (LSDC) that are the focus of this volume share these workflows, utilising automated processes to ensure efficient throughput of materials. Entire libraries can be digitised, albeit at nowhere near the scale of Google Book Search. In considering the difference between large-scale and mass digitisation, I refer to Hazen, Horrell and Merrill-Oldham, who propose the following criteria for defining digital resources:

> The judgements we must make in defining digital projects involve the following facts: the intellectual and physical nature of the source materials; the number and location of current and potential users; the current and potential nature of use; the format and nature of the proposed digital project and how it will be described, delivered and archived; how the proposed product relates to other digitisation efforts; and the projection of costs in relation to benefits.
>
> (1998)

With this in mind, the following non-exhaustive list of shared features will provide a working definition of large-scale digitised collections for this book:

• They are defined collections of a set of primary and/or secondary materials drawn from national library collections.

- They are accessible to the public through a website, either commercially or for free.
- They provide a searchable interface with which to discover and view digitised materials.
- Their web platform allows readers to interrogate a larger amount of content than could be feasibly achieved by an individual in a physical archive.
- They utilise time-saving methods of digitisation and metadata creation, including scanning, OCR and automated layout recognition.
- They have an explicitly or implicitly defined user base which interacts with the collection via the web.

Methods for assessing impact

When evaluating the "impact" of digitised collections, it is important to consider exactly what this most nebulous of terms means. Impact now draws to mind the metric-driven demands of the Research Excellence Framework in academia, or indeed the shift in government towards demonstrating the relevance of public services through easily quantifiable outputs (Hesmondhalgh, 2015). Martin Eve notes that the REF is associated with aspects of neoliberalism in Higher Education, arguing that "it is about measurement, it introduces formal competition into university research and it is framed through the rubric of transparency and accountability" (Eve, 2013). As a result, impact is frequently associated with the perceived encroachment of neoliberalism into academia and the cultural heritage sector. Given the pressure on library services, it is perhaps unsurprising that impact has also become a key research topic in Library and Information Science (LIS). To date, a number of projects have examined the impact of digital collections in the United Kingdom, including the LAIRAH project (Warwick *et al.*, 2008) and the influential Toolkit for the Impact of Digitised Scholarly Resources (TIDSR) (Meyer *et al.*, 2009). I will explore these in more detail later, but it is worth noting that most studies to date have focused on a specific material, collection or resource type and have applied their methods to smaller scale digital resources. As the scale of digitisation increases, we must interrogate existing work to ask whether the impact of smaller collections remains relevant, or whether increased scale drives different types of impact. It is here, in the ways in which user and institutional practices may have been changed by large-scale digitisation, that this book situates impact. Simon Tanner provides an aspirational definition for how impact should be considered in the library sector:

> The measurable outcomes arising from the existence of a digital resource that demonstrate a change in the life or life opportunities of the community for which the resource is intended.
>
> (Tanner, 2012)

The problem for libraries, though, is that there is no single way of measuring the impact of collections. As leading researchers have indicated, the sector lacks established metrics for undertaking rich analysis of the impact of digital resources. This means that studies can exist in isolation, leading to narrow insights, when a more diverse methodological toolset and unified approach could provide greater significance. The problem is sector-wide: a recent Online Computer Library Centre (OCLC) report, for instance, noted that:

> A lack of established metrics limits collecting, analysing, and comparing statistics across the special collections community. Norms for tracking and assessing user services, metadata creation, archival processing, digital production, and other activities are necessary for measuring institutions against community norms and for demonstrating locally that primary constituencies are being well served.
>
> (2015)

There have been attempts to address this problem. Meyer *et al.* (2009), for instance, produced a suite of methodological tools which could be applied to measuring impact. Having noted that existing studies lacked a concrete way for collection managers, developers and funding bodies to collect data for measuring the impact of digital resources, they created the Toolkit for the Impact of Digitised Scholarly Resources (http://microsites.oii.ox. ac.uk/tidsr/). Intended to provide a best practice toolkit for assessing the impact of digitisation projects, it provides information on some of the most commonly used methods for evaluating impact and user behaviour. In a separate study, Tanner (2012) proposed the Balanced Value Impact Model. Intended to aid the thinking and decision making of those engaged in impact assessment, it guides institutions through the process of considering the impact of their own collections. Despite their efforts, there is still little evidence of work which applies rich methodological models for evaluating the impact of digitised collections. This leaves no widely adopted conceptual framework for understanding how contemporary researchers will use digital collections or for identifying how far resources go in achieving the aim of widening digital participation. Here, Tanner bemoans the lack of evidence for the positive benefits of digitisation on user communities:

> Many previous efforts to assess digital resources have either been limited to number-crunching visitor numbers without much segmentation and analysis, or the use of anecdotal or survey evidence to try to find out about value and benefits. We remain in a situation where the creative, cultural and academic sectors are not able to demonstrate from a *strong* enough evidence-base that they are changing lives or having a positive impact with regard to digital content in the way that

other sectors have found it possible to do for their services, activities or products.

(2012)

The lack of this framework for evaluating digital resources, alongside the mythologising tendency of commentary on technological innovations, is a dangerous combination if we intend to make progress in assessing the users of digitised collections. This book therefore suggests that using robust qualitative and quantitative methods holds the potential to remedy this and to provide a basis for this progress to be made. I approach the core themes of this book by making explicit my understanding that the interaction of humans and technology is complex and relies on tacit knowledge and external frameworks as much as the nature of the technology. By contrast, the critical debate surrounding large-scale digitisation has often limited our understanding of this relationship by ignoring the human context of technological innovations. The methods described in Chapter 3, and expanded upon in Chapters 4 and 5, therefore reflect a desire to distance this work from the rhetoric of disruption. Thus, methodological flexibility (Gorman and Clayton, 2005) and a theoretical pragmatism towards subsuming methods to the research question (Tashakkori and Teddlie, 1998) are both vital to underpinning approaches to evaluating impact.

The increased availability of online digitised resources places digital media at the centre of contemporary research practices. Their ubiquity means that, regardless of the input of the library sector, users and critics are already defining how these collections are used and perceived. This book is my attempt to intervene in the debate, understanding it as a product of the mythology that surrounds new, underexplored technologies. It presents the findings of one of very few studies which look specifically at the use and users of LSDC. Previous studies have tended to focus on smaller scale resources or have applied a more limited range of methods to exploring their impact and usability. This book intervenes in the debate by providing an insight into the impact of digitised newspaper collections, informed by a theoretical framework which argues that our understanding of digitisation is influenced, to a large extent, by a process of mythologisation which clouds the true impact of technological innovation. I attempt to make sense of the theoretical underpinnings of technological debates, while exploring the benefits of adopting a critical approach to evaluating the impact of digitised resources, which consciously rejects the hyperbolic in favour of a user-driven approach that is empirically grounded in mixed methods user studies.

The remaining three sections of this introduction set out the main themes of this book. The first section situates historical newspapers within the wider context of large-scale digitisation, making the case for their relevance as an exemplar case study which can address the media-specific aspects of newspaper digitisation while also informing the wider critical debate. The following section deals with the theoretical basis for the critical debate, developing a framework for understanding discussions around digitisation in terms of Mosco's (2004) theory of the digital sublime. Over the course of the book, I use this framework to contextualise the wider findings, placing the need for mixed methods approaches as a strategy for dealing with the tendency of technological debates to shift towards the hyperbolic. I argue that empirically driven user studies have a role to play in grounding this debate, using observed behaviour and discussion with users to provide a more nuanced evaluation of the ways in which digital resources have influenced researchers, institutions and society alike. Finally, the third section explores how these themes merge to tell us more about the practical ways in which user studies in LIS can contribute to increasing our understanding of the use and users of digitised resources. The introduction concludes with an overview of how these varied critical approaches to large-scale digitisation have been combined in the remainder of the book. It explains the focus of the remaining chapters, drawing the argument together as a whole which focuses on the wider significance of digitised newspaper collections in helping us to understand issues relating to user behaviour, research practices, institutional roles and social equality in the digital age.

User studies in the age of large-scale newspaper digitisation

Nunberg (1993) argues that the rhetoric of technological determinism suggests that technological innovations will inevitably disrupt that which they replace, and this viewpoint is still alive in the technocentric criticism of the media discourse. Chris Anderson, for instance, claims that big data methods spell the end for academic theory:

> The new availability of huge amounts of data, along with the statistical tools to crunch these numbers, offers a whole new way of understanding the world. Correlation supersedes causation, and science can advance without coherent models, unified theories, or really any mechanistic explanation at all.
>
> (2008)

This is problematic for many reasons, not least because it is clear that mass digitisation has yet to exert its own unique identity. There is a tension between the potential impact of digital media and how they have been substantiated. Google Books embodies this tension: while its "electronic card catalogue" (Schmidt, 2005) provides an immense database of textual information, the sources remediated within still owe their representational basis to the printed form. Bolter and Grusin (2000) have noted that new technologies commonly reference previous media in their developmental stage, before their own identity is fully formed. Such close remediation is driven by an assumption that older media remain relevant, and so digitisation still closely remediates the bibliographic codes of print that are so familiar to users. The marketing of eBooks to the public provides evidence of our reliance on existing intellectual paradigms, as it focuses primarily on those aspects of the new technology which it shares with print books. While digital media provides opportunities for change, the reality is that the print form still dominates how we choose to present text online. The scale of the endeavour has changed, but the activities undertaken remain the same. For the majority, digitised collections still operate "not as a radical break but as a process of reformulating, recycling, returning and even remembering other media" (Garde-Hansen *et al.* 2009).

This book views the wider context for large-scale digitisation through the particular lens of newspapers. Newspapers can tell us much about large-scale digitisation. They have been routinely collected by libraries for over 200 years and represent an important historical source which has long been considered worthy of preservation. I do not intend to provide a thorough account of the material context of digitised historical newspapers. James Mussell (2012) has already done this with thoroughness and style, while Deegan and Sutherland (2009) explore the future of print forms more widely. This volume focuses more on how the digitised nature of contemporary usage affects our institutions and researchers. The formative centuries of the medium now exist in public domain collections, which provide an abundant and readily available resource which is increasingly separated from its material physicality. Where, previously, researchers of historical newspapers attended their local archive or braved the Northern Line to visit the British Library's Colindale reading rooms, they now experience newspapers largely online. The number of researchers accessing them has therefore increased significantly, as evidenced by the wide variety of disciplines not only citing historical newspapers but the digital platforms where they are hosted. Newspapers provide a valuable contemporary view of historical opinion, allowing modern researchers to access useful information on diverse topics, including: the opinions of a particular readership, or views from across the political spectrum, about local, national and international events; evidence of journalistic responses to contemporary issues; a record of historical commercial activity; genealogical information; and insights into the textuality and periodicity of the newspaper medium.

Newspaper digitisation allows institutions to increase access to these valuable resources, which are often physically vulnerable or simply inaccessible. This improved access has been a factor in broadening the research base which draws upon them as evidence; digitised newspapers have been used by researchers studying tourism history, literary studies and even ophthalmology. In this sense, digitisation extends the reach of historical materials to researchers for whom physical archival research would have represented a significant barrier, as Laurel Brake vividly explains:

> Prior to digitization, newspaper research was primarily undertaken by historians – political, local, cultural, art, scientific, legal or literary – who had reason and time to travel slowly through bound volumes of unwieldy and desiccated broadsheets or, when paper copy was unavailable, to manage microfilm.
>
> (2012)

The role of digital surrogates in alleviating problems with the physical form can be easily overlooked. Large-scale digitisation removes researchers from the unflatteringly described "wearing tyranny of microfilm" (Leary, 2004), allowing them to answer questions more quickly, consult a wider breadth of material and interrogate it in different ways than were possible in the physical archive. There are also opportunities for using digitised newspapers in the teaching process. James-Gilboe (2005) notes that digitised newspapers can help promote scholarship through the development of primary research skills, addressing a perceived knowledge gap among current students who may interact less frequently than previous generations with newspapers as a print form. The potential for teaching extends to the changing methodological context, allowing students to combine historical sources with digital humanities approaches. Hawkins and Gildart have written of their attempt to integrate digitised newspapers into an undergraduate-level history module, with student outputs showing the rich potential for combining data in innovative ways:

> One student, who answered a question on nineteenth-century prostitution, used articles on brothels in Victorian Wolverhampton to create a map showing their location using Google Maps. This is an excellent example of the potential for data mashing.
>
> (2010)

The opportunities also extend beyond academia. The team behind Utah Digital Newspapers cite the example of a commercial food industry representative using their resource to research the history of tofu and soy food production in the Western world (Herbert and Estlund, 2008). Those engaged in research in genealogy, local and national history, and other topics can also find enormous value in digitised newspaper collections. Despite these benefits, the impact of digitised newspapers has not been received with universal positivity. To date, the academic community has been the focus of many digitisation efforts. Investment from organisations such as Joint Information Systems Committee (JISC) and close consultation with academics in the development of digital resources ensure their needs are served to some extent. While this shows an admirable commitment to one of the core audiences for historical materials, other audiences have often represented a low priority. Recent years have seen both commercial and open access collections begin to address this problem: the British Newspaper Archive has fostered excellent links to the non-academic community through its customer-facing activities in social media forums. Despite this, there is still a clear need to address the under-representation of audiences from outside academia in impact evaluation.

Many writers have expressed concern that digital remediation of newspapers could damage both usability and meaning. Digitisation projects, as Mussell explains, demand editorial decisions to be made about representation:

> Identifying which aspects of a printed object are to be reproduced in the new media is … an important interpretive process, but one easily overlooked in projects where the final edition closely resembles whatever it is that it models. For instance, in books that model works previously published as books, many of the formal aspects are simply reproduced and so editorial scrutiny is focused upon the meanings in the letterpress. As the digital is completely different from that which it models, the scope of this hermeneutic process is made explicit. The entire object is available for translation, forcing editors to identify the significant aspects that must be modelled in digital form.
>
> (Mussell, 2012)

This interpretive process has been alternately labelled "media translation" (Hayles, 2005) and "remediation" (Bolter and Grusin, 1999). Bolter and Grusin's seminal work refers to the incorporation or representation of one medium in another medium and provides a cornerstone account of the digital representation of physical media. This process of representation is a particular challenge for digitised newspapers: their material form does not translate easily to the screen, due to their often enormous pages, multiplicity of editions, ephemerality and challenging layouts. The process of adapting media into digital formats is envisioned by Mussell as an editorial one, which is further complicated by the need, for identifying some forms of meaning, to view the newspaper as a complete artefact. Newspapers are fundamentally tied to their place, time and means of production, and to formal features. This form balances novelty and familiarity: content changes to some extent with each edition, whereas formal features such as presentation, tone, typeface, layout and genre can often remain reasonably stable through time for each title. The *Guardian*'s (2014) relatively recent switch to a Berliner paper format[1] illustrates the strong editorial reasoning for deciding formal presentation within newspapers. The switch in paper size came as a result of a series of internal discussions, which centred upon benefits to the company in editorial decisions, advertising income and production costs. This careful assessment of features, such as page size, emphasises the importance of the visual aspects of newspapers, yet the workflow for large-scale digitisation is predicated on understanding print as a primarily textual medium, thereby asserting a "spurious symmetry between the digital transcript and the printed text while subordinating any non-linguistic elements" (Mussell, 2012). This has manifested itself in the common editorial decision to display newspapers in digital resources at article-level rather than as a single element within a page. Users are forced to navigate menus to view articles within their original material context, moving the focus of their relationship with the material away from the artefact and towards the interface. In doing so, users and resource creators alike begin to understand digital remediation in terms of re-presenting textual information, while inadvertently diminishing the influence of the physical object. Removing white space, which occurs when margins are excised by content viewers, has a similar effect. White space on a screen can be seen as wasted space, if we assume that the text consists solely of the printed words on the page. But while there is no textual information in white space, it provides important information about a publication's attitude to readability while also allowing readers to contribute to the text through marginal annotations (Borgman, 2007).

Thus, rather than acting as a neutral technical process for digitising newspapers as surrogates for the printed text, digitisation appears to fundamentally shift the representational forms of newspaper to fit within the constraints of a digital resource. The default visual language of digital resources generally incorporates a Google-inspired search bar and immediately recognisable layouts which revolve around keyword searching. Bingham takes issue with this approach, arguing that the textual identity of newspapers is undermined by shallow, wider searching:

> Keyword searching treats the newspaper archive as a repository of discrete articles; those relevant to the search are identified and plucked out of their context for the scholar to read. There is a danger in this process of forgetting that newspapers were material objects that were bought, read and passed around, and that the location and presentation of individual articles is of central importance in understanding how these articles were received by readers.
>
> (2010)

Brake expands upon this point, arguing that removing articles from their context transforms the reader into a user who "sees the content inextricably embedded in the matrix of the newspaper pages, which are not comfortably accommodated on the computer screen or by software" (2012). Indeed, there are signs that users view content differently when it is viewed online, and researchers have sometimes noted that readers' interest is in discovering relevant information rather than viewing a particular newspaper. Some researchers therefore rely on the authority of the resource, rather than the source material, without making their own critical judgements about individual newspaper titles. This flattening of information structures leads to the assumption that all information is equally valuable and asserts a symmetry between sources which ignores the social and material aspects of each source.

I will argue in this book, though, that this kind of behaviour is adopted consciously by users as a way to cope with the information overload that large-scale digitisation has caused. I will demonstrate that users are not browsing through editions of newspapers but instead are using search tools to find what they need before moving on to another search query. This means that the connection between the textual artefact and the content within is abstracted by the interface. Lanier (2011) claims that the act of decontextualising a text through user interfaces that obscure content and authorship will result in only one book. When texts are deconstructed, as they are through the search interface, there is in fact no book or newspaper. Instead there is a massive corpus of words which is given meaning only through interactions with computers. The thematic and structural elements of text are stripped away, to be replaced by a modern interpretation of the meaning of information which understands texts as carriers of word-level information. There are obvious similarities to the concept of the intertext: a work that exists as part of an intertextual network, its meaning mediated through links, citations, influences drawn from other texts and the knowledge of each reader. But whereas the intertext places each text in a wider cultural network, digitisation acts to place texts in a more literal networked environment where users are reliant entirely upon computers to give their interactions meaning. Online behaviour therefore makes sense precisely because computers are central to the experience of users of large-scale digitised collections.

While users are unanimous in their agreement that large-scale digitisation has changed their research practices, I will argue that these changes are restricted to specific aspects of user behaviour. We can certainly point to novel quantitative uses of digitised collections which would be almost impossible using the originals. In particular, users are enabled to use methods which rely upon the processing of large datasets. The most high profile projects have been undertaken with books (Michel and Shen, 2010), but there have been smaller scale attempts to utilise digitised newspapers in similar ways (Liddle, 2012; Nicholson, 2012). There is, however, little sign that underlying researcher behaviour has shifted away from the scholarly primitives, as defined by Unsworth (2000). Here, I will argue for the social life of the city as a corollary for user behaviour in LSDC: each demands extended searching and filtering of information through external platforms, the use of multiple resources simultaneously, and an increased exposure to a multitude of different interactions. The pattern of prolonged information seeking using web interfaces is therefore a deliberate approach on the part of researchers. What has been labelled as an erosion of existing intellectual paradigms is in fact a conscious reaction from users to the demands caused by the proliferation of available inputs.

The big challenge for libraries is to ensure that we are not constraining user behaviour by creating interfaces that solely address the need to process external inputs efficiently. To date, libraries have created interfaces which are immediately familiar to users of other web resources, but I will argue that web interfaces are themselves responsible for constraining the potential impact of large-scale digitisation. The standard search-based approach to digital resources is widely accepted, but it is not neutral in its influence on user behaviour. Providing researchers with only one possible platform for interacting with digitised content already shapes research rather than enables it. Open Access resources provide the opportunity for libraries to avoid this trap and will require our institutions to re-appraise how content is licensed during digitisation. Providing scanned pages under an open licence, with open metadata and full text corpora, will make the entire resource open and flexible for potential future usage. This approach is important because it allows researchers to go beyond the constraints of the interface:

> Open Access also creates exciting new opportunities for academic research. The methodological possibilities of an archive are defined by the parameters of its interface: the searches we construct, the way we filter data, and the forms in which results are displayed all shape the questions we can ask of an archive.
>
> (The Digital Victorianist, 2013)

I will argue that libraries remain relevant in the digital age, but that this relevance will come at the cost of removing their gatekeeper role and opening up collections to the masses. I will refer to Whitelaw's concept of "generous interfaces" (2015) in suggesting that LSDC must adopt open data and open platforms in order to truly engage with digital media as a distinct intellectual entity which will create new opportunities for research. Digitisation creates the potential for users not only to access materials, but to build tools, shape new forms of interaction and perform innovative research. I hope to reframe our understanding of user behaviour, in order to argue for institutional thinking that prioritises open, abundant sharing, which builds on the strengths of digitised materials, instead of referring back to its imperfect re-creation of material forms.

Summary

Newspapers are widely digitised, yet Stroeker and Voegels (2012) reported that just 17 per cent of newspapers in European libraries had been digitised. Question marks also remain about the strategic direction for digitisation at national and global levels. However, the expectations surrounding mass digitisation are huge for libraries as well as users. The BL, for instance, aims to open up its collections online through digital resources, increased usage and support for innovative research methods. The National Library of Wales (2009) similarly hopes to "take the Library's digitised collections to existing and new users regardless of their location", while also encouraging new forms of research and learning. The core goal of widening participation with library collections underpins the digitisation programmes of libraries around the globe. It is problematic, then, that the extent of impact for digitisation is limited to those within these intended communities. There is a growing body of work that demonstrates that social inequalities can persist from the physical world to the digital (e.g. UNESCO, 2015). In LIS, the majority of research has focused on the capability of libraries to assist in bridging the digital divide (Vahid Aqili and Isfandyari Moghaddam, 2008), but there have been some studies which report a different story. Real, Bertot and Jaeger (2014), for instance, have reported on the challenges for rural libraries in ensuring digital inclusion across all demographic groups. The academic need for digitised content is often the focus of research, but we must also recognise that newspapers are an important source for those who reside beyond the information-rich environs of the Western university. Modern users are diverse, diffuse and often anonymous, and their behaviour is poorly understood. We have yet to meaningfully address whether collections are creating opportunities for those outside a particular resource's intended community. This is tied to the common technocentric mistake of assuming that digitisation is an inherently democratising activity, rather than a complex technical process. The clarion call of techno-utopianism is that "information wants to be free"; but the man credited with coining the phrase, Stuart Brand (1989), provides a far more nuanced account of what this means in reality. He notes the tension between the infinite reproducibility of digital information and its value to the owner and recipient. This book attempts to explore these tensions, using the specific case of large-scale newspaper digitisation as an indicative case of institutional and user practices, from which wider insights into the phenomenon can be drawn.

In Chapter 1, I explore the wider public debate around digitisation, concentrating particularly on the tendency for technology to be the subject of exaggerated and emotionally driven reactions. In doing so, I will analyse the reasons for this mythologising tendency, drawing extensively on a wide theoretical base to argue that the polarised nature of discourse around this technological development is far from unprecedented. Indeed, it can be traced through key theoretical texts across the humanities and social sciences: the debate surrounding mechanisation and digital technologies; our understanding of the role of the sublime in modern representations of technology; the similarities between the sociology of city life and digital information overload; and the way in which innovations are diffused throughout society. I will argue that this theoretical framework explains why the debate has become so hyperbolic, concluding that mass digitisation is conceptually stuck between two conflicting rhetorical movements, and that as a result it is necessary to move the debate forward through empirical observation and analysis of particular cases.

In Chapter 2, I will provide a history of newspapers in the United Kingdom, looking at how national library collections grew in light of the development of the medium in the seventeenth century onwards. I will establish the common ground between physical and digital manifestations of historical newspapers, introducing existing research into user behaviour with both physical archives and digital resources. Although it is illuminating to look at how the popular discourse has presented web-based reading as an inherently diminishing activity, we cannot easily reconcile the idea of loss that permeates the literature of digitisation with the shift among users towards online resources. That chapter therefore makes the case that, while digital resources can easily be viewed as inadequate surrogate materials, their status as digital materials provides value that makes them essential to readers. Authors such as Birkets (1994) and Carr (2010) have argued that the internet is changing the way we read, and indeed our intellectual abilities, in comparison to the way we engage with printed text. In their arguments, though, we do not see the full range of usage to which the physical artefact is subjected. The model of deep reading in physical texts is representative of only one facet of a complex information behaviour. Inevitably, users must engage in filtering behaviour, regardless of whether they access the material text or the digital resource. As a result, I will suggest that online user behaviours, such as filtering, allocating less time to reading and using web discovery interfaces, are in fact logical reactions to a huge increase in the scale of information they must navigate. The technocentric view that technology inevitably changes our intellectual capacity, normally for the worse, ignores the conscious way in which technologies are diffused and adopted for a specific purpose. As a result, I will argue that the "scholarly primitives" (Unsworth, 2000) are still extremely relevant to online user behaviour.

Chapter 3 explores the methodological grounding for user studies of large-scale digitised resources. It will explore the methods that can be used to evaluate online user behaviour. It will cover a number of major methods, including Google Analytics, web log analysis, and survey- and interview-based studies, establishing how each method has been used in Information Science. I will also attempt to situate the methods as part of a suite of possible approaches to user analysis, addressing the major strengths and weaknesses of particular methods. These insights will form the basis for arguing for the importance of mixed methods research, and for adopting appropriate methods based on the needs of a particular research question.

Chapters 4 and 5 give practical examples of the insights that these methodological approaches can provide. They refer directly to two case studies undertaken with UK national libraries, using the evidence gathered from these studies to explore ways in which libraries and users are affected by large-scale digitisation. Chapter 4 presents evidence of how mass digitisation has begun to change institutional practices in the cultural heritage sector. It explores the ways in which UK national libraries are adapting to meet the challenges of providing a hybrid library service which increasingly relies on digital services to reach a growing online user community. The demands of supporting a diffuse, and often anonymous, user base must now be balanced with the task of making digital materials available in a way that supports library objectives and ensures that users understand the relevance of library services in the digital age. Chapter 5 explores the ways in which users have been affected by mass digitisation. It covers the benefits, challenges and shifting research landscape for users, presenting findings which link online user behaviour to that of archival researchers. Its central argument is that, while users of digitised newspapers exhibit behaviour which has been characterised as "dumbing down", they are in fact responding rationally to the specific challenges of the digital realm in ways which allow them to extract value from online library collections.

Chapter 6 presents the findings of an experimental study into the wider social impact of mass digitisation, arguing that the assumption that making digitised collections available online represents an inherently democratising activity is flawed. Drawing on my work in utilising geodemographic methods to explore subscription patterns for digitised collections, I will argue that the theoretical democratisation of information is precisely that: a theoretical construct that ignores the reality of information networks in the real world. The potential for moving to truly open access to information is in fact limited by the reality of funding models, commercial interests and legislative frameworks, in ways which underline that mass digitisation is not a disruptive social movement but a process which is defined by the social context of its era.

I will conclude in Chapter 7 by summarising the book's central themes, situating the impact of mass digitisation in the gap between theoretical and empirical research. I will summarise the major findings as they relate to user behaviour with digitised collections, suggesting that the true potential of large-scale digitisation has not, to date, been achieved. There are many reasons to conclude that the impact has not been as disruptive as some would claim: other than a few early adopters, the behaviour of the majority of the user community can be more accurately described as adapting existing behaviours to work more effectively with digitised collections than a paradigm shift in user behaviour; the true extent of democratisation, in comparison to the utopian ideal of digital access, is limited and in fact remains delineated according to existing divides, and digitised collections still exist as part of a hybrid library where users and institutions are engaged with both physical and digital resources. I will make the case that openness is vital to library services in the digital age: open interfaces, open access collections and open dialogue with users.

The extent of the digital library has grown dramatically in the last 15 years. Significant benefits have been realised by the large-scale digitisation of heritage collections, including newspapers. Access has been transformed for some communities, allowing researchers unprecedented access to these valuable collections in a medium that provides the potential for new ways of working. The largest gains have been made in freeing researchers from the confines of the library building: archival research has become a mobile activity, done at home, on the train, or in cafes. Collections can be accessed more easily by those in other countries, and new research questions can be asked as a result. Yet digitised resources exist largely as an extension of users' existing research practices: the bolder predictions of change have not yet been realised. There is certainly the potential, theoretically, for large-scale digitisation to go further in providing truly transformative benefits to users, but my central argument is that these benefits cannot be realised through technological change alone. Social, institutional and regulatory barriers exist which ensure that the benefits of large-scale digitisation are felt most keenly by those who are already privileged in their ability to engage with cultural heritage. I recognise this not as a failure but an area for future work by heritage institutions: when faced with a mythologising theoretical discourse, in fact, only a critically engaged approach to both the strengths and the weaknesses of digitisation in the cultural heritage sector will ensure that we can achieve transformative change. There are therefore two vital challenges for memory institutions in the coming years. The first is to continue our efforts to support existing communities while expanding them to new, previously excluded users, by evaluating how digital technologies can facilitate innovative research in the academy and support new ways of learning. The second is to successfully move impact evaluation beyond merely considering these existing communities and to start facing the big questions that sit at the intersection of libraries and society: how far do our activities go to increase digital participation? What is the role of the library in an age of online, distributed access to historical materials? And, indeed, how can we achieve the grand ambitions which are contained within library strategy documents the world over? As more of our cultural heritage is made available online, we must address these questions to ensure the relevance of library collections in the digital age.

Note

1 The Berliner, or midi, is a newspaper format with pages measuring 315 mm by 470 mm. To put this page size into context, it is slightly taller and wider than the tabloid format, but still narrower and shorter than the broadsheet format.

Bibliography

Anderson, C. (2008) 'The end of theory: the data deluge that makes the scientific method obsolete', *Wired*. Retrieved from: www.wired.com/science/discoveries/magazine/16-07/pb_theory.

Battles, M. (2004) *Library: An Unquiet History*. London: Vintage.

Bingham, A. (2010) 'The digitization of newspaper archives: opportunities and challenges for historians', *Twentieth Century British History*, **21**(2), pp. 225–231.

Birkets, S. (1994) *The Gutenberg Elegies: The Fate of Reading in an Electronic Age*. New York: Ballentine Books.

Bolter, J. D. and Grusin, R. (2000) *Remediation: Understanding New Media*. Cambridge, Mass.: MIT Press.

Borgman, C. L. (2007) *Scholarship in the Digital Age: Information, Infrastructure, and the Internet*. Cambridge, Mass.: MIT Press.

Brake, L. (2012) 'Half full and half empty', *Journal of Victorian Culture*, **17**(2), pp. 222–229. doi: http://dx.doi.org/10.1080/13555502.2012.683151.

Brand, S. (1989) *The Media Lab: Inventing the Future at M.I.T.* New York: Penguin Books Ltd.

Brin, S. (2009) 'A tale of 10,000,000 books', *The Official Google Blog*, 9 October 2009. Retrieved from: http://googleblog.blogspot.com/2009/10/tale-of-10000000-books.html.

Carr, N. (2010) *The Shallows: How the Internet Is Changing the Way We Read, Think and Remember*. London: Atlantic Books.

Coyle, K. (2006) 'Mass digitization of books', *Journal of Academic Librarianship*, **32**(6). Retrieved from: www.kcoyle.net/jal-32-6.html.

Crane, G., Bamman, D., Cerrato, L., Jones, A., Mimno, D., Packel, A., Sculley, D. and Weaver, G. (2005) 'Beyond digital incunabula: modeling the next generation of digital libraries', *Lecture Notes in Computer Science*, 4172, pp. 353–366.

Deegan, M. and Sutherland, K. (2009) *Transferred Illusions: Digital Technology and the Forms of Print*. Farnham: Ashgate Publishing.

Digital Victorianist (2013) 'Welsh newspapers online', *The Digital Victorianist*, blog post, 15 March 2013. Retrieved from: www.digitalvictorianist.com/2013/03/welsh-newspapers-online/.

Eve, M. (2013) 'Open access, "neoliberalism", "impact" and the privatisation of knowledge'. Retrieved from: www.martineve.com/2013/03/10/open-access-neoliberalism-impact-and-the-privatisation-of-knowledge/.

Fleming, P. and Walravens, H. (2011) 'The British Library newspaper strategy: developing collaboration with publishers to digitise back runs and to ingest born digital newspapers', in *Newspapers: Legal Deposit and Research in the Digital Era*. The Hague: IFLA Publications, pp. 21–30.

Garde-Hansen, J., Hoskins, A. and Reading, A. (Eds) (2009) *Save as...* Basingstoke: Palgrave MacMillan.

Gorman, G. E. and Clayton, P. (2005) *Qualitative Research for the Information Professional* (2nd edn). London: Library Association Publishing.

Guardian (2014) 'The Berliner format', *Guardian*, 12 May 2009. Retrieved from: www.theguardian.com/gpc/berliner-format.

Hawkins, R. A. and Gildart, K. (2010) 'Promoting the digital literacy of historians at the University of Wolverhampton using nineteenth century British Library newspapers online'. Retrieved from: www.heacademy.ac.uk/assets/documents/ subjects/history/cs_hawkins_digitalliteracy_20100426.pdf.

Hayles, N. K. (2005) *My Mother Was a Computer: Digital Subjects and Literary Texts*. Chicago: University of Chicago Press.

Hazen, D., Horrell, J. and Merrill-Oldham, J. (1998) 'Selecting research collections for digitization'. Washington D.C.: Council on Library and Information Resources. Retrieved from: www.clir.org/pubs/reports/hazen/pub74.html.

Herbert, J. and Estlund, K. (2008) 'Creating citizen historians', *Western Historical Quarterly*, **39**(3), pp. 333–341.

Hesmondhalgh, D. (2015) *Culture, Economy and Politics: The Case of New Labour*. London: Palgrave MacMillan.

Hughes, L. M. (Ed.) (2012) *Evaluating and Measuring the Value, Use and Impact of Digital Collections*. London: Facet Publishing.

James-Gilboe, L. (2005) 'The challenge of digitization: libraries are finding that newspaper projects are not for the faint of heart', *Serials Librarian*, **49**(1–2), pp. 155–163.

Jeanneney, J.-N. (2007) *Google and the Myth of Universal Knowledge*. London: Chicago University Press.

Keegan, V. (2005) 'A bookworm's delight', *Guardian*, 21 October 2005. Retrieved from: www.guardian.co.uk/technology/2005/oct/21/comment.bookscomment.

Lanier, J. (2011) *You Are Not a Gadget*. London: Penguin.

Leary, P. (2004) 'Victorian studies in the digital age', in Taylor, M. and Wolff, M. (Eds) *The Victorians Since 1901*. Manchester: Manchester University Press, pp. 201–214.

Liddle, D. (2012) 'Reflections on 20,000 Victorian newspapers: "distant reading" *The Times* using *The Times* digital archive', *Journal of Victorian Culture*, **17**(2), pp. 230–237. doi: http://dx.doi.org/10.1080/13555502.2012.683151.

Meyer, E. T., Eccles, K., Thelwall, M. and Madsen, C. (2009) 'Usage and impact study of JISC-funded phase 1 digitisation projects & and the Toolkit for the Impact of Digitised Scholarly Resources (TIDSR)'. Oxford: Oxford Internet Institute, University of Oxford. Retrieved from: http://microsites.oii.ox.ac.uk/tidsr/sites/ microsites.oii.ox.ac.uk.tidsr/files/TIDSR_FinalReport_20July2009.pdf.

Michel, J.-B. and Shen, Y. K. (2010) 'Quantitative analysis of culture using millions of digitized books', *Science Magazine*, **331**(6014), pp. 176–182.

Mosco, V. (2004) *The Digital Sublime: Myth, Power, and Cyberspace*. Cambridge, Mass.: MIT Press.

Mussell, J. (2012) *The Nineteenth-Century Press in the Digital Age*. Basingstoke: Palgrave MacMillan.

National Library of Wales (2009) *Digitisation Strategy: 2008/09–2010/11*. Retrieved from: www.llgc.org.uk/fileadmin/documents/pdf/2009_Digi_Strat.pdf.

Nicholson, B. (2012) 'Counting culture; or, how to read Victorian newspapers from a distance', *Journal of Victorian Culture*, **17**(2), pp. 238–246. doi: 10.1080/13555502.2012.683331.

Nunberg, G. (1993) 'The place of books in the age of electronic reproduction', *Representations*, **24**, pp. 13–37.

OCLC Research (2015) *Making Archival and Special Collections More Accessible*. Dublin, Ohio: OCLC Research.

Ranganathan, S. R. (1931) *The Five Laws of Library Science*. Bombay: Asia Publishing House.

Real, B., Bertot, J. C. and Jaeger, P. T. (2014) 'Rural public libraries and digital inclusion: issues and challenges', *Information Technology and Libraries*, **33**(1). Retrieved from: http://ejournals.bc.edu/ojs/index.php/ital/article/view/5141.

Schmidt, E. (2005) 'The point of Google Print', *Official Google Blog*, 19 October 2005. Retrieved from: http://googleblog.blogspot.com/2005/10/point-of-google-print.html.

Stroeker, N. and Vogels, R. (2012) 'Survey report on digitisation in European cultural heritage institutions 2012'. ENUMERATE Thematic Network. Retrieved from: www.enumerate.eu/fileadmin/ENUMERATE/documents/ENUMERATE-Digitisation-Survey-2012.pdf.

Tanner, S. (2012) 'Measuring the impact of digital resources: the Balanced Value Impact Model'. London: King's College London. Retrieved from: www.kdcs.kcl.ac.uk/fileadmin/documents/pubs/BalancedValueImpactModel_SimonTanner_October2012.pdf.

Tashakkori, A. and Teddlie, C. (1998) *Mixed Methodology: Combining Qualitative and Quantitative Approaches*. Thousand Oaks, California: SAGE Publications Ltd (Applied Social Research Methods Series).

Terras, M. (2005) 'Reading the readers: modelling complex humanities processes to build cognitive systems', *Literary and Linguistic Computing*, **20**(1), pp. 41–59.

UNESCO (2015) 'Keystones to foster inclusive knowledge societies: access to information and knowledge, freedom of expression, privacy, and ethics on a global Internet'. UNESCO.

Unsworth, J. (2000) 'Scholarly primitives: what methods do humanities researchers have in common, and how might our tools reflect this?', in *Humanities Computing: Formal Methods, Experimental Practice*, King's College London. Retrieved from: http://people.brandeis.edu/~unsworth/Kings.5-00/primitives.html.

Vahid Aqili, S. and Isfandyari Moghaddam, A. (2008) 'Bridging the digital divide: the role of librarians and information professionals in the third millennium', *The Electronic Library*, **26**(2), pp. 226–237.

Warwick, C., Terras, M., Huntington, P. and Pappa, N. (2008) 'If you build it, will they come? The LAIRAH study: quantifying the use of online resources in the arts and humanities', *Literary and Linguistic Computing*, **23**(1), pp. 85–102.

Whitelaw, M. (2015) 'Generous interfaces for digital cultural collections', *Digital Humanities Quarterly*, **9**(1). Retrieved from: www.digitalhumanities.org/dhq/vol/9/1/000205/000205.html.

1   The myth of the new
Theories of technological discourses

In the Discworld, where the librarian of the most prestigious library in the world is an orangutan, L-Space represents the magical manifestation of what happens when large quantities of books are put in close proximity. L-Space is accessed via portals which follow the layout of the floor and ceiling of the library used to access it and links every library throughout space, time and the multiverse. A well-prepared librarian, armed with enough bananas, can find any book ever written and return it to their users. This magical manifestation of the universal library has but three simple rules:

> 1.) Silence; 2.) Books must be returned by the last date stamped; 3.) Do not interfere with the nature of causality.
>
> (Pratchett, 1989)

In Pratchett's vividly imagined world, strange things happen when large quantities of books are grouped together. Books bend space and time, warping the world around them as a result of the magical power they exert. When reading the discourse around large-scale digitisation, one could be forgiven for assuming that a similar bending of the rules of space-time was occurring in our world. The effects of digital media on our social, cultural and intellectual practices are profound, certainly, but this impact must be considered in relation to a wider discourse which exaggerates the impact of digital technologies. Evgeny Morozov has provocatively argued that this discourse has co-opted the term "Internet" to create an all-encompassing technology which defies rational debate: "instead of debating the merits of individual technologies and crafting appropriate policies and regulations, we have all but surrendered to catchall terms like 'the Internet', which try to bypass any serious and empirical debate altogether" (2013). But the way in which internet technologies influence our social and intellectual structures is not an inevitable result of an overarching technology: indeed, I will argue in this chapter that the tendency to overstate the impact of large-scale digitisation is part of a wider trend towards building a mythology around new technology, and that the reality of technological adoption and impact is far more complex.

There is, in the discourse which surrounds large-scale digitisation, a consensus that digitising huge swathes of public domain historical materials will drive significant changes in access, research methods and institutional practices. It is certainly true that there has never been more historical material available for those who possess an internet connection and the necessary individual or institutional subscriptions. The unprecedented growth in digital availability of historical materials, which have remained inaccessible for hundreds of years, is a cause for excitement. Yet the enthusiasm for the possibilities offered by large-scale digitisation is in fact part of a larger cultural interrogation of the impact of digital technologies on our social practices and the intellectual paradigms which underpin research, reading and engagement with historical artefacts. As such, it is difficult to focus on the cultural heritage sector without considering their wider significance. While it is certainly true that many critics have been realistic in their assessment of the transformative potential of digital technologies, their claims contrast with grandiose statements of epochal change. The growing scale of digital collections has caused some critics to overstate their benefits and exaggerate any negative impacts. This chapter explores the ways in which theoretical discourse has been subject to a process of exaggeration and how this constrains our efforts to consider the impact of large-scale digitisation in a more nuanced way. It begins with a brief consideration of the most influential project in this debate, the Google Books project. Without understanding how Google's enormous digitisation project was received, it is difficult to assess how public and critical opinion has been shaped in the last decade. On the one hand, some have claimed digitisation as a democratising force which will ensure the survival of our cultural heritage and allow us all to access the world's knowledge without leaving our homes; others are already developing research projects that rely upon the existence of the massive literary datasets that are a product of Google's digitisation efforts. Michel and Shen (2010), for instance, coined the term "Culturomics" to describe their quantitative literary analysis of linguistic and cultural phenomena in the English language from 1800–2000, claiming that their work allows them to observe quantitative trends in a corpus of over five million books taken from Google's digitised vaults. The inspiration for the term comes from a self-declared identification with computational approaches to scientific problems:

> Various fields with the suffix "-omics" (genomics, proteomics, transcriptomics, and a host of others) have emerged in recent years ... These fields have created data resources and computational infrastructures that have energized biology. The effort to digitize and analyse the world's books has proceeded along these lines.
>
> (Culturomics, 2010)

These computational methods have led *Wired* contributor Chris Anderson to declare that the big data era renders theoretical models obsolete. He comments that "correlation supersedes causation, and science can advance without coherent models, unified theories, or really any mechanistic explanation at all" (2008). While these arguments introduce a spurious claim for objectivity, based on the idea that media which is widely understood to be subjective somehow defies interpretation when considered at scale, the academic community has tempered their language. Moretti observes that:

> Quantitative data can tell us when Britain produced one new novel per month, or week, or day, or hour for that matter, but where the significant turning point lies along the continuum – and why – is something that must be decided on a different basis.
>
> (2007)

Despite many such cautionary notes, this excitable media coverage has tended towards overstatement of the significance of aspects of digital media. Castells sums this tendency up accurately, noting that:

> The media, keen to inform an anxious public, but lacking the autonomous capacity to assess social trends with rigor, oscillate between reporting the amazing future on offer and following the basic principle of journalism: the only news is bad news.
>
> (2002)

The chapter is divided into a number of sections which are intended to take the reader through the theoretical basis for this work. First, I explore the role of the technological sublime in framing cultural discourses around digitisation. Next, I explore how this mythology of the digital interacts with the diffusion of innovations, which explains how technology is communicated through cultural channels. The role of the medium in shaping meaning is explored further, providing a critique of the extent to which older theories of media specificity remain relevant in the digital age. I also consider how city life and online information behaviour relate to emerging methods such as corpus analysis. The chapter finishes by considering the remediation of print materials online, concluding that our skeuomorphic digital surrogates belie the idea that digitisation represents a significant divergence from what has come before. This being established, there is a need to more carefully consider the subtler impacts of large-scale digitisation. Through a critical awareness of the role of technological discourse in framing and constraining our understanding of new technologies, we can develop methodological approaches to reframe this discourse and begin to explore the pressing question of how users interact with digitised materials in reality.

Google Books: the universal library reimagined

> Whatever is fitted in any sort to excite the ideas of pain, and danger, that is to say, whatever is in any sort terrible, or is conversant about terrible objects, or operates in a manner analogous to terror, is a source of the sublime; that is, it is productive of the strongest emotions which the mind is capable of feeling.
>
> (Burke, 1998)

Commercial companies have, more than the heritage sector, been responsible for dramatically accelerating the rate of digitisation at a global level. Public institutions face decreasing levels of funding, to the extent that Google Book Search (GBS) would have struggled to gain such momentum within the constraints of the contemporary heritage sector. Google has shaped demand for digitised content and user expectations for how it will be presented online. The influence of GBS is such that it is almost impossible to address technological discourses around digitisation without considering the project and its reception. Initially branded Google Print when it was announced in 2004, GBS was inspired by a desire to digitise the world's knowledge in full. At the Frankfurt Book Fair in October 2004, Google announced the start of Google Print, followed in December 2004 by the announcement of the Google Print Library Project. In partnership with the New York Public Library and the Universities of Stanford, Oxford, Michigan and Harvard, Google announced its intention to digitise an estimated 15 million texts from the internationally significant collections of these libraries. The aims of the project were simultaneously extremely simple and hugely ambitious: to make the full text of all the world's books searchable online by anybody with an internet connection. As the project developed, other institutions also signed up to become library partners, recruiting its first non-English-speaking partners in 2006.

The New York Times (Heyman, 2015) estimates that around 25 million books have been digitised by Google to date, the majority of which are now available through GBS for searching and, in the case of public domain materials, reading. Due to copyright restrictions, GBS is based largely around search and discovery, quite severely limiting access to copyrighted materials in what has been quite accurately described as the equivalent of a giant card catalogue. Despite the limitations in access, Google's evangelical approach has inspired a techno-utopian interpretation of its impact. For instance, in an interview with Ken Auletta, Google co-founder Eric Schmidt described the moment that he was introduced to the book scanner that would be the catalyst for the project:

> It had been inspired by the Great Library of Alexandria, erected around 300 B.C. to house all the world's scrolls. Page had used the equivalent of his own 20 percent time to construct a machine that cut

off the bindings of books and digitized the pages. "What are you going to do with that, Larry?" Schmidt asked. "We're going to scan all the books in the world", Page said. For search to be truly comprehensive, he explained, it must include every book ever published. He wanted Google to "understand everything in the world and give it back to you." Sort of a "super librarian," he said.

(2009)

This anecdote bears all the hallmarks of the self-mythologising tendency of the tech sector: the association with the Library of Alexandria, which itself has become the semi-mythological originator of contemporary librarianship; the dismissal of librarians and the assumption that digital materials at scale will replace existing information infrastructures; and a grand belief that technology will inevitably change the world. In reality, this utopianism has been challenged by consistent criticism of Google's work from rights holders and critics alike. This critical split will prove illuminating in understanding the theoretical framework within which large-scale digitisation exists. While there is a clear distinction between GBS and the more selective approach of large-scale digitisation practised by libraries and archives, the corporation's work has profoundly informed the development of interfaces for digitised collections and the debate around their impact.

Criticism of the project has concentrated primarily on Google's digitisation of copyrighted texts; unlike many others, Google has sought to digitise texts regardless of their copyright status. For its part, Google has consistently argued that its efforts fall under the traditional definition of "fair use",[1] a point that has been hotly contested. Lawsuits brought separately by The Authors Guild and the Association of American Publishers in 2005 alleged that Google was infringing copyright and, furthermore, was failing to properly compensate rights holders for reusing their work. This led directly in 2009 to the Google Books Settlement, a wide-ranging document in which Google agreed to compensate publishers and authors in exchange for permission to make copyrighted works searchable in the GBS database. The question of fair use has been revisited in court since, with the latest ruling in the US Appeals Court in October 2015, declaring that Google did not violate copyright law. There is no need to go into the legal intricacies of the case here, and indeed others have already done so in great depth (Band, 2008; Grimmelmann, 2009). Google (2015) provides its own legal guide, which focuses on the company's interpretation of the "fair use" exception in copyright law. In reality, a number of controversial points remained even after the settlement was reached: the lack of progress in deciding the legality of mass book scanning; concerns that this poorly legislated domain would be dominated by "private law" (Hetcher, 2006) that favours the companies involved; allegations that the settlement created a de facto monopoly in the area of orphan works, thus creating an almost insurmountable barrier to entry for Google's rivals (Gibson, 2008); continued disagreement over the validity of the fair use argument, and whether digital indexing should in fact be considered transformative; and the global implications of a class action suit that nominally took place within the exclusive purview of US copyright law (Guo *et al.*, 2010).

These global concerns go beyond the legal ramifications of US jurisdiction being used to decide the validity of a resource which provides international material to a global audience; there has also been sustained concern that GBS will further undermine the cultural output of nations that fall outside dominant Anglo-American circles. One of the most outspoken critics to date has been Jean-Noël Jeanneney, former president of the National Library of France. He suggests that the US is exerting a form of cultural dominance over the rest of the world and that Google's actions are exacerbating the problem. At the heart of his argument are two main anxieties. The first is the effect that American market forces exert on the project. He cites the negative impact of advertising on Google products and the bias towards the English language in Google's products. The foreign language instructions for GBS, for instance, had been machine-translated: "they were filled with gobbledygook, some of it hilarious" (Jeanneney, 2007). Anthony Grafton portrays GBS as an undemocratic exercise, with the envisioned universal library taking shape as "a patchwork of interfaces and databases, some open to anyone with a computer and Wi-Fi, others closed to those without access or money" (2007), while Hetcher points out that universality cannot be achieved because libraries have already preselected materials for their collections. With each institution focusing its collection development strategy on its own user community, certain types of text will be historically under-represented, regardless of Google's success: "if none of these libraries carries pulp fiction, for instance, then these texts will not be available for searching" (2006).

Beyond the systemic problems associated with large Western corporations taking control of the public domain, there has also been overwhelming criticism of the lack of quality control exerted during digitisation. Many users were underwhelmed by their early experiences of Google Books; scan quality was ridiculed, and a variety of negative factors led Townsend to suggest that "the project is falling far short of its central premise of exposing the literature of the world" (2007). The specific criticisms have been diverse and scathing, covering a variety of failings: flaws in the GBS search functionality (Nunberg, 2009); the rejection of established library metadata standards in favour of a flawed, automated metadata creation system, which produces irrelevant keyword lists (Jackson, 2008); sloppy name authority implementation and an inability to distinguish between bibliographic data and incidental information (Nunberg, 2009); poor quality control in workflows for scanning (Conway, 2013b) and OCR (Tanner *et al.*, 2009); and concerns that a "good enough" (Pope and Holley, 2011) attitude to quality control exists. Conway (2013b) has attempted to provide empirical evidence of the proportion of errors in the GBS database, concluding that while the severity of errors varies, only a minority of volumes are entirely error-free. He points out that minor errors are becoming an embedded feature of large-scale digitisation, but that more serious errors threaten the long-term trustworthiness of digitised collections. These complaints are not directed exclusively at Google, though. The Burney Collection, the British Library's collection of newspapers and news pamphlets gathered by the Reverend Charles Burney, represents a significant collection of early English news media, available online through Gale Cengage. Tanner *et al.* (2009) undertook an analysis of the collection's OCR accuracy; they reported an average character accuracy of around 75.6 per cent, while significant word accuracy was less than 50 per cent. In practical terms, significant words are those which are most important for aiding discovery, and users of the Burney Collection are faced with a situation where these are returned wrongly more than half the time. Where OCR or automated extraction has also been used for metadata creation, this has led to a doubling up on errors, exacerbated by the poor quality of scans in some collections.

The GBS controversy is significant for several reasons. Jeanneney's warning of bias towards English and American outputs is relevant to Michel and Shen's work. They focus is primarily on English words drawn from the English and American corpora, an act which privileges dominant Anglo-American historical accounts. For an illuminating example, we can look to their brief consideration of the word "slavery". They demonstrate that the word appears more frequently in the corpus at important points in the American history of slavery and civil rights (Michel and Shen, 2010). Their reliance on American culture to contextualise their examples exemplifies the way in which non-American cultures can be implicitly marginalised. Datasets, and the assumptions we make about them, are inevitably biased, because universality is an unobtainable goal:

> In spite of what nineteenth-century publishers sometimes imagined, there can be no universal library, only specific ways of looking at what is universal. Choices are always made, and must be made.
>
> (Jeanneney, 2007)

Library collections have been formed over decades or centuries and reflect the particular power structures, biases and assumptions of each era and therefore cannot truly represent a universal human truth. Regardless, the glittering promise of the universal archive still inspires awe and influences thinking on digitisation. We can thus place calls to universality alongside other extreme critical reactions to digital media. If it is impossible to consider large-scale digitisation without referring to Google, it is similarly difficult to separate it from the reception for digital reading technologies more widely. Each informs the other, building an overall account which argues for the negative intellectual impact of the shift towards digital consumption. Sven Birkets, writing in 1994, predicted the emergence of such a shift in reading behaviour. He claimed that exposure to large quantities of digital media would destroy our attention spans, our ability to read deeply, our willingness to engage with a text for extended periods and even the survival of our literary and historical narratives. The emotional pull of his argument is strong, over 20 years later:

> On bad days I think ... that it is inevitable that generation by generation all independence and idiosyncrasy and depth will be worn away; that we will move ever more surely in lockstep, turning ourselves into creatures of the hive, living some sort of diluted universal dream in a perpetual present.
>
> (1994)

Birkets reaches this conclusion by presenting the intellectual activity of reading as a natural act undermined by digital technologies, referring to the "deep time" spent considering a text, inhabiting its words and concentrating solely on its content in order to understand it on a deeper level. Maryanne Wolf reaches a similarly negative conclusion, arguing that reading is not a normal human activity, possible only because of the brain's ability to adapt and create new connections in its existing structure. As differing forms of reading may produce different connections within the brain, she posits that new media forms may rewire the human brain in ways that we don't yet understand. Like Birkets, though, she appears to assume that this rewiring process is inevitably negative:

> Will the present generation become so accustomed to immediate access to on-screen information that the range of attentional, inferential and reflective capacities in the present reading brain will become less developed?
>
> (Wolf, 2008)

Jaron Lanier takes this negativity a step further, providing a dystopian view of the impact of digital media. He portrays the potentially damaging outcome of a shift towards distant reading, suggesting that the dominance of machines as communications platforms has deadened personal interactions and will impact negatively on our intellectual capacity. Referring to digital reading, he argues that words "will be scanned, rehashed, and misrepresented by crowds of quick and sloppy readers into wikis and automatically aggregated wireless text message streams" (2011). The emotional power of these arguments is superficially persuasive, but obscures their speculative nature. The complaints of these three authors, whose work spans 27 years, bear remarkable similarities which show that the debate around digital technologies has progressed slowly, with little evidence to substantiate or refute their claims. Too little is known about digitisation, and digital technologies more widely, for a definitive understanding of digital media to emerge, if one were ever possible. For this reason, claims about the impact of digital media can go unchecked for many years, allowing them to gain wide acceptance in the absence of contradictory evidence. This deficiency is enabled by the inflated rhetoric that surrounds the discourse. Media history has a tendency to forget what has come before, with the huge significance of contemporary digital mass media obscuring the fact that previous innovations have met with similar fascination and fear. Carolyn Marvin elaborates on this point in her account of nineteenth-century electronic technologies:

> This artefactual notion is pervasive and not much debated, for it seems simple, obvious, and convenient. But it has rendered invisible important aspects of electric media history, and perhaps of mediated communication generally. It does this in part by fixing the social origin of electric media history at the point where media producers began to service and encourage the appliance-buying demand of mass audiences. Everything before this artefactual moment is classified as technical prehistory, a neutral boundary at which inventors and technicians with no other agenda of much interest assembled equipment that exerted negligible social impact.
>
> (1988)

Many technologies have followed a similar course, where inflated claims about its positive and negative aspects fail to take into account the importance of what the given technology will nominally replace. The contemporary debate surrounding large-scale digitisation can be characterised in this manner, defined as it is by overstatement to fill the void left by a relative absence of empirical evidence. Theoretical debate is essential, but it can support the creation of a myth instead of illuminating the true utility of a new technology. We can therefore learn much about contemporary debates by studying the formation of technological discourses. The rest of this chapter explores the theoretical foundations of this discourse, seeking to explore why this tendency is manifested and how we can address it through a critical approach to user studies methodology.

The role of the technological sublime

In the absence of evidence that would inform theory, we are in a transitional phase where the wider impact of digital media technologies is not fully understood. Deegan and Sutherland point out that:

The representational structures of any and all technologies … have implications for the formulation of knowledge and the reformulation of our critical engagements; that means of storage and reproduction are related; that the medium is, after all, the message.

(2009)

Technological discourses thus share a structural basis and tend to follow a familiar trajectory as language and critical understanding adapts to new demands. Within this transition is a "historical development of social language itself" (Williams, 1977). Our theoretical understanding of new technologies is inherently incomplete and therefore subject to the same social imperatives that have historically influenced the adoption of other innovations. Yet public perceptions of technological innovations are still fundamentally shaped by this emerging discourse.

Mosco's (2004) theory of the digital sublime successfully unifies the ideas that underpin this familiar diffusion process. His work reimagines Edmund Burke's (1998) treatise on the sublime as relevant to the disruptive influence of social discourse on technological adoption. Computer technology, he argues, can only be fully understood by recognising some of the myths with which it is associated. This mythological status is common across many innovations: promoters tell us it will improve our lives and render obsolete what has gone before, while critics imagine the cataclysmic effects that the new technology will wreak upon humanity. The resultant critical environment is a powerful postmodern narrative of ruptures and dramatic change, which is rarely reflected in reality. The true status of an innovation is therefore clouded by this social process, and recognising that it tends towards the hyperbolic is an important first step in addressing this problem. Similar narratives have developed in previous eras, portraying a new technology as something that threatens to engulf older methods of knowledge production and mediation. The invention of the steam-powered rotary press in the nineteenth century prompted the *London Times* to declare that "a system of machinery that almost organic has been devised and arranged, which, while it relieves the human frame of its most laborious efforts in printing, far exceeds all human powers in rapidity and dispatch" (Deegan and Sutherland, 2009). *The New York Times* claimed in 1938 that "the heavily engineered typewriter would do away with the simple pencil" (Duguid, 1996), yet the portability and convenience of the pencil ensures it remains useful long after typewriters have become obsolete. Indeed, when Apple advertised the iPad in 2013, it wasn't the typewriter which provided the comparison but the timeless technology of the leaded pencil. These are just two of many stories from which we can identify a common theme: with the arrival of an innovation comes a belief in the inevitability of an emergent social paradigm to match it. Indeed, Nunberg comments that "the past can come to seem an unbroken stream of proclamations that man is living in an epochal moment" (1996). These claims originate in a desire to see the past as simple and obsolete and the future as complex, meaning that we tend to assume the innate superiority of more intricate new technologies. This is further complicated by other factors: the process of technology diffusion and adoption; the mythology that surrounds technological innovation; and the theoretical discourses that explain the impact of cultural heritage.

Diffusion of innovations

Diffusion, in the context of technological adoption, is "the process in which an innovation is communicated through certain channels over time among members of a social system" (Rogers, 2003). There have been several accounts of how diffusion can shape the period between the invention of a technology and its widespread acceptance but, in essence, they argue that the success of a particular technology relies not upon its technical characteristics but on social factors that occur alongside the development of our understanding:

> Technologies do not have a momentum of their own at the outset that allows them ... to pass through a neutral social medium. Rather, they are subject to contingency as they pass from figurative hand to hand, and so are shaped and reshaped.
>
> (Hutchby, 2001)

The transition to a new technology is thus far from a deterministic inevitability, instead resembling a social process built largely upon the influence of an early group of innovators. More precisely, human factors are vital to an adoption process which relies both on the utility of a given technology and the influence of opinion leaders and change agents. Opinion leaders are individuals who play a vital part in the diffusion process, earning and maintaining a position in the centre of their communication system through "technical competence, social accessibility, and conformity to the system's norms" (Rogers, 2003). They are responsible for influencing those within their social network and, as a result, affecting the rate of uptake. In the case of large-scale digitised collections, these opinion leaders come from many overlapping sectors: academia, publishing, librarianship and the technology industry, for example. The role of the change agent differs because they look to influence the decision-making process in a manner that benefits their own agency, whereas opinion leaders are more likely not to have direct links to the technology under development. The professional affiliation of a participant in the critical debate therefore shapes their input. When a traditional publisher argues against digitisation, or a Google employee extols the virtues of their book search, they seek to influence public perception in a way that favours their own agency. Even when we balance these different voices, though, there are common and shared assumptions which help to frame the terms of the discourse.

With digital technologies, in line with McLuhan's (1964) famous slogan, we are faced with the enduring truism that the medium is, indeed, the message. His words continue to define a debate that accepts that the medium of representation plays a role in giving meaning to cultural expression. This furthermore entails an acceptance that the medium must therefore act as a transformative force. Knowledge has always been mediated by the social and technological framework in which it resides, from the primarily oral tradition of pre-literate societies, to the scribe-written texts of the pre-print era, followed by the transition towards the solitary consumption of a work written by a defined authorial figure. But when a medium becomes accepted, even commonplace, Mosco argues that this sense of familiarity obscures our awareness of the mediation that unavoidably occurs:

> Electricity and radio broadcasting are, of course, still powerful forces in the world. But the Age of Electricity, like the Age of Radio, is over. Both electricity and radio have passed into powerful banality.
>
> (2004)

Instead of banality, though, some representations of the print medium have become almost fetishistic in their portrayal of the book as a pleasurable physical object (Sartre, 1967; Scarry, 2001). By doing so, they contradict the idea that the print medium can ever represent a neutral, or even natural, medium of expression. The pleasure that derives from the contemporary physical form of what was once a revolutionary technology, the mass printed book, tells us that the medium does affect the transfer of knowledge precisely because it "is itself an actor in the shaping and reshaping of experience" (Van Dijck, 2005). Duguid (1996) suggests that the print medium's specific combination of technology and social process continues to exert a strong influence on contemporary society. This does not invalidate the argument that digital technologies may change our reading habits; rather, by recognising that media have a complex relationship with social and intellectual practices, we can see that they are more likely to be part of a multifaceted negotiation between the technology, the medium and the individual than the cause of paradigmatic shifts in our intellectual structures.

Mechanical reproduction and the end of the age of the author

Williams theorises that "our culture, being materially formed, is subject to change through the changing technologies which always constitute its fundamental processes" (1977). Thus, as poetry was associated with orality, and novels with print, digital technology can influence our perceptions of cultural artefacts and shape the ways in which we relate to them as a society. Walter Benjamin approached this process from the perspective of mechanical reproduction, and in doing so foreshadowed the issues that relate to the mass digitisation of our culture. Benjamin raised important questions about where the authenticity of cultural experience lies in a reproduction:

> Even the most perfect reproduction of a work of art is lacking in one element: its presence in space and time, its unique existence at the place where it happens to be. This unique existence of the work of art determined the history to which it was subject throughout the time of its existence.
>
> (2007b)

When a cultural artefact is removed from its original form, Benjamin claims that there is a danger it will be shorn of its context, its history and thus its authenticity. The physical artefact therefore gains importance as an authentic historical record at the same time that its ritualistic aura is eroded by reproduction. Yet the process of reproduction is vital in ensuring the suitability of artefacts for mass public viewings, linked as it is with increased education and cultural awareness and a widespread desire to experience culture first-hand. As a result, the public are frequently exposed to a representation rather than an original artefact. When art is separated from the physical in this manner, Benjamin claims that a transformation of the object's nature occurs. This transformation is vital in defining the author's relationship with their audience:

> The film actor lacks the opportunity of the stage actor to adjust to the audience during his performance, since he does not present his performance to the audience in person. This permits the audience to take the position of a critic, without experiencing any personal contact with the author. The audience's identification with the actor is really an identification with the camera.
>
> (2007b)

Rather than providing us with an unmediated cultural experience, then, each translation of an artefact to a new medium acts to mediate the original in ways that are meaningful to its reception. The medium is indeed the message, in so far as it helps to shape our cultural understanding of its content.

McLuhan's words continue to exert an influence on the contemporary debate. Based on the observation that medium defines meaning, his narrative makes the case that print forced humanity into a state of conformity and consumption, which the technologies of the twentieth century had the power to reverse, thus leading humanity towards a technology-driven recreation of the oral tradition. He sees the digital destruction of physical space and time as a way to lead humanity back to what he saw as a more natural communication structure:

> We are back in an acoustic space. We have begun again to structure the primordial feeling, the tribal emotion from which a few centuries of literacy divorced us.
>
> (1967)

But at the heart of his work is a flawed understanding of what this digital space would come to resemble. His notion of the digital space as a global village, "a single constricted space resonant with tribal drums" (1962), is at odds with our experience of the web in contemporary society, more accurately described by Castells (2002) as the "Internet Galaxy". Whereas the village operates in a semi-closed system with clear boundaries, the information infrastructure of the internet is enormous in its complexity, scale and openness. It more accurately represents the loose structures of a modern city in this regard. The next section therefore turns to look at how individuals experience the city and the social experience of information overload, in order to understand how this distinction from McLuhan's work influences our understanding of the likely impact of digitised materials.

The city and information overload

City life has provided distinct cultural benefits, including massively increasing the effectiveness of human interactions in comparison to smaller settlements. Deutsch describes this effectiveness as the increased probability of an individual carrying out a specific interaction regardless of its cost. The greater proximity of other citizens means that any desired human interaction is more likely to be possible in a city. Not only is each interaction easier, but inhabitants of a city experience a very particular kind of freedom:

> If freedom is the opportunity to choose, then the metropolis, in so far as it is an engine for facilitating change, is also one of choice. This liberation may be physical, in terms of the visits, the meetings, the sights now possible, or psychological and vicarious, in terms of the choices and experiments which can be made in the imagination.
>
> (Deutsch, 1961)

The internet shares this freedom with cities. In the specific sense that people have a greater choice of available interactions, being online increases the freedom of users. This freedom comes at a cost, though, in a huge increase in the number of external stimuli, which could lead to information overload. Milgram defines information overload as "an inability to process inputs from the environment because there are too many inputs for the system to cope with" (1970). He argues that the phenomenon can impact on daily life in a number of ways, damaging work performance and the evolution of social norms. Deutsch further notes that when an individual is confronted by increased choice, the opportunity cost of any chosen course increases, unless an effective mechanism exists for filtering excessive information:

> Whatever he does will necessarily imply forgoing something else that has also appeared relevant and in a sense attractive ... we are quite likely to also have increased his vague but nagging sense of self-doubt and misgivings as to whether he has made the best choice.
>
> (1961)

In this aspect of city life, we hear echoes of the high profile critics of digital media, but with the key difference that the behaviours they describe as an erosion of our intellectual capabilities are in fact a necessary reaction to an increased range of stimuli to which we are exposed. The behavioural traits of internet users must thus begin to resemble those of city residents, at least when it comes to processing information. Palfrey and Gasser write that city residents develop a lower capacity for reacting to new inputs with the same energy they once had, noting that they become desensitised as they "shield themselves from external stimuli in the form of media, ideas, communications and so forth" (2008). This desensitisation is expressed in a number of practical ways which compensate for individual opportunity cost. Milgram (1970) suggests several characteristics which arise, including the allocation of less time to each piece of information, the use of filtering devices to discover pertinent sources, and the creation of specially designed platforms or institutions to externalise the absorption of inputs. These features are also present in descriptions of web usage, described colourfully by Nicholas *et al.* (2004) as a promiscuous and diverse reading style that bounces horizontally between various sources while spending less time with each.

In a sense then, the manner in which researchers interrogate the massive datasets produced by large-scale digitisation recalls the behaviour of overloaded city inhabitants. Recognising the impossible task of reading millions of digitised texts, researchers begin to adopt computational methods to discover themes and patterns at scale, an approach that Franco Moretti (2007) has labelled "distant reading". Quantitative analysis has been readily adopted in some fields, partly because it allows researchers to utilise digital texts that exhibit poor readability:

> As the size of a collection grows, you can begin to extract information and knowledge from it in ways that are impossible with small

collections, even if the quality of the individual documents in the giant corpus is relatively poor.

(Cohen, 2006)

With the sheer scale of digitised corpora, and the number of errors present in scanned documents, it is therefore unsurprising that emerging methods of large-scale corpus analysis rely on methods that operate at a layer of abstraction from the original documents. This abstraction is at the heart of quantitative analysis in the humanities; when textual information is collated at scale, it no longer necessitates close reading to interrogate it for certain types of meaning. But the meaning produced by these methods differs from that of close textual analysis, focusing instead on networks, trends, automated document classification, genre analysis and pattern analysis. While an excitable press suggests that these approaches can replace close reading of textual materials, the reality is that the majority of digital humanities researchers recognise that distant and close reading are complementary methods.

Despite this, there has been resistance to quantitative methods in the humanities. Because data-driven methods can rely on interrogating existing human knowledge, there is concern that they are vulnerable to being nothing more than derivative work, which Lanier rather dramatically labels "fragmentary reactions to first-order expression" (2011). This seems a strange criticism, given that the researchers involved in implementing these methods have been quite open in recognising this aspect of their work. For instance, Allison *et al.* developed a software tool which was capable of recognising the genre of literary texts in a sample database with a high degree of accuracy. Despite this success, the researchers identified that the innovation within their research was found in the technology, not the findings:

> Striking as these results were, did we think they had produced new knowledge? The answer, of course, was no: Docuscope had corroborated what literary scholars already knew.
>
> (Allison *et al.*, 2011)

This by no means invalidates the work being done on software tools for textual analysis, and indeed it is likely that these tools will develop over time given that methods are still in the process of being created and defined. Yet it is one reason for the cynicism afforded to high profile attempts at quantitative literary analysis. Michel and Shen's immodest claims to have identified the "cultural genome" (2010) met with resistance from existing researchers for their claims to have revolutionised literary research. It is certainly true that the technological scale of their analysis is almost unprecedented: "Of course there is a jump in scale, not just in the size of the corpus but also in the staggering processing power that researchers can throw at it" (Nunberg, 2010). The problems identified with the GBS corpus are emblematic of wider issues with digitised collections: difficulties with poor OCR and metadata; problems with legitimate but irrelevant data; changes in typography such as the demise of the long 'S' rendering results inaccurate; the problem of decontextualised data being stripped of meaning; and the difficulty these issues create for drawing reliable conclusions. Furthermore, some critics have pointed out methodological flaws that demand human expertise in the areas being studied. Nunberg takes issue with a graph that judges the relative fame of a selection of scientists based solely on the flawed notion that frequency of mention necessarily correlates to levels of fame:

> It defies belief that Freud is vastly better known than Darwin among the authors of books in a corpus that was drawn from the collections of research libraries. We simply mention Freud more often ... The data don't wear their cultural significance on their sleeves; they need cultural historians to speak for them.
>
> (2010)

A recent article by Pechenick *et al.* (2015) goes further, showing that the growing presence of scientific texts since the 1900s has caused a surge of phrases typical to academic articles but less common in general. Their findings suggest that only the English fiction dataset from the second version of the Google Books corpus is not heavily affected by such texts, concluding that the skewing of the texts towards particular types of writing, and specific prolific authors, calls into question the vast majority of claims drawn from the Google Books corpus. These findings confirm the concerns of writers like Nunberg, who argue that the concept of a cultural genome is not easily identified solely by counting word frequency.

Moretti's (2007) work has also received widespread media attention, and focuses on illuminating literary networks. He argues that literary history requires a quantitative treatment because of the impossibility of understanding huge swathes of writing based solely on close reading of a small and unrepresentative sample. The literary canon of the nineteenth century, for instance, contains less than 1 per cent of the novels published in that period. His research is therefore concerned with illuminating the wider knowledge systems that encompass all texts. Rather than using data to derive seemingly objective meaning in the manner of Culturomics, his work reflects Chartier's (1992) notes on book historiography, which concentrate on the network by identifying the alliances, hierarchies and patterns that emerge from analysis and thus provide a starting point for more detailed analysis. This approach, applied quantitatively, creates models to make sense of literary history: graphs of the growth of the novel in various countries; maps that show the nature of space in narrative; and taxonomic trees of novelistic genres. Moretti's work is arguably more intellectually coherent than initial forays into Culturomics and hints at the true value of quantitative analysis as a way of solving new problems while also identifying questions for closer analysis. It is just one high profile example of the work that has been facilitated by large-scale digitisation, none of which would be feasible without it.

The concerns of critics of distant reading centre on the idea that it exists in opposition to close reading, in a reflection of the polarised debate that we would expect around technological innovations. The outspoken author Jaron Lanier claims that quantitative researchers "care about the abstraction of the network more than the real people who are networked, even though the network by itself is meaningless" (2011). Like much of Lanier's polemic, it is not fairly representative of the majority of researchers, but it does hint at the problems that are caused by the tension between close and distant reading. One of these problems is the undoubted pressure that institutions face in adapting collections to deal with quantitative analysis. It can seem difficult to reconcile the need for high quality scans, metadata and OCR with the need for high throughput digitisation to facilitate data-driven approaches. Small digital collections have generally relied upon human intervention to ensure quality and have therefore adopted time-consuming methods to maintain standards. These methods can also be intellectually intensive, designed to ensure that digitised content is presented in its most suitable form. The rigorous nature of these methods renders them unsuitable for cost-effective digitisation at a large scale, meaning that larger projects must rely upon scalable technologies, such as page scanning and OCR to produce searchable texts and retrieve metadata. In this manner, large quantities of textual information can be digitised extremely quickly, but at the expense of the highly granular approach associated with some smaller projects. Degraded quality is found in several respects: problems with incomplete or incorrect metadata, particularly relating to name authority; the poor quality of individual scanned pages; unreliable OCR that produces a high proportion of errors in the machine-readable text; and the proliferation of editions that results from scanning multiple copies of an individual work. These errors become magnified at scale, creating noise that must be filtered by the user. As we have seen, corpus analysis offers a strategy for copying with the proliferation of errors, but discoverability and readability are negatively affected as a result. Therefore, a digitisation strategy that prioritises either distant reading or close reading risks damaging the usability of collections for other researchers.

The difficulties of supporting different types of research behaviour can lead to the assumption that innovative approaches are privileged at the expense of traditional methods. Indeed, it can seem that distant reading changes the fundamental nature of information. Lanier's comments recall a tradition where information was defined in a particularistic sense; deriving meaning from an individual text, or imparting facts about specific people, opinions or events. In separating form from content, information instead becomes an abstract entity with human characteristics and a distinct personality:

> People treat information as a self-contained substance. It is something that people can pick up, possess, pass around, put in a database, lose, find, write down, accumulate, count, compare, and so forth.
>
> (Brown and Duguid, 2002)

Brown and Duguid's comment pre-empts the contemporary situation where texts exist simultaneously as readable artefacts and carriers of word-level data, demanding new methods of interaction. One such demand is that all information must be equally valuable and must therefore be freely available. But such a viewpoint entails a selective reading of the famous maxim that "information wants to be free", for which Stewart Brand is widely credited. His original quote is in fact far more considered, pointing out that the desire for free information emerges from its technological characteristics, which are oppositional to social and commercial pressures:

> Information wants to be free. Information also wants to be expensive. Information wants to be free because it has become so cheap to distribute, copy, and recombine – too cheap to meter. It wants to be expensive because it can be immeasurably valuable to the recipient. That tension will not go away. It leads to endless wrenching debate about price, copyright, "intellectual property", the moral rightness of casual distribution, because each round of new devices makes the tension worse, not better.
>
> (1989)

Digital technologies *theoretically* flatten these existing information hierarchies while in reality still operating within them. Here, there are obvious echoes of the intertext: a work that exists as part of an intertextual network, its meaning mediated through links, citations, influences drawn from other texts, and the knowledge of each reader (Barthes, 1977). We will see, though, that the intertext provides an inadequate metaphor for the digital corpus.

Reality and remediation

Baudrillard warns that the process of reducing cultural objects to components in a digital network threatens the boundary between truth and falsehood. Whereas current critics have related this threat to the growing popularity of big data, he sees a damaging form of abstraction which originates in the technology itself:

The real is produced from miniaturized cells, matrices, and memory banks, models of control – and it can be reproduced an infinite number of times from these. It no longer needs to be rational, because it no longer measures itself against either an ideal or negative instance. It is no longer anything but operational.

(1994)

Baudrillard's scepticism extends to theorising that electronic media are not real in a meaningful sense, existing only as "a hyperreal, produced from a radiating synthesis of combinatory models in a hyperspace without atmosphere" (1994). While it is hard to endorse such radical scepticism, he is correct in the specific sense that a digitised artefact is indeed purely operational, impossible for humans to engage with unless parsed through automated tools or reconstituted into a simulacrum of the original. It is more accurate to suggest that, rather than representing digitised materials as a disconnected hyperreal, they can be more usefully compared to a poor translation in need of tools to reincorporate it to some form of meaning:

What does a literary work "say"? What does it communicate? It "tells" very little to those who understand it. Its essential function is not statement or the imparting of information. Yet any translation which intends to perform a transmitting function cannot transmit anything but information, hence, something inessential. This is the hallmark of a bad translation.

(Benjamin, 2007a)

Digitised information, whether represented by the large-scale corpus or the scanned image, is a pure manifestation of what I have discussed in this chapter. Not only does it require that filtering and analysis tools are created to navigate its digital form, but it is only through digital technologies that it can provide any meaning. This goes one step further than the intertext, which exists as part of a wider network that reduces the author to a cipher for cultural ideas and focuses attention on the text (Barthes, 1977). Instead, the digitised artefact in its abstract form shifts meaning away from author and text and towards the network. Meaning resides in the words, which become both literally and figuratively a form of computer data, and the ways in which that data is presented to users for discovery and analysis. While the network is central to users of large-scale digitisation, the individual textual artefact is not. This is problematic because it is increasingly clear that large-scale digitised collections must perform multiple functions, operating both as vehicles for creating literary corpora and as authoritative digital surrogates for textual sources that are interrogated by researchers from many disciplines. Referring to Bolter and Grusin's (1996) dismissal of the notion that digital remediations are

somehow less real than the physical, we are ultimately left with a technology that is stuck between two competing theoretical movements: one that
prioritises fluid, freely available digital corpora of information, and one
that clings to the representational codes of print because it considers these
existing bibliographic norms to be vital to the intellectual process.

Twenty years ago, Nunberg (1996) suggested that the rhetoric of
technological innovation assumes the inevitable destruction of its prede-
cessors. The reaction to mass digitisation has been inflamed by this aspect
of technological discourse, leading the abstraction inherent in quantitative
methods to be interpreted as disruptive to existing knowledge paradigms,
rather than additive. This futurological rhetoric claims that it is enough to
discover that something is true without attempting theoretical explana-
tions. The dismissal of the old is total: "There's no reason to cling to our
old ways. It's time to ask: What can science learn from Google?" (Anderson, 2008). Anderson's theory of the Death of Theory is linked to the
humanities through the close methodological identification with scientific
research found in the work of scholars such as Michel and Shen. But such
powerful faith in computational methods does the wider community a dis-
service because it suggests that big data leaves no questions or gaps to
worry about. Effectively, it creates a myth of the power of big data and the
digitisation processes that make it possible in the humanities.

Heralding a new paradigm is problematic in itself because mass digitisation is still concerned with closely remediating the existing print paradigm. New technologies commonly reference previous media in their
development stage, and this close remediation is driven by an assumption
that older media do in fact remain relevant. The contrast between the
public discourse about paradigm shifts in information structures, and the
continued dominance of the skeuomorphic digital object which refers to
the norms of print culture, is stark. The close attachment to print is particularly evident in the language commonly used to market technology to
the general public. Rather than assert the unique features of new technologies, technology companies prefer instead to emphasise their familiarity
and their adherence to previously understood media:

> Reading on iPad is just like reading a book. You hold iPad like a book
> and flip the pages like a book. And you do it all with your hands – just
> like a book.

> (Apple, 2011)

This fetishisation of the familiar is driven by an assumption that the bibliographic codes of print are easily understood by readers and hold ongoing
relevance. There is, though, a contradiction between the way that digital
media are simultaneously understood to be disruptive and the desire to
faithfully reproduce existing models of publication and form online.
Hayles (2005) points out that digital copies differ more from print in their

materiality than unique print forms do from each other, and so large-scale digitisation does hint at the possibility of a cultural shift. I will argue though, that the close link between usage of LSDC and physical archival behaviour shows that this shift has not yet occurred.

Summary: waiting for the paradigm shift

The presence of error has, Conway argues, become one of the defining features of large-scale digitisation. As a result, it has defined the standards to which digitised material are held:

> Digital surrogates produced by Google (and likely by other large-scale digitization efforts) carry with them transparent evidence of scanning techniques and post-scan enhancement procedures, including visible fingers and clamps, subtle page warp, and inconsistent typography. In this way, large-scale digitization has established a new ethical norm that varies quite dramatically from the digitization norms pioneered in research libraries over 25 years ago.
>
> (2013a)

Large-scale digitisation, at this technical level, offers benefits and drawbacks: digital resources excel at allowing users to interrogate large quantities of material, access heritage resources from outside traditionally defined spaces and use computational methods to explore them in new ways. This makes them intellectually distinct from the physical materials which they remediate. The biggest mistake we can make when considering digitised artefacts is assuming that they represent nothing more than a surrogate object, because then they can only ever represent an inferior surrogate, shorn of context and placed in a distributed network in such a way that our understanding of it shifts in subtle but vital ways. Allowing digitised artefacts to become intellectual products in their own right helps us to identify their strengths and weaknesses and to understand more clearly their position in a hybrid print/digital information infrastructure.

As we have seen in this chapter, the intellectual nature of the digitised artefact shifts subtly away from the textual artefact and towards the network within which it exists. Digitised materials represent a new form, which has the potential to create its own knowledge structures through understanding them as a unique form in need of its own representational and analytical approaches. Our methods for understanding this shift are likely to lie in a combination of distant and close reading and of a critical engagement with the artefact in its physical and digitised forms. What is less clear is how this digital medium will supplant what has gone before. I have argued in this chapter that there is a gap between the reality of technological innovations and their reception, which has led to the dominance of a polarised critical debate, which can be explained with reference to Mosco's theory of the digital sublime. Our theoretical understanding of large-scale digitisation is therefore incomplete, demanding that researchers adopt an evidence-based approach to impact evaluation, to intervene in creating a more rational technological discourse. I will argue in the following chapter that, despite the abstraction which occurs through digitisation, user behaviour online is in many respects similar to archival research. Scholarly research in archives is a complex process involving several activities that do not occur in a predetermined order. Researchers use filtering devices and external finding aids, in the same way that city inhabitants use external aids when exposed to excessive stimuli. The behavioural commonality of this otherwise very different environment predicts the types of behaviour we can expect to see online, and I will therefore approach the impact of large-scale digitisation with the understanding that user strategies for coping with huge amounts of data are founded in existing practices.

Although new research methods are being facilitated by large-scale digitised collections, digital media is still widely understood in comparison to the bibliographic codes of print. This is shown in the way that digitisation aims to closely remediate the printed text and the theoretical view that the digitised object is merely an inferior surrogate version of the original. We do not yet view digitised materials as intellectually distinct products in their own right, and as such the extent of change is unlikely to be as extensive as the more extreme predictions would suggest. The theoretical framework of this chapter therefore fuels a number of proposals: first, that the majority of users of large-scale digitised collections do not view their contents as intellectually distinct from physical newspapers; second, that we do not, as a result, have a clear idea of how this intellectual distinction will manifest itself, beyond some early examples of research methods which are emerging from the products of large-scale digitisation; third, that the reality of usage is obscured by the polarised debate around digital media in general; and finally, that digitised materials should be expected to perform an additive role, rather than a disruptive one.

This chapter demonstrates that the mythologising tendency of technological discourse provides an inaccurate view of the true impact of digitisation. The most strident claims regarding large-scale digitisation are supported by little evidence either supporting or contradicting the author's assertions. This lack of evidence allows claims to go unchecked for long periods of time, allowing them to gain authority and remain in circulation for many years. I will argue in the next chapters that the study of digitised resources would benefit from a more realistic evaluation of their impact, based upon observation of, and discussion with, users. Rather than framing the debate in oppositional terms, impact analysis can help to build our understanding of an additive technology with genuine real-world benefits. As such, I will present an approach to methodology which is based upon discovering both the benefits and drawbacks of large-scale digitisation. These arguments are presented through the focal lens of digitised newspapers. But in a sense this book is not about newspapers: it is about understanding how issues from varied domains, including large-scale digitisation of newspapers, carry over into the way that LSDC are conceived by libraries and received by users. I will argue that in order to achieve the rich potential offered by large-scale digitisation, libraries must not look to those techno-futurist discourses which position users as passive recipients of disruptive innovation. Instead, by understanding that the discourse tends towards the mythical, we need to look to the past. Specifically, we need to look back to models of librarianship which drew upon the transformative role of libraries in providing access to their users. In the rush to create digitised collections and meet an undoubted demand among users, libraries need to re-align themselves to remember the service aspect of their role. Large-scale digitisation offers many opportunities, but these exist in a state of conflict with existing regulatory, commercial and social structures, which define how resources are conceived. I will argue that the emergence of open access digital newspaper collections represents a first step in aligning their impact more closely with the need to widen participation and address the digital divide as it relates to online library resources.

Note

1 The US Copyright Office provides a clear guide to the legal doctrine of "fair use", which includes the reproduction of copyrighted works for purposes such as criticism, scholarship and research. Google has consistently maintained that it adheres to the regulations, comparing the activity of indexing complete copies of a book to the way that their search engine automatically indexes billions of web pages for the purpose of discovery (Schmidt, 2005).

Bibliography

Allison, S., Heuser, R., Jockers, M., Moretti, F. and Witmore, M. (2011) 'Quantitative formalism: an experiment', p. 28. Retrieved from: http://litlab.stanford.edu/LiteraryLabPamphlet1.pdf.

Anderson, C. (2008) 'The end of theory: the data deluge that makes the scientific method obsolete', *Wired*. Retrieved from: www.wired.com/science/discoveries/magazine/16-07/pb_theory.

Apple (2011) 'iBooks: a novel way to buy and read books', *Apple*. Retrieved from: www.apple.com/ipad/built-in-apps/ibooks.html.

Auletta, K. (2009) *Googled: The End of the World as We Know It*. London: Random House.

Band, J. (2008) 'A guide for the perplexed: libraries and the Google Library Project Settlement', policybandwidth. Retrieved from: www.arl.org/bm~doc/google-settlement-13nov08.pdf.

Barthes, R. (1977) 'The death of the author', in Heath, S. (tran.) *Image-Music-Text*. London: Fontana Press.

Baudrillard, J. (1994) *Simulacra and Simulation*. Glaser, S. F. (tran.). Ann Arbor: University of Michigan Press.

Benjamin, W. (2007a) 'The task of the translator: an introduction to the translation of Baudelaire's *Tableaux Parisiens*', in *Illuminations*. New York: Schocken Books, pp. 69–82.

Benjamin, W. (2007b) 'The work of art in the age of mechanical reproduction', in *Illuminations*. New York: Schocken Books (Penguin Great Ideas).

Birkets, S. (1994) *The Gutenberg Elegies: The Fate of Reading in an Electronic Age*. New York: Ballentine Books.

Bolter, J. D. and Grusin, R. A. (1996) 'Remediation', *Configurations*, **4**(3), pp. 311–358.

Brand, S. (1989) *The Media Lab: Inventing the Future at M.I.T.* New York: Penguin Books Ltd.

Brown, J. S. and Duguid, P. (2002) *The Social Life of Information*. Boston, Mass.: Harvard Business School.

Burke, E. (1998) *A Philosophical Enquiry into the Origin of Our Ideas of the Sublime and Beautiful*. Oxford: Oxford University Press.

Castells, M. (2002) *The Internet Galaxy: Reflections on the Internet, Business, and Society*. Oxford: Oxford University Press.

Chartier, R. (1992) *The Order of Books: Readers, Authors, and Libraries in Europe between the Fourteenth and Eighteenth Centuries*. Cochrane, L. G. (tran.). Stanford: Stanford University Press.

Cohen, D. (2006) 'From Babel to knowledge: data mining large digital collections', *D-Lib Magazine*, **12**(3). Retrieved from: www.dlib.org/dlib/march06/cohen/03cohen.html.

Conway, P. (2013a) 'Preserving imperfection: assessing the incidence of digital imaging error in HathiTrust', *Digital Technology and Culture*, **42**(1), pp. 17–30.

Conway, P. (2013b) 'Validating quality in large-scale digitization: findings on the distribution of imaging error'. University of Michigan. Retrieved from: www.unesco.org/new/fileadmin/MULTIMEDIA/HQ/CI/CI/pdf/mow/VC_Conway_28_C_1440.pdf.

Culturomics (2010) 'FAQ – Culturomics'. Retrieved from: www.culturomics.org/Resources/faq.

Deegan, M. and Sutherland, K. (2009) *Transferred Illusions: Digital Technology and the Forms of Print*. Farnham: Ashgate Publishing.

Deutsch, K. W. (1961) 'On social communication and the metropolis', *Daedalus*, **90**(1), pp. 99–110.

Duguid, P. (1996) 'Material matters: the past and the futurology of the book', in *The Future of the Book*. Berkeley and Los Angeles: University of California Press. Retrieved from: www2.parc.com/ops/members/brown/papers/mm.html.

Gibson, J. (2008) 'Google's new monopoly? How the company could gain by paying millions in copyright fees', *The Washington Post*, 3 November 2008. Retrieved from: www.washingtonpost.com/wp-dyn/content/article/2008/11/02/AR2008110201721.html.

Grafton, A. (2007) 'Digitization and its discontents', *The New Yorker*. Retrieved from: www.newyorker.com/reporting/2007/11/05/071105fa_fact_grafton?printable=true.

Grimmelman, J. (2009) 'The Google Book Search settlement: ends, means, and the future of books', ACS Issue Brief. Retrieved from: http://works.bepress.com/cgi/viewcontent.cgi?article=1024&context=james_grimmelmann.

Guo, Y., Liu, Y. and Yu, Z. (2010) ' "Google Library": some copyright infringement concerns in China', in *2010 International Conference on E-Business and E-Government*. Guangzhou, China, pp. 2053–2056.

Hayles, N. K. (2005) *My Mother was a Computer: Digital Subjects and Literary Texts*. Chicago: University of Chicago Press.

Hetcher, S. (2006) 'The half-fairness of Google's plan to make the world's collection of books searchable', *Michigan Telecommunications and Technology Law Review*, **13**(1).

Heyman, S. (2015) 'Google Books: a complex and controversial experiment', *The New York Times*, 28 October 2015. Retrieved from: www.nytimes.com/2015/10/29/arts/international/google-books-a-complex-and-controversial-experiment.html?_r=0.

Hutchby, I. (2001) 'Technology, texts and affordances', *Sociology*, **45**(1), pp. 441–456.

Jackson, M. (2008) 'Using metadata to discover the buried treasure in Google Book Search', *Journal of Library Administration*, **47**(1), pp. 165–173.

Jeanneney, J.-N. (2007) *Google and the Myth of Universal Knowledge*. London: Chicago University Press.

Lanier, J. (2011) *You Are Not a Gadget*. London: Penguin.

Marvin, C. (1988) *When Old Technologies Were New: Thinking about Electric Communication in the Late Nineteenth Century*. New York: Oxford University Press.

McLuhan, M. (1962) *The Gutenberg Galaxy: The Making of the Typographic*. Toronto: University of Toronto Press.

McLuhan, M. (1964) *Understanding Media: The Extensions of Man*. London: Routledge and Kegan Paul.

McLuhan, M. (1967) *The Medium Is the Message*. Harmondsworth: Penguin.

Michel, J.-B. and Shen, Y. K. (2010) 'Quantitative analysis of culture using millions of digitized books', *Science Magazine*, **331** (6014), pp. 176–182.

Milgram, S. (1970) 'The experience of living in cities', *Science*, **167**, pp. 1461–1468.

Moretti, F. (2007) *Graphs, Maps, Trees: Abstract Models for Literary History*. New York: Verso.

Morozov, E. (2013) *To Save Everything, Click Here*. London: Penguin.

Mosco, V. (2004) *The Digital Sublime: Myth, Power, and Cyberspace*. Cambridge Mass.: MIT Press.

Nicholas, D., Huntington, P., Williams, P. and Dobrowolski, T. (2004) 'Reappraising information seeking behaviour in a digital environment: bouncers, checkers, returnees and the like', *Journal of Documentation*, **60**(1), pp. 24–39.

Nunberg, G. (Ed.) (1996) *The Future of the Book*. Berkeley and Los Angeles: University of California Press.

Nunberg, G. (2009) 'Google's Book Search: a disaster for scholars', *The Chronicle of Higher Education*. Retrieved from: http://chronicle.com/article/Googles-Book-Search-A/48245/.

Nunberg, G. (2010) 'Counting on Google Books', *The Chronicle of Higher Education*. Retrieved from: http://chronicle.com/article/Counting-on-Google-Books/125735.

Page, B. (2010) 'Government slammed by authors over Google', The Bookseller, 4 February 2010. Retrieved from: www.thebookseller.com/news/111639-government-slammed-by-authors-over-google.html.

Palfrey, J. and Gasser, U. (2008) *Born Digital: Understanding the First Generation of Digital Natives*. New York: Basic Books.

Pechenick, E. A., Danforth, C. M. and Dodds, P. S. (2015) 'Characterizing the Google Books corpus: strong limits to inferences of socio-cultural and linguistic evolution', PLoS ONE, **10**(10).

Pope, J. T. and Holley, R. P. (2011) 'Google Book Search and metadata', *Cataloging and Classification Quarterly*, **49**(1), pp. 1–13.

Pratchett, T. (1989) *Guards! Guards!* London: Corgi.

Rogers, E. M. (2003) *Diffusion of Innovations* (5th edn). New York: Simon & Schuster.

Sartre, J.-P. (1967) *Words (Les Mots)*. Clephane, I. (tran.). London: Faber and Faber.

Scarry, E. (2001) *Dreaming by the Book*. Princeton, NJ: Princeton University Press.

Schmidt, E. (2005) 'The point of Google Print', *Official Google Blog*, 19 October 2005. Retrieved from: http://googleblog.blogspot.com/2005/10/point-of-google-print.html.

Tanner, S., Munoz, T. and Ros, P. H. (2009) 'Measuring mass text digitisation quality and usefulness: lessons learned from assessing the OCR accuracy of the British Library's 19th century online newspaper archive', *D*, **15**(7/8). Retrieved from: www.dlib.org/dlib/july09/munoz/07munoz.html.

Townsend, R. B. (2007) 'Google Books: what's not to like?', *AHA Today*, 30 April 2007. Retrieved from: http://blog.historians.org/articles/204/google-books-whats-not-to-like.

Van Dijck, J. (2005) 'From shoebox to performative agent: the computer as personal memory machine', *New Media and Society*, **7**(3), pp. 311–332. doi: 10.1177/1461444805050765.

Williams, R. (1977) *Marxism and Literature*. Oxford: Oxford University Press.

Wolf, M. (2008) *Proust and the Squid: The Story and Science of the Reading Brain*. Cambridge: Icon Books Ltd.

2 Digitised newspapers

Histories, contexts, behaviours

In 2001, Nicholson Baker (2001) courted controversy in the library sector by criticising the trend of libraries disposing of printed copies of newspapers once they had been microfilmed. This was not his first rodeo: he had previously written about the destruction of printed card catalogues after they had been transferred to Online Public Access Catalogues (OPACs). Baker, strident in his criticism of librarians in both cases, took issue not only with the technological shift but with the destruction of potentially significant sources of information about the history of information discovery:

> We can't blame Saracen sackers, B-52s, anarchists, or thieves; nor can we blame propagandist politicians intent on revising the past, moralistic book banners, or over-acidic formulations of paper. The villains, instead, are smart, well-meaning library administrators, quite certain that what they are doing is right for their institutions.
>
> (1994)

In the first instance, his ire was targeted at the destruction of the card catalogues, but he also took issue with problems in early OPACs such as poor authority control in newly created records, difficulties in searching the catalogues, irrelevant search results and greater noise being returned from searches. Digital resources have come a long way since then, but the problems associated with their implementation remain remarkably similar. Baker's later book is more relevant here, as it analyses the decision taken by some libraries to destroy historical newspapers, either by disposing of the originals after microfilm surrogates were made or through destructive scanning processes. Historical newspapers are often bound in large volumes which contain multiple editions of a particular title ordered by date. These are extremely unwieldy and difficult to scan, and destructive scanning is sometimes used to save time when such inconvenient source material is not considered worth keeping. In the case of newspapers, the pages are cut from the binding, leaving a sheaf of loose-leaf pages which can be loaded en masse into an automatic document feeder for scanning.

This has a number of operational benefits, not least of increasing efficiency, saving money and removing the need for careful handling. Of course, it also means that the original is destroyed, and the process is therefore quite unsuitable for unique or vulnerable items.

The decision to destroy newspapers arose from a belief that the original newspapers were no longer worth keeping, which Baker blamed upon two mistaken ideas: that the paper they were made of was of poor quality and therefore unsuitable for long-term preservation, and that microfilm, due to its longevity, provided a suitable preservation format. His argument against destroying newspapers focused on the "double fold" test he alleges was used to aid disposal decisions. (The double fold is a recognised test of paper folding endurance; it is used more commonly in the paper production process to determine the material's fold number, a numeric guide to its durability.) When testing newspapers, the process consisted simply of folding the corner of a page over twice: any pages which tore were considered to be damaged beyond repair. Baker claimed that not only did the test not replicate genuine reading conditions, but that "the damage to the paper didn't extend to the printed area of the page in the vast majority of cases" (2001). These allegations triggered a passionate response from librarians around the world, who were angered by Baker's confrontational style and his weak grasp of the realities of library practice. Zelden, for instance, took issue with the tone of the book:

> His book's distortions, half-truths and mischaracterizations are so offensive to so many cultural resource professionals and scholars, that his partly meritorious message gets lost in the controversy.
>
> (2001)

Despite the derailing effect of Baker's polemical approach, a useful discussion emerged regarding the gap between how the library profession views its role and how it is represented more widely. Baker, for instance, argues that all texts are essential cultural artefacts, and that libraries are the means to preserve them:

> Lest we become confused and forgetful, the function of a great library is to store obscure books ... Libraries are repositories for the out of print and the less desired, and we value them inestimably for that. The fact that most library books seldom circulate is part of the mystery and power of libraries.
>
> (Baker, 1994)

Yet in reality, preservation is only one of many library functions. As institutions, libraries are under pressure to balance preservation with access and user service, under tight financial constraints, in order to provide a rounded service which goes beyond acting as a static storage facility for old books. While Baker shows little awareness of the library's wide remit, his concern with preserving physical media after digitisation was met with some reactions that were equally dismissive of the complex negotiation between media forms and content: "Content matters, not format. Format only matters when it affects the endurance and transmission of content" (Quint, 2001). Quint's attitude betrays a worrying lack of understanding of the importance of the physical medium in codifying certain types of meaning, and mirrors recent pronouncements that "putting things on dead trees" (Toobin, 2007) is now obsolete. Yet these comments lead us towards the polemical framework which is a feature of technological discourse, by creating an either/or relationship between media. The specificity of physical and digital media alike makes them distinct and suggests that each will remain relevant for certain tasks or research questions. Darnton is typically insightful when identifying the underlying point that printed media are never neutral carriers to begin with: "newspapers are not transparent windows into a world we have lost, as Baker seems to think. They are collections of stories, written by professionals within the conventions of their craft" (2001). The difference for libraries in the digital age is that, instead of acting to preserve and facilitate access to physical texts, they are now directly involved in thinking through how our cultural heritage will be remediated online. The decisions that libraries make regarding presentation, access and digital formats will therefore play a huge role in defining how digitised materials are used online. Librarians increasingly fulfil the editorial role of which Mussell (2012) speaks but do so as part of a desire to meet one or more of a variety of library functions, and digitisation must therefore be viewed in terms of whether it achieves these aims.

This chapter will explore the issues for the identity of libraries in the digital age, using digitised newspapers as a focal point. To account for this focus, I have split this chapter into two sections. The first deals with the specific case of digitised newspapers. It will explore how newspapers grew as a medium in the United Kingdom and how libraries were involved in collecting them in a reasonably systematic way from an early point. The development of newspapers as a mass market medium shares characteristics with the contested spaces of the digital era, drawing parallels between how the physical record was created and the way in which news delivery has increasingly moved online in recent years. The second section deals with the ways in which digitisation has impacted upon conceptions of library identity, purpose and roles and then how Library and Information Science has already explored the question of researcher behaviour in physical archives. In Chapter 1, I made the case that the nature of online user behaviour in fact shares several similarities to researcher behaviour in physical archives. Here, I refer to previous studies into user behaviour in these differing environments to draw out the specific similarities. While digitised resources exist in abstraction from the physical artefact, this has not stopped their widespread uptake. There are facets of information behaviour which have been carried over from the physical text which are particularly well-supported by digital technologies. In order to understand why users have been so willing to use digitised newspapers, then, we must understand what those features are, while understanding the ways in which the specificity of digital media might impact negatively on other aspects of user experience.

The history of newspapers in the United Kingdom

> Where all the newes of all sorts shall be brought,
> And there be examin'd, and then registred,
> And so be issu'd under the Seale of the *Office*,
> As *Staple Newes*; no other newes be currant.
>   (Jonson, 1631)

Jonson's *The Staple of News* satirised the newspaper and news agency industry that emerged; from their origins in the seventeenth century, through their rise to prominence in the eighteenth century, to increased readership and mainstream popularity in the nineteenth and twentieth centuries, the social importance of newspapers has made them a vital primary historical source for modern researchers. They developed quickly from being niche publications to becoming culturally significant sources of news and contemporary information. But the history of newspapers is also the history of newspaper preservation. In the United Kingdom, certainly, we can trace the systematic collection of newspapers back to the early nineteenth century: libraries began to preserve newspapers well before their significance was recognised by scholars, meaning that the historical record while no means complete, spans the entire range of their history as a medium. The transfer of newspapers from physical form to electronic code is therefore just one part of the history of newspapers in libraries, a history filled with challenges in indexing, storing and providing access to hundreds of miles of densely printed materials. Digitisation is the latest step in transferring newspapers into a medium fit for twenty-first century consumption, but it is just the latest in a series of remediations that newspapers have undergone as a result of technological shifts in library service provision. This is not a history volume, and the history I provide below therefore relies on existing texts for its necessarily incomplete overview, but many authors that I have drawn on for this introduction provide high quality accounts which go into much more depth. Somerville (1996) and Raymond (2005) provide an excellent introduction to the development of the newsbook in these early years, while I have relied heavily upon Curran and Seaton (2010) as a guide to the development and character of the nineteenth century press.

Before 1600, little consideration seems to have been given to creating regularly scheduled news for public consumption, although printed news existed in the form of ballad books and government broadsides (Somerville, 1996). The earliest recurrently printed news sheets in England were printed by a handful of publishers in the 1620s. These precursors to the modern newspaper were inspired by continental *corantos*, the name of which referred to the current of information provided within, but the form of which more closely resembled existing book quartos (Deegan and Sutherland, 2009). By the 1640s, these publications had evolved into newsbooks which were generally published at least once a week. The right to print news was, with some exceptions, tightly controlled by the Crown. By the eighteenth century, though, the loosening of regulations preceded a growth in the number of newspapers available and a shift towards a form which was both revolutionary and more directly comparable to today's medium:

> Newspapers were different to other forms of printed news or commentary, such as pamphlets and prints, because they were regular and frequent. They therefore offered a predictable sequence of communication for which the only real counterpart was the weekly sermon.
>
> (Black, 2001)

The newspaper industry grew steadily throughout the eighteenth century amid continuing government attempts to control production, with many large cities gaining their own publications. As a result, there were over 150 newspaper titles in the UK by the early nineteenth century (Somerville, 1996). As newspapers became more common, the government found it increasingly difficult to control the industry through regulation. The burgeoning radical press, which was credited with bringing news to a huge working class readership, often avoided paying stamp duty. These publications were frequently anti-establishment, gaining a large readership through being read aloud and shared widely within communities; they could therefore claim a huge share of the total circulation of newspapers:

> By 1836 the unstamped press published in London had an aggregate readership of at least two million. According to government estimates, its circulation exceeded that of the respectable, stamped press.
>
> (Curran and Seaton, 2010)

This huge market grew further in the mid-nineteenth century due to improvements in transport infrastructure and literacy. Contemporary news became more accessible to a mass audience, which led to newspapers being viewed by the establishment as sources of radical opposition that allowed for continuity of the connection between press freedom and civil liberty (ibid.).

The government therefore attempted to censor the radical press via taxation and regulation throughout the nineteenth century, but radical newspapers continued to ignore stamp duty and taxation on advertising income. Instead, a combination of industrialisation and market forces eventually limited the reach of the radical press. This was due to the increasing cost of newspaper production: in the early and mid-nineteenth century, it cost just a few pounds to launch a small periodical, but the rising cost of machinery and materials to serve the mass market created a financial barrier which excluded those who were unable to meet prohibitive setup costs. *The Daily Mail,* for instance, required £500,000 in 1896 to cover "the initial costs of machinery, buildings, ink factories and the like, and this was altogether apart from the capital required for daily working expenses" (Curran and Seaton, 2010).

Despite the importance of newspapers as a communications medium, Stoker claims that "the recognition that they contain a mass of valuable information not available elsewhere is only a comparatively recent phenomenon" (1999). He refers here to their significance as an academic source, but their importance as an archival artefact has in fact been long recognised. Even as early as the nineteenth century, there were many attempts to catalogue and record newspaper publications, so that the information contained within could be retrieved in perpetuity. Individuals created directories and indexes of contents to aid discovery (Jones, 1996), while libraries were already involved in systematically collecting the stamped press at a relatively early date. Such efforts fell under the remit of the British Museum, and its library, which were established in 1753 by the Royal Assent of King George II. For over 200 years, the library remained part of the British Museum, with responsibility for collecting printed publications in Britain. It grew in size and significance in the nineteenth century under the supervision of Anthony Pazzini and became increasingly recognised as the national library of Britain. It wasn't until 1873 that the British Museum library became a separate institution, though: as a result of the British Library Act, its collections formed the basis of the newly formed British Library. In 1833, the British Museum arranged for copies of newspapers deposited with the Stamp Office in London to be transferred to the British Museum for permanent storage. By 1848, this arrangement had already been extended to include English and Welsh provincial newspapers, and latterly Irish and Scottish newspapers (Jones, 1996). The agreement was formalised under the legal deposit legislation of 1869, meaning that the majority of newspapers from the UK and Ireland were deposited directly with the British Museum library (King, 2007). The history of other national library newspaper collections is, sadly, less thoroughly documented. The National Library of Wales (NLW), established by Royal Charter in 1907, based its collections upon the holdings of the Welsh Library at the recently founded University of Wales in Aberystwyth, and books were first collected in 1873 with the intention of founding a national library. It has since become one of six legal deposit libraries in the United Kingdom, with a special remit to collect and preserve Welsh cultural outputs and therefore purchase printed materials of Welsh and Celtic interest. The library holds roughly 40 newspaper publications from the nineteenth century, all with direct relevance to Wales, with a total size of around a million newspaper pages. The National Library of Scotland is the main repository for Scottish newspapers, although it does not publicise the precise extent of its collections. Its predecessor was the Advocates Library, which was founded in the seventeenth century and served as the national deposit library for Scotland until 1925. The Advocates Library, in common with so many other institutions, did not have the room to store its newspaper collections. They therefore did not collect newspapers during the nineteenth century, despite their entitlement to do so, and this has led to uneven coverage of older newspapers in the NLS collections.

As a result of these historical differences, the BL's collections represent the largest single source of historical newspapers in the UK. In total, the library houses an estimated 750 million newspaper pages within its physical collections, comprising 53,198 unique titles and 370,000 reels of microfilm on nearly 50 kilometres of shelf space (Fleming and Walravens, 2011). The scale of this collection and the potential online audience contrast strongly with the facilities that were available at the BL's newspaper reading rooms at Colindale. The reading rooms consisted of just 77 desks, serving roughly 30,000 annual visitors (British Library, 2011). In late 2013, the Colindale facility closed to the public, to be replaced by a state-of-the-art storage facility in Boston Spa and a dedicated reading room at the BL's St. Pancras headquarters.

The BL's modern, multimedia-news research space is the latest solution to the problem of processing huge amounts of newspapers. Unprecedented growth in the volume of newsprint being produced led to storage difficulties which have persisted to the modern day. By the late nineteenth century, the British Museum library found the situation so urgent that they sought to dispose of their collections of provincial newspapers using the British Museum Bill of 1900. This proposal met with fierce opposition, and an alternative plan was implemented to build a newspaper repository on a new site in Colindale. The first repository building contained no facilities for readers and again filled swiftly to capacity. A new building was created in 1932, the first to contain onsite reader facilities; after being destroyed by bombing in 1940, alongside an estimated 6,000 volumes of English provincial and Irish newspapers, it was eventually replaced in 1957 by a second building (British Library, 2012). Space, access and preservation of newspaper materials have clearly been longstanding problems for institutions. The British Library has invested considerable resources into addressing these problems, particularly in widening access by creating surrogate versions of newspaper materials. As a result, the physical archive has undergone many changes since its nascent collections were begun centuries ago.

Large-scale digitisation of newspapers occurs at a time when contemporary news media has been profoundly affected by online consumption. The market for print newspapers shrinks every year; traditional journalism has come under threat from citizen journalists, start-up media platforms and social media's role in disseminating news. Franklin sums these challenges up in with the pithy phrase, "the contraction of legacy media continues apace" (2014). He elaborates on the shift from print news to digital delivery:

> In the United Kingdom ... the larger, city-based, daily local papers have suffered disproportionate losses of titles, circulation and staff, compared to the traditional weekly paid newspapers. The loss of advertising revenues has been critical in shaping this decline. By 2017 newspaper advertising in the United Kingdom is projected to have fallen to £1.9 billion (11.2 per cent of market share), while significantly, digital advertising spend will grow from £7 billion (47.5 per cent) in 2014 to a prominence above all legacy media at £9 billion (53.8 per cent) in 2017.
>
> (Franklin, 2014)

The encroachment of new media organisations signals a shift in the way that news is presented online. Franklin refers to digital advertising, much of which is distributed not by sales of copies of newspapers but by the number of hits that news websites receive. This has led to the "BuzzFeedification" of the news media (O'Neil, 2013), a term coined to address the influence of the successful website BuzzFeed in pushing viral content out via social media platforms in order to draw large audiences. The tension between the push culture of media corporations, intent on garnering large audiences, and the desire of the sovereign user to produce and consume content on their own terms means that the internet is a contested space. But this challenging environment for news production is not new. The transition to digital media has led to comparisons between the nineteenth century press and the internet, with both becoming contested forms where market forces and ideology collide. Chase claims that "something about the character of the internet is reminiscent of Chartism – sprawling, undisciplined, democratic and open yet dominated by a handful of leading players" (2009). Curran and Seaton expand on this analogy, in language which reinforces the influence of the digital sublime in our technological discourses:

> In the nineteenth century, people were so awed by the emancipatory power of the newspaper and periodical that it became the convention to refer to the press with an upper case "P". When this awe gave way to familiarity, the press was denoted by a lower case "p", and commentary about the press became more sensible. Convention requires that the internet be designated with an upper case "I" ... The wonderment of this convention goes some way towards explaining why so much current discussion of the net is so inadequate.
>
> (Curran and Seaton, 2010)

Our sense of wonderment at the possibilities of innovative media, or indeed technologies, is a constant thread throughout this book. Newspapers sit in this conceptual space: the early years of the nineteenth century were characterised by a mistrust of newspapers and news reporting, based upon their novelty. This can be traced at least as far back as Jonson's *The Staple of News*. Jones (1996) writes that the cheap newspaper was regarded as a new untested form of communication, important because of the freshness of the form and the changing social world in which it existed. Like the internet, social change from newspapers was partly driven by market forces. In the case of the nineteenth century press, popular newspapers were gradually forced to concentrate on entertainment rather than in-depth political issues, and as the working classes were priced out of the means of production, they were increasingly viewed as consumers rather than producers of newsprint. As a result, ownership of the press transferred to wealthy businessmen, and a commercial reliance on advertising meant that controversial titles found growth difficult. The present discourse around large-scale digitisation is therefore shared with the historical discourse around the newspaper medium. That newspapers have been heavily digitised in recent years is just one of the reasons for their contemporary importance as a focal lens for exploring wider issues around digitisation, including user behaviour, access and the impact of digitisation on libraries as institutions.

Issues for the identity of libraries in the digital age

The definition and value of libraries as cultural institutions are not fixed and are therefore liable to be affected by technological and cultural shifts. National libraries are a unique part of the library sector, in the sense that their contemporary activities are largely shaped by the question of posterity. Library services commonly plan for the long term, but national libraries are positioned in the difficult space between serving contemporary information needs through the provision of rich collections based upon legal deposit, the need to ensure that contemporary rights holders are not financially inconvenienced by the reuse of national library collections, and the need to secure the long-term survival of the ever-growing collections that they hold. Peter Brophy provides a strong definition for the role of the national library in contemporary society:

> The national library provides a cultural focal point which transcends the present and reaches into the past, in terms of the "stuff" it secures, and into the future, in terms of transmitting human knowledge to future generations. It fulfils these roles by collecting a representative, although never comprehensive, set of records and by ensuring that they are organized and preserved so as to remain of use in the future.
>
> (Brophy, 2007)

Brophy sensibly emphasises the long-term nature of national library activities. The commercial sector, for all its involvement in large-scale digitisation, has a long history of high profile failures and cancelled projects. Google has an extensive tradition of closing resources which many users still find essential, while there are examples of large-scale digitisation programmes which have been closed due to commercial pressures. Microsoft, for instance, launched their Live Book Search service in 2006. Despite working with a number of libraries to digitise books and make them searchable, they were unable to compete with the dramatic scale of Google Book Search and closed the project in 2008. In this case, Microsoft ensured the longevity of their work by donating digital copies of all books to their partner libraries and depositing the entire collection with the Internet Archive, but there is no guarantee that other companies would ensure such a favourable outcome when mothballing a project. There is significant risk of data loss in the event that a company ceases trading or simply chooses to stop supporting a particular resource. Such high profile cancellations show that national libraries still provide a more stable repository of human knowledge in the long term.

But the efforts of national libraries do not exist in isolation. Google and its peers have increased the pressure for libraries to digitise their collections through commercial digitisation activity. Google Books has signalled a sea change in the expectations of users, who are now used to being able to access huge amounts of information from any device with an internet connection. Tech companies are thus seen as competitors to libraries. The differing priorities of these sectors, though, ensure that this is not the case at a conceptual level. Commercial companies shape the service that users demand and drive competition with cultural heritage organisations for the attention of audiences, but their interest in providing information does not transcend the contemporary. The question of access is the key driver of competition and is a fundamental concern for libraries in the early twenty-first century. Brophy comments that "the idea that the library's *primary* role is to provide access to books, journals and other sources of information is relatively modern" (2007), and yet this role is now integral to how libraries are viewed in society. Increased availability of information from other online sources, facilitated by internet technologies which have in turn fuelled the ability to reach a larger audience, has positioned access as one of the key benefits of cultural heritage digitisation. Indeed, Lankes notes that access has now become a service in itself:

> The way something is organized, displayed, and addressed is a service that varies by the community that puts up the content. It used to be said that content was king, but on the web it seems context rules the castle.
>
> (2011)

It is here that libraries have not yet reached the mass audience with the message of their continued relevance in the digital age. Even the huge advances in scale achieved by Google are built on the collections that have been carefully constructed, curated and preserved over many centuries by the major libraries of the world. An increasing number of major collections from libraries have reached the public domain online and have been used in transformative ways which clearly demonstrate the value that libraries continue to offer, and yet the popular discourse is dominated by the marketing machines of tech companies which effectively marginalise, even malign, the contribution made by libraries. The idea that Google can produce better results through the sheer brute force of their programming teams has come to be accepted, despite high profile failings in Google Books which could have been addressed with careful attention to existing standards and quality controls. The vital difference between the activities of libraries and the wider heritage sector, engaged in long-term preservation of the human record and the commercial aims of tech companies is therefore widely misunderstood.

In reality, commercial input has been vital in supporting large-scale digitisation activities in the public sector. The savings made by mitigating costs through commercial partnerships can therefore be considerable. The National Archives, for instance, offered commercial companies the opportunity to work in partnership to create co-branded online services under its Licensed Internet Associates Programme. It estimates that commercial partners have invested the equivalent of £53 million into digitising and providing ongoing support for National Archives content. In return, commercial partners are free to monetise the digitised materials under the terms of their agreement. Similarly, the Bodleian Library was an early UK library partner for Google Books, providing books for scanning in return for free archival copies. One of the primary benefits was the creation by Google of a dedicated website where scanned copies were made immediately available online to accredited Bodleian users. Other institutions have benefited from allocating specialist work to expert contractors. The NLW outsourced the OCR scanning of its digitised newspapers, complicated by the bilingual source material, allowing it to access cutting edge technology without the potential inefficiency of investing in staff and infrastructure for the short duration of the project. These factors ensure that the overall costs of large-scale digitisation can be considerably lower through involving commercial partners than for projects funded through project-based programmes.

Guaranteeing sustainability for internally funded projects is also difficult. Many projects are funded for a specific period of time to create a digital resource, and there have been longstanding questions over what happens to these resources after the cessation of the project period. Sustainability in this context is the ability to maintain, update and provide continued access to the digital resource in the long term. This commitment requires ongoing time and finance, and we cannot assume that open access is achievable merely because a resource receives public funding in the first instance.

Griffiths and Maron (2009), for instance, note that when the National Archives undertakes projects internally, it sometimes has to plan to cover its costs by charging for access. This naturally causes a substantial drop in access and, indeed, in opportunity for those without the resources to pay. In this respect, agreements which promise open access can be problematic for institutions in the long term:

> The free at the point of use and open access objectives are currently time limited. No-one yet knows how costly it is going to be to keep the collections going, to develop them technically, to improve their interfaces, and in some cases to add more content.
>
> (Sykes, 2008)

Even so, the presence of external partners has received a great deal of criticism. The majority of items in research and national libraries are of limited financial value when digitised, regardless of their historical or scholarly importance. They largely resemble a long tail of little-used texts that are retained on grounds that would please Nicholson Baker – that somebody will find them useful, some day. Commercial partners, on the other hand, require profitable collections and thus tend to prioritise materials which meet the public appetite for genealogy and family history. A bias is therefore instilled in digitised resources towards the profitable, the mainstream, the paid-for, and public institutions are still left with responsibility for digitising difficult or niche materials. There are doubts over the willingness of business to support digital resources beyond their commercial viability. The long-term responsibility for sustaining resources can fall upon institutions once any profitable life has expired, along with the commercial value of selling access or even actively maintaining the resource. As Deegan and Sutherland comment:

> There needs to be an active will to preserve digital content ... and constant intervention will be required for the foreseeable future to ensure that all necessary preservation tasks are carried out.
>
> (2009)

Without this will, we risk the so-called "digital dark age", where responsibility for preserving digital cultural heritage is concentrated in the hands of corporations which have no duty to act in the public interest. Preservation is an ongoing cost, with no guarantee that commercial companies will reach a favourable outcome when their interest in supporting the resource ends. The question of ownership is particularly important. Google, for instance, retains all original scans, metadata and algorithms relating to GBS, providing libraries with a derivative library copy with limited reuse rights for archival purposes. The National Archives has previously admitted that much of the metadata relating to its digitised collections remains the intellectual property of the commercial partner, and there is a continued sense that the quality of commercially produced metadata can be inferior to public sector efforts.

It has become essential not just for libraries to provide digital services to their users, but to simultaneously interrogate how their efforts interact with those of commercial providers to reflect emerging trends in access to information. Increasing the openness of library collections is one way of achieving this. The act of transmitting collections beyond library walls is increasingly trivial in a purely technical sense, yet the librarian's role in providing expert assistance is harder to translate. Therefore, the problem for libraries is not the relevance of their collections to modern users but adapting their service models to support users who may be unaware of the origins of the material that they access. MacLeish, writing in 1971, claimed:

> The fact is, of course, that these new facilities for the dissemination of information became available precisely at a time when the great human need is not for additional information or more rapid information or more universally available information but for the comprehension of the enormous quantities of existing information the scientific and other existing triumphs of the last several generations have already dumped into our minds.
>
> (1971)

The underlying need for libraries to facilitate high quality information sources, as well as make them available at scale, remains despite seismic technological shifts since the 1970s, and the huge increase in material available online from other sources makes this more pressing. As a sector, we can be guilty of assuming that merely providing huge digitised databases is an end in itself, but a dramatic increase in the scale of resources demands a deeper engagement with how library services deal with the changing research context that comes with such an endeavour. The role of the librarian is one of mediator between "man and book, where book is a generic term that includes all graphic records" (Shera, 1972); in the era of large-scale digitisation there remains a need for the mediator, but this need must be approached sensitively. Torkington (2011) has forcefully argued that some libraries have mistaken gatekeeping for mediation, and unless they match their undoubted success in digitising collections with an improvement in access to their online collections, they risk undermining their value in the public eye when compared to otherwise extremely different organisations.

Existing research into online user behaviour

It is, then, perhaps unsurprising that the LIS community has often been absent from the wider social discourse on the impact of digitisation and digital resources. There have been a number of important studies in the discipline which have presented evidence for the impact of digitisation, but the focus has been on the use and users of digital resources rather than a wider consideration of the intellectual and cultural implications. This body of research uses a variety of approaches to evaluating the impact of digital resources, with impact often poorly defined as a concept. Here I return to Tanner's definition of impact, introduced in Chapter 1:

> The measurable outcomes arising from the existence of a digital resource that demonstrate a change in the life or life opportunities of the community for which the resource is intended.
>
> (2012)

His definition underlines the importance of moving away from solely statistical studies, which focus upon quantitative measures such as the number of users and the size of the digital network surrounding resources, to demonstrate the tangible impact of resources. As he points out (2012), many LIS studies have relied purely on quantitative metrics to successfully indicate the popularity of a resource without necessarily demonstrating how this translates into a genuine impact for its users. Meyer (2011) makes a similar point, noting that the metric-based approach adopted by many studies has not been conducive to clearly defining the impact that digital resources are having on cultural institutions. For this reason, a critical approach to research methods is vital: there are methodological steps that we, as researchers, can take to overcome the limitations of our work which make it fall short of more widely applicable significance.

The concept of value for users has been severely underexplored for digital resources, although there has been some work which attempts to address this. Tanner and Deegan, for instance, have advocated for the benefits of digital resources for the academic community. Their 2010 report, entitled "Inspiring research, inspiring scholarship", gathers and synthesises evidence from JISC-funded digital resources and beyond to build a case for their importance in teaching, learning, research, leisure and supporting the Digital Britain agenda. The result is a wide-ranging report which argues that digital resources continue to transform the research process, supporting users in asking new, increasingly complex questions and enhancing learning and teaching. It proposes that the key consideration for impact assessment must be to look at value in terms of the core principle of how a resource changes people's lives. The authors provide the following example, demonstrating the benefit of the BL's digitised newspapers for authorial research:

> Author Kate Summerscale's best-selling book *The Suspicions of Mr. Whicher* draws heavily on contemporary newspaper reports of the famous Nineteenth Century murder trial. Kate found that the BL's digitised archive added new dimensions to her story.
>
> (Tanner and Deegan, 2010)

The use of such a high profile example is instructive because, by its very nature, it is not representative of the majority of users of large-scale digitised collections. The benefits for other user groups largely centre on huge leaps in access to digital resources, the availability of materials outside library walls, the volume of material available to users, and the ways in which that material can be used to undertake new research questions and support emerging methods. In a sense, then, identifying high profile examples of impact risks undermining the more prosaic but equally important examples of impact that many other researchers have found, for better or worse. Taken individually, these examples are instructive; taken across the entire LIS discipline, the seductiveness of the high profile impacts can lead to an unrealistic expectation of the extent of change. One way in which this has been manifested is in the mistaken assumption that the digitised record is in any way comprehensive, or even representative, in its current state. Bingham, for instance, overestimates the comprehensiveness of digitised newspaper collections when he asserts that:

> Historians can be far more confident that content will not elude them and that they will track down obscure and potentially revealing articles. Biographers can ensure that they have read every mention of their subject in the press.
>
> (2010)

On the contrary, there is no way of knowing to what extent a particular topic is represented in the digitised archive: the lack of interoperability and the huge amount of uncatalogued and undigitised material in libraries suggest that comprehensiveness is an unrealistic goal. Indeed, it is potentially harmful for the way that we view the impact of digitisation.

James Mussell (2012) addresses these changes at length, applying the question of academic value to the case of digitised newspapers. He notes that digitising large tracts of the nineteenth century press has transformed how material is discovered and recovered. The sheer amount of material available entirely changes the profile of the press in scholarly research and teaching. It has become less frequently ignored by academics due to the increased ease of access, while also being more representative of the historical record than was possible previously. Mussell argues that the digital form has always represented a transformation of the source material and reiterates the importance of recognising the editorial elements of any digitisation project:

> Identifying which aspects of a printed object are to be reproduced in the new media is thus an important interpretive process ... the entire object is available for translation, forcing editors to identify the significant aspects that must be modelled in digital form.
>
> (2012)

A full consideration of the impact of digitisation must inevitably consider what the nature of the material transformation is, while recognising the possibility that this transformation manifests itself in both positive and negative ways. Understanding digital media as separate intellectual forms, with their own particular strengths and weaknesses, can help us to cut through the polemic and more deeply understand impact in terms of the reality of contemporary usage. Mussell argues that the digital form demands a critical reader of the nineteenth century press and a critical user of digital resources. While we gain a multitude of information online, we now lack details of who produced and contributed to the press and some of the shared cultural resources which come from being a historical contemporary, as he notes:

> We struggle to realize the meanings and effects such texts had for their readers: the pleasure of reading, the surprise or shock of their appearance, the nuances of description, the familiarity or novelty of what was under discussion, or glancing references and allusions.
>
> (2012)

Mussell's work stops short of applying this critical approach directly to specific cases of digitised collections, but he provides a reminder of the importance of a critical approach to impact evaluation. This can be usefully positioned within the idea of change in comparison to previous technologies and practices. I will therefore turn to consider our current understanding of how users currently interact with resources.

The critical debate around newspaper digitisation has often focused on the impact of web technologies on the textual artefact. The trend towards article-level representation in digitised newspaper collections foregrounds the partial textual manuscript, even though the article is just one element of a larger whole. The loss of context is therefore one of the primary effects of newspaper digitisation, as materials shift away from physical artefacts and towards web interfaces. Brake sounds a note of caution about the negative impact of this shift, arguing that:

> Digital representation of nineteenth-century copy denaturalizes it and transforms the *reader* who is rapidly scanning the *content* of the print page (and looking past the naturalized medium) into a *user* who sees the content inextricably embedded in the matrix of the newspaper pages, which are not comfortably accommodated on the computer screen of by software.
>
> (Brake, 2012)

Her concerns are intimately linked to the perception that digital media could have a detrimental effect on our intellectual capabilities. When Sven Birkets (1994) mourned the perceived shift away from the printed text towards the mediated digital form, he embedded the idea of loss into his argument, framing his work as an elegy for a threatened form. This evocation of the social language of death provides a metaphor for digital media, which immediately presents them as oppositional to the survival of existing forms. He argues that this alleged metaphorical death is worrying because the inherent characteristics of each medium ensure that readers are more deeply engaged with physical books than the digital text. To Birkets, our experience of the physical text is one of deep, uninterrupted engagement with individual texts in a sustained and intellectually rewarding manner that is diminished by the characteristics of the digital media which threaten it. Digital texts, in this account, not only demand a new form of interaction from the reader, but actively erode the reader's ability to interact deeply with physical texts as a result. Critics of digital media more recent than Birkets draw on this oppositional relationship: the digital, these critics claim, is both different from and worse than the physical because it threatens to diminish and replace existing intellectual paradigms. Nicholas Carr, for instance, anecdotally describes the insidious effects of digital technologies on his own attention span and intellectual abilities.

> I'm not thinking the way I used to think. I feel it most strongly when I'm reading. I used to find it easy to immerse myself in a book or a lengthy article. My mind would get caught up in the twists of the narrative or the turns of the argument, and I'd spend hours strolling through long stretches of prose ... Now my concentration starts to drift after a page or two. I get fidgety, lose the thread, begin looking for something else to do. I feel like I'm always dragging my wayward brain back to the text.
>
> (Carr, 2010)

He claims that these behavioural changes signal a wider change in our ability to read deeply, caused by the proliferation of digital media. In doing so, he sets up the same oppositional relationship as Birkets; reading the physical text is a deep, intellectually rewarding experience, while digital reading is intellectually diminishing. This diminishing aspect is evident in other accounts. Edwards (2013), for instance, argues that making historical manuscripts available to the public damages their intellectual foundations, by opening up scholarly sources to people who cannot approach them in an informed way. The behaviours that these critics place in opposition to the supposedly dangerous encroachment of digital technologies are in fact just one small subset of user behaviour: sustained scholarly engagement with one particular text, where the reader is dedicating significant periods of time to inhabiting and understanding the text. But they propose a media-centric understanding of technological diffusion, implying that the specific impact of the digital medium is inevitable. Leaving aside the question of how far the evidence supports claims of the internet fundamentally rewiring our brains, this position ignores the complex cultural processes by which technologies are adopted, as well as the external influences upon user behaviour online. Bawden and Robinson argue that Information Science researchers "while being fully involved with technology … should avoid being consumed by it" (2013). The same charge can equally be levelled at high profile theorists who appear in thrall to the concept of technological determinism and thus assume the position of the audience as passive consumers of disruptive innovations, rather than as engaged participants in a larger cultural negotiation.

The diminishing representation of digital media and the overwrought tone are evident in other accounts, which argue that the widespread availability of historical manuscripts to the general public removes barriers to access to the academic field which risk the possibility of sub-standard scholarship emerging. Harking back to Walter Benjamin's account of mechanical reproduction, the *aura* of the physical artefact shapes these concerns. But it is this focus on the aura that places physical editions in opposition to digital media, precisely because it is so difficult to translate any medium with its context intact. These passionate attacks on digital representation carry an inherent defence of existing intellectual paradigms; or rather, they defend an idealised intellectual paradigm which does not represent the full range of scholarly behaviour. In defending an idealised representation of just one aspect of information behaviour, the focus of these accounts on the reading experience effectively disallows the possibility that there may be other clear benefits to digital media that make any potential loss for the user worthwhile. Edwards argues that digitisation is negative for those who study or edit books in their material forms, claiming that "a willingness to trust surrogates is a willingness to abandon scholarly responsibility" (2013). Within the specific case of material book studies this may be the case, but for other purposes audiences already rely upon surrogates. Whether scholarly editions, digitised manuscripts, translated texts or microfilmed newspapers, researcher engagement with surrogates is a longstanding reality for many. The relationship between researcher and text is a mediated one, with an individual or group tasked with translating the text from one form or another acting as the mediator. There is a person, or people, behind each surrogate, and therefore the scholarly effort occurs not in tracking down the original but in critically evaluating the surrogate. Researchers have not moved directly from physical originals to digitised remediations but have, in fact, applied this criticality to a series of format changes which have influenced the research experience. Binding, for instance, has played an essential role in preserving newspapers for considerable time. When reader facilities were added to the original Colindale newspaper repository in 1932, a bindery was also created. It remained in operation until 2001, by which time it had preserved thousands of newspapers in a variety of styles of bound volumes (Ryan, 2014). The shift to microfilm occurred after the shift to bound volumes, and the format of many newspapers of archival record has not fully resembled the original artefact for many years: instead, it has moved from the original to bound volumes of newspapers, to microfilm and now to digitised files. As Nicholson notes, "by the time we access them, many digital newspapers have been remediated three times ... each step serves to distance us from the original text" (2013).

With newspapers, then, the physical ideal has not been accessible for a long time, and researchers are in fact adapting to another in a long line of format changes which have been undertaken to facilitate either preservation or increased access to collections. This latest adaptation has led to improvements in working conditions for some, given that digitised collections have relied frequently on microfilm as a source material. Darnton provides a particularly vivid description of the trials of using microfilm for research:

> Reading microfilm is hell. Hours spent cranking blurry images under a hot light and staring at a screen can turn you off research and even turn your stomach ... Entire years are missing from important newspapers, and there are no complete sets of the originals anywhere in existence, because librarians have got rid of them.
>
> (2001)

This unflattering description of microfilm illustrates that, while digitised remediations can work to distance readers from the physical text, they still offer distinct benefits which must be recognised to understand why researchers use them so heavily. Mainstream debates about the impact of digitisation upon scholarly practices often lack this understanding, ignoring the literature around scholarly information behaviour. The ideal to which writers such as Carr refer bears little resemblance to how physical newspapers are used for research, according to the research that exists. These accounts tell us that researchers use newspapers very differently; even with physical newspapers, the lack of indexes and complete publication records require researchers to spend significant periods of time browsing and visually scanning newspapers and surrogates to find relevant information. Large-scale digitised collections are excellent vehicles for facilitating this form of user behaviour, allowing users to adopt the filtering and automation that I have argued are key strategies for navigating information overload.

Sue Stone noted in 1982 that the literature regarding the information needs and uses of humanities and scholars was piecemeal and confusing. Undoubtedly, the literature in this area has grown in quality and usefulness since then, but there remains a gap in knowledge of how people interact with particular media. The body of work which relates most closely to newspapers is that which explores the information seeking behaviour of historians in physical archives. Levy (1997) notes that digital resources are a locus for search, acquisition and reading, and my argument for the rest of this chapter is twofold: first, that user behaviour in digitised collections in fact resembles archival information seeking to a large degree; and second, that we must widen our understanding of online user behaviour to take into account that the web interface provides a single focus for complex information behaviour that previously took place across a variety of sources. My exploration of user behaviour is therefore, by necessity, a whistle-stop tour. Others have already given thorough accounts. Dalton and Charnigo (2004) provide an excellent review of the literature relating to pre-digital information seeking, but the most relevant studies assess user behaviour within historical archives. Duff and Johnson, for instance, consider the information seeking behaviour of historians. They present the findings of a qualitative study which focuses particularly on archival research, using interviews and questionnaires to discover patterns of behaviour. They emphasise the vital importance of information seeking to researchers before they access printed sources:

> Examining finding aids was a key strategy to reduce uncertainty when visiting a new archive or starting to look at a new collection. Some participants suggested they used the finding aids to get a sense of the whole ... of the collection.
>
> (2002)

The centrality of finding aids and their importance for orientating scholars predate the introduction of online discovery. Even as researchers rely increasingly on the web, filtering strategies remain vital to physical and digital resource discovery alike, alongside the need for researchers to orientate themselves to a new archival environment. Even for users familiar with the norms of the reading room, there is a need to familiarise oneself with each new environment which shortens the effective time available for research.

Reading is an important archival discovery strategy which involves reading primary and secondary sources in order to note patterns and frequent occurrences of particular names and places and to identify other sources that may be useful in future. Historians therefore read vast quantities of material in their research, even if this more accurately resembles skim reading in the first instance. And while reading remains essential, it does not occur as an isolated phenomenon but as part of a wider series of activities that can occur at any time. Ellis (1993) and Uva (1977) de-emphasise the importance of sequential stages of research, focusing on the multiple activities in which a researcher may be engaged at any point. Case outlines the various stages which can occur:

Choosing and refining topics, planning and conducting studies, gathering and interpreting evidence, and writing and revising manuscripts can go on concurrently, both within and across projects.

(1991)

This bears more in common with online behaviour than allowed for by the narrative of technological disruption. In particular, it suggests that the bouncing behaviour of online users (Nicholas *et al.*, 2004) is not unprecedented. Instead, digitised resources represent an acceleration of the scholarly primitives of discovering, annotating, comparing, referring, sampling, illustrating and representing that Unsworth (2000) has argued form the basis for all scholarly projects. In his influential article, Unsworth points out that these functions would logically form the basis for computer-based scholarship. Many of these behaviours are actively supported by the facilities which digitised collections provide, meaning that historians commonly suggested that options such as keyword searching would prove useful to their research in physical archives (Duff and Johnson, 2002). The importance allocated to reading in the debate around digital media is therefore not borne out in reality. The multifaceted nature of research emphasises the importance of multiple routes to discovery, while underscoring that deep reading, if it does occur, is not strongly represented in the information seeking phase of research. It is therefore unsurprising that the most significant studies undertaken by LIS researchers do not share the negative views of writers such as Birkets and Carr. Instead, as I argued in Chapter 1, they have been positive about the overall impact of digitisation, instead focusing on aspects of its implementation that provide difficulties for users.

Summary: concurrent discourses of digitisation

While the wider debate around digitisation and digital media shows no obvious sign of consensus and tends towards the polemic, researchers in LIS have presented generally positive evidence for the impact of digitisation. To date, the focus has not been on large-scale digitisation as a specific phenomenon but on the use and users of digital resources in general. In this chapter, I have argued that there is a disconnect between these two critical discourses, with the mainstream debate tending towards the mythical account of technology and thus closely resembling the model of Mosco's digital sublime. The benefits of digitised collections over physical collections are clear and numerous. In the archive, the lack of indexes and complete publications, the presence of extraneous information and the sheer scale of the newspaper archive necessitate significant periods of browsing and scanning original newspapers and surrogates in order to identify relevant information. In this particular respect, digital remediation can provide an excellent surrogate for archival information seeking practices. The extent to which this represents a change from existing practices and the methods by which we can track this change form the focus of the remaining chapters of this book. Chapters 2 and 3 have argued for the relevance of a theoretical framework which understands technological discourse in terms of its mythologising tendency and has noted the presence of this tendency in arguments around digital media. Brake's contrast between the value-laden concepts of *reader* and *user* are vital. The shift from physical to digital media has necessitated a shift in our understanding of the text which moves us away from the artefact and towards the interface. Our interactions with material in the large-scale digitised archive are mediated primarily through the web interface, which provides the locus for discovery, browsing, reading and analysis. Yet, in doing so, it recreates many of the features of the physical archive with a great deal of success.

The process of technological adoption is not an inevitability. Instead, the desire of users to adopt a new technology is driven by social and cultural factors, but also by the utility of the new technology for their purposes. The widespread adoption of LSDC demonstrates their value to researchers. Rather than framing the debate in oppositional terms, searching for what has changed in the transition to digital, impact analyses can help to build our understanding of an additive technology which has clear real-world benefits by adopting an evidence-driven approach to evaluating the extent of change wrought by digitisation. Research methods for evaluating impact must therefore be devised with this in mind, and with the aim of discovering both benefits and drawbacks. The following chapter will consider some methods by which this can be achieved. It presents the case for using mixed methodology as a conscious response to the hyperbolic debate around digital technologies and provides a brief description of how some of the most popular impact evaluation methods can be utilised together to achieve this aim.

Bibliography

Baker, N. (1994) 'Discards', *The New Yorker*, 4 April 1994. Retrieved from: www.newyorker.com/magazine/1994/04/04/discards.

Baker, N. (2001) *Double Fold: Libraries and the Assault on Paper*. New York: Random House.

Bawden, D. and Robinson, L. (2013) 'No such thing as society? On the individuality of information behaviour', *Journal of the American Society for Information Science and Technology*, **64**(123), pp. 2587–2590.

Bingham, A. (2010) 'The digitization of newspaper archives: opportunities and challenges for historians', *Twentieth Century British History*, **21**(2), pp. 225–231. doi: 10.1093/tcbh/hwq007.

Birkets, S. (1994) *The Gutenberg Elegies: The Fate of Reading in an Electronic Age*. New York: Ballentine Books.

Black, J. (2001) *The English Press 1621–1861*. Stroud, Gloucestershire: Sutton Publishing.

Brake, L. (2012) 'Half full and half empty', *Journal of Victorian Culture*, **17**(2), pp. 222–229. doi: http://dx.doi.org/10.1080/13555502.2012.683151.

British Library (2011) 'Knowledge, inspiration, innovation: thirty-eighth annual report and accounts 2010–11'. British Library. Retrieved from: www.bl.uk/aboutus/annrep/2010to2011/annualreport10_11.pdf.

British Library (2012) 'History of British Library newspapers', British Library. Retrieved from: www.bl.uk/reshelp/findhelprestype/news/historicalblnews/index.html

Brophy, P. (2007) *The Library in the Twenty-First Century* (2nd edn). London: Facet Publishing.

Carr, N. (2010) *The Shallows: How the Internet Is Changing the Way We Read, Think and Remember*. London: Atlantic Books.

Case, D. O. (1991) 'The collection and use of information by some American historians: a study of motives and methods', *Library Quarterly*, **61**, pp. 61–82.

Chase, M. (2009) 'Digital chartists: online resources for the study of chartism', *Journal of Victorian Culture*, **14**(2), pp. 294–301. doi: 10.3366/E135555020900085X.

Curran, J. and Seaton, J. (2010) *Power without Responsibility* (7th edn). London and New York: Routledge.

Dalton, M. S. and Charnigo, L. (2004) 'Historians and their information sources', *College and Research Libraries*, **65**(5), pp. 400–425.

Darnton, R. (2001) 'The great book massacre', *The New York Review of Books*, 26 April 2001. Retrieved from: www.nybooks.com/articles/2001/04/26/the-great-book-massacre/.

Deegan, M. and Sutherland, K. (2009) *Transferred Illusions: Digital Technology and the Forms of Print*. Farnham: Ashgate Publishing.

Duff, W. M. and Johnson, C. A. (2002) 'Accidentally found on purpose: information-seeking behavior of historians in archives', *The Library Quarterly*, **72**(4), pp. 472–496.

Edwards, A. S. G. (2013) 'Back to the real?', *The Times Literary Supplement*, 7 June 2013. Retrieved from: www.the-tls.co.uk/tls/public/article1269403.ece.

Ellis, D. (1993) 'Modeling the information-seeking patterns of academic researchers: a grounded theory approach', *Library Quarterly*, **63**, pp. 469–486.

Fleming, P. and Walravens, H. (2011) 'The British Library newspaper strategy: developing collaboration with publishers to digitise back runs and to ingest born digital newspapers', in *Newspapers: Legal Deposit and Research in the Digital Era*. The Hague: IFLA Publications, pp. 21–30.

Franklin, B. (2014) 'The future of journalism in an age of digital media and economic uncertainty', *Journalism Practice*, **8**(5), pp. 469–487.

Griffiths, R. and Maron, N. L. (2009) 'The National Archives (UK): digitisation with commercial partnerships via the Licensed Internet Associates Programme', London: The National Archives. Retrieved from: http://sca.jiscinvolve.org/wp/files/2009/07/sca_bms_casestudy_natarchives.pdf.

Jones, A. (1996) *Powers of the Press: Newspapers, Power and the Public in Nineteenth-Century England*. Aldershot: Scholar Press.

Jonson, B. (1631) *The Staple of News*. Lincoln, Nebraska: University of Nebraska Press. Retrieved from: https://archive.org/details/staplenews00jonsgoog.

Lankes, R. D. (2011) *The Atlas of New Librarianship*. Cambridge, Mass.: The MIT Press.

Levy, D. M. (1997) '"I read the news today, oh boy": reading and attention in digital libraries', in *Proceedings of the Second ACM International Conference on Digital Libraries*. New York, pp. 202–211. Retrieved from: http://renu.pbworks.com/f/p202-levy.pdf.

MacLeish, A. (1971) 'Changes in the ritual of library dedication', in *Champion of a Cause: Essays and Addresses on Librarianship*. Chicago: American Library Association.

Meyer, E. T. (2011) 'Splashes and ripples: synthesizing the evidence on the impact of digital resources'. London: JISC. Retrieved from: http://ssrn.com/abstract=1846535.

Mussell, J. (2012) *The Nineteenth-Century Press in the Digital Age*. Basingstoke: Palgrave MacMillan.

Nicholas, D., Huntington, P., Williams, P. and Dobrowolski, T. (2004) 'Reappraising information seeking behaviour in a digital environment: bouncers, checkers, returnees and the like', *Journal of Documentation*, **60**(1), pp. 24–39.

Nicholson, B. (2013) 'The digital turn: exploring the methodological possibilities of digital newspaper archives', *Media History*, **19**(1), pp. 59–73.

O'Neil, L. (2013) 'The year we broke the Internet', *Esquire*. Retrieved from: www.esquire.com/news-politics/news/a23711/we-broke-the-internet/?src=spr_FBPAGE&spr_id=1456_36858863.

Quint, B. (2001) 'Don't burn books! Burn librarians!! A review of Nicholson Baker's *Double Fold: Libraries and the Assault on Paper*', *Searcher*, **9**(6). Retrieved from: www.infotoday.com/searcher/jun01/voice.htm.

Raymond, J. (2005) *The Invention of the Newspaper: English Newsbooks, 1641–1649*. Oxford: Oxford University Press.

Ryan, S. (2014) 'Read all about it #2: building a future', *Collection Care Blog*, 13 January 2014. Retrieved from: http://britishlibrary.typepad.co.uk/collection-care/2014/01/read-all-about-it-preserving-the-national-newspaper-collection-2-building-a-future.html.

Shera, J. H. (1972) 'Toward a theory of librarianship and information science', Centre for the Study of Democratic Institutions, 1 November 1972. Retrieved from: http://revista.ibict.br/ciinf/index.php/ciinf/article/viewFile/1643/1251.

Somerville, C. J. (1996) *The News Revolution in England: Cultural Dynamics of Daily Information*. New York and Oxford: Oxford University Press.

Stoker, D. (1999) 'Should newspaper preservation be a lottery?', *Journal of Librarianship and Information Science*, **31**(3), pp. 131–134.

Stone, S. (1982) 'Humanities scholars: information needs and uses', *Journal of Documentation*, **38**(4), pp. 292–313.

Sykes, J. (2008) 'Large-scale digitisation: the £22 million JISC programme and the role of libraries', *Serials*, **21**(3). Retrieved from: http://eprints.lse.ac.uk/21045/1/Large_scale_digitisation%28LSEROversion%29.pdf.

Tanner, S. (2012) 'Measuring the impact of digital resources: the Balanced Value Impact Model'. London: King's College London. Retrieved from: www.kdcs.kcl.ac.uk/fileadmin/documents/pubs/BalancedValueImpactModel_SimonTanner_October2012.pdf.

Tanner, S. and Deegan, M. (2010) 'Inspiring research, inspiring scholarship: the value and benefits of digitised resources for learning, teaching, research and enjoyment', London: King's College London. Retrieved from: www.kdcs.kcl.ac.uk/fileadmin/documents/Inspiring_Research_Inspiring_Scholarship_2011_SimonTanner.pdf.

Toobin, J. (2007) 'Google's moon shot: the quest for the universal library', *The New Yorker*, 5 February 2007. Retrieved from: www.newyorker.com/reporting/2007/02/05/070205fa_fact_toobin?currentPage=all.

Torkington, N. (2011) 'Libraries: where it all went wrong'. Blog post, 23 November 2011. Retrieved from: http://nathan.torkington.com/blog/2011/11/23/libraries-where-it-all-went-wrong/.

Unsworth, J. (2000) 'Scholarly primitives: what methods do humanities researchers have in common, and how might our tools reflect this?', in *Humanities Computing: Formal Methods, Experimental Practice*. London: King's College London. Retrieved from: http://people.brandeis.edu/~unsworth/Kings.5-00/primitives.html.

Uva, P. A. (1977) 'Information-gathering habits of academic historians: report of the pilot study'. ERIC ED 142 483. Syracuse: State University of New York, Upstate Medical Center.

Zelden, C. (2001) 'H-Net book review: *Double Fold: Double Trouble*'. Retrieved from: http://h-net.msu.edu/cgi-bin/logbrowse.pl?trx=vx&list=H-Law&month=0106&week=d&msg=%2bOC3qO3tRcvD7of/3dsDCA&user=&pw=.

3 Exploring methods for evaluating user behaviour

Researchers in Library and Information Science have, for many years, been extremely successful in adopting diverse research methods from other fields. In recent years, ethnographic studies, webometric analyses and data-driven studies of user behaviour have been used to develop significant insights into users of online library resources. Yet there are sizeable skill barriers that may stop users from adopting complex quantitative approaches. The academic literature discusses methodology in enough detail for expert readers to make a judgement on the validity of an approach and to understand the extent of the insights which it is likely to support. Other researchers without the same level of expertise, though, can be confused about how to implement these methods. This difficulty inspired creation of the Toolkit for the Impact of Digitised Scholarly Resources (TIDSR) in 2011. Freely available online, TIDSR provides a suite of evaluative methodologies for measuring and understanding the impact of digital collections. Its guides are extremely useful but, in common with any such resource, its aim to trigger a contributory culture to build content around the resource has not been fully achieved. I have attempted here to draw several introductory methodological approaches together to provide an idea of how each could best be used to increase the significance of findings and to allow us to produce research which is more easily generalisable. Given the myriad ways in which data about online users can be collected, my intention is not to provide a textbook for undertaking these methods. Indeed, such texts already exist for qualitative research in LIS (Gorman and Clayton, 2005; Pickard, 2007), and I would recommend that readers start with the two cited here. Instead, I have tried to provide an insight into the major approaches available to librarians and researchers and to suggest where they may, or may not, provide significant insights into the use of digital resources online. As such, I have adopted a warts-and-all approach: an honest account of where these methods are most useful and, indeed, where they may not provide meaningful insights. These methods are applicable to case study approaches, where an in-depth investigation of a particular website or digital resource is undertaken to gain specific knowledge of the resource and of the wider phenomenon which it represents.

This book addresses key communities that have been influenced by large-scale digitisation most strongly. Chapters 4 and 5 address two of these stakeholders. The first, covered in Chapter 4, are libraries. The primary stakeholders in the library sector are large research libraries with public collections, and in particular national libraries which have created, or are in the process of creating, large-scale digitised collections of historical material for use via the web. These digitised collections are primarily drawn from their existing physical collections, but they may include other material from other libraries under licence or reciprocal agreements. This includes libraries which have public collections that could potentially be used by researchers from a variety of backgrounds. These institutions are most commonly funded by public taxation or through their charitable status. Thus personal libraries, corporate and commercial libraries, and subscription libraries are not directly considered. I will explore two levels at which these institutions are affected by large-scale digitisation: the institutional, where the legal, regulatory, strategic, economic and cultural effects of digitisation are most relevant; and the individual, where professional practice is likely to be affected. As such, two primary stakeholders are considered. The first is the library as a public-facing institution which makes collections available to the public through large-scale digitisation. This includes large research libraries, legal deposit libraries and national libraries but can encompass any memory institution which intends to make its collections available online to the public. The second group is library staff: employees of libraries with public collections, who are directly or indirectly affected in their professional practice by large-scale digitisation. The impacts could include changes in professional practice, job titles and training, and professional redundancy or new job assignment. Secondary stakeholders in the library sector are libraries which purchase access to collections from the primary stakeholder libraries or receive access as part of a wider negotiated agreement. This includes Higher Education (HE) and Further Education (FE) Libraries and public libraries. Large organisational libraries and commercial libraries fall outside the scope of this discussion.

The research community has also been heavily influenced by large-scale digitisation. I refer to researchers variously in this book as researchers, readers or users but each should be understood to be an individual or community which is engaged in some form of research using digitised newspaper collections online. While I recognise the inherent individualism of each researcher, and I indeed advocate for creating resources which allow individual approaches to be more strongly supported, here I primarily interpret research as a universal activity meant to encompass all activities undertaken by researchers, who have the aim of gathering data and information to advance knowledge relating to a specific task or question. As Bawden and Robinson (2013) explain, this allows us to study the information behaviour of groups which share a commonality in their research behaviour, as the majority of users of digitised newspaper collections do. This said, the user community of researchers is diverse: a large proportion of users undertaking research would not be traditionally identified as "scholars", including family historians and genealogists drawn from the general public. I understand "researchers" to encompass both the academic community and the wider user base, all of whom share a need for digitised newspapers for their own individual research agenda.

Although many studies have focused on a specific group of users, such as academic researchers or family historians, the British Library has stated that one of its strategic drivers for extensive digitisation is to "make the Library's collection available to as wide a range of users as possible" (2008). They share this aim with other libraries of a similar status. I therefore envisage a number of stakeholder groups that may be affected by large-scale digitisation: academic researchers, including those employed in academic positions, those who identify as academics but are not currently in permanent paid employment, students and other researchers who identify as academics; members of the public engaged in research into topics relating to genealogy, family history or other topics which are facilitated by archival research using newspapers; local historians, who may be working individually or as part of a larger local history network; and professional non-academic researchers, who are undertaking word-based research using archival resources. The potential audience for digitised newspapers is extremely wide, and while I have attempted to consider this diverse group thoroughly, the difficulties associated with researching diffuse online user communities have not made this possible in some cases. The two groups most thoroughly represented in this book are therefore academic researchers and non-academic genealogists and family historians.

The final group to be considered is more general and can most accurately be described as those who may benefit from access to digitised collections but currently face barriers to participation. Libraries play a key role in widening participation, whereas impact evaluation generally looks to address existing communities. There are good reasons for this, not least the difficulty in defining a potential audience and thereby accessing it for the purposes of research. However, there is a need for research which considers whether the aims of existing large-scale digitisation programmes go far enough in addressing the key question of access. This chapter presents some of the most common methods of impact assessment and discusses their relevance for investigating the impact of digital resources on the stakeholder communities I have outlined. The findings are contextualised by case studies from my own research, which provide insights into the wider phenomenon of large-scale digitisation.

Methods for case study research

Case studies have been variously defined, but Gorman and Clayton's definition is pertinent to their use in LIS research:

> An in-depth investigation of a discrete entity ... on the assumption that it is possible to derive knowledge of the wider phenomenon from investigation of a specific case or instance.
>
> (2005)

For this reason, case studies are commonly used to analyse, among other things, aspects of library service including digital tools, digitised collections and OPACs. The case study has been refined and modelled in-depth over recent decades, but it is commonly based on the following steps: defining the research question; collecting data; and using an iterative process of analysis which allows the researcher to investigate emerging themes. This process is valuable when description of phenomena and development of theory is necessary, when the experience of individuals and the context of actions are important and when grounded theory approaches are implemented, allowing theoretical concepts to emerge through data collection and analysis (Darke and Shanks, 2002). By catering to continuous refinement of the research question and encouraging a flexible approach to data collection and analysis, case studies are particularly valuable for research projects which must adopt an inductive approach to developing theoretical insights. Inductive methods are an essential component of research where little is known about the phenomenon in question and they therefore represent a methodological response to the inflamed rhetoric of discourses around technological innovations.

Inductive research allows theoretical and practical insights to emerge from data collection and analysis. Rather than testing an overarching hypothesis, researchers instead look to answer a specific research question. For instance, a deductive approach would put forward a hypothesis that digital resources have caused researchers to read fewer primary sources and then test that hypothesis through the development of an appropriate methodology. An inductive approach would ask what impact digital resources have had on reading habits and then devise a methodology which allows the hypothesis to emerge from the data. Grounded theory is a high profile example of the inductive approach, where the researcher is concerned with developing new theory based upon the data they collect. Many writers have covered the theory and practice of grounded theory since Glaser and Strauss (1967) developed it in the 1960s. It utilises a process of qualitative analysis that works without a driving hypothesis, and the term can be used in two ways. It can be indicative of a strictly adhered-to research method, largely in line with the substantive approach established over the last 50 or so years, or of an approach which is grounded in data but may not itself have strictly adopted grounded theory in its entirety. The latter approach, which can still be profoundly influenced by evidence from the literature, is more accurately described as inductive. Indeed, the theoretical context presented in the previous chapters is in itself strong justification for the adoption of an inductive approach. The most insightful research to date has drawn upon self-collected data to provide meaningful insights, whereas the character of the debate that I have previously outlined could be described as a series of hypotheses in need of testing. The adoption of inductive data analysis should be seen as a conscious rejection of hypothesis-driven theory in relation to digital media, which I have argued occurs in areas where understanding lags behind adoption. This requires an open mind on behalf of the researcher, who should be flexible not only in their data collection and analysis but also in responding to areas of insight which emerge in the course of their analysis.

Gorman and Clayton, in their excellent guide to qualitative research for information professionals, make the following comment on flexibility in research:

> Flexibility in any approach to problem-solving permits information professionals to understand complex organizational and social phenomena more clearly. Indeed, this is a particular strength of the qualitative approach, which, with its interpretivist focus, permits a more flexible understanding of complex and evolving social constructs.
>
> (2005)

It is this flexibility that we have found missing; we can trace the same arguments emerging over a period of decades through the evolution of the discourse around digital media. Their position has become entrenched, with the result that very little data has been gathered to test their claims. This is in comparison to research in LIS, which has been characterised by incremental and limited insights into the phenomenon. It is my belief that case study research is vital to the development of overarching theories for large-scale digitisation, and it is most effectively done through a mixed methods approach through which theoretical insights emerge from observed behaviour, quantitative insights gained from users, and extant datasets which can contextualise these qualitative findings. In order to allow for the development of more widely applicable theoretical insights, there is a need to adopt a diverse approach to data collection, which relies on multiple data sources viewed in conversation with each other. Many past LIS projects have relied on a narrow data collection strategy, which has borne insights into specific research questions or collections but has not provided a strong basis for generalising these findings to the wider phenomena under discussion. This is not to say that LIS is unwilling to adopt new research techniques; far from it, researchers in the field are extremely receptive to new ideas. But these techniques are used in isolation;

surveys of small groups of users are common, as are studies which interview members of an immediately accessible user community. As a result, our knowledge of user behaviour with online digitised collections grows slowly, with an evidence base that is too narrow to draw conclusions about wider social and cultural trends. Thelwall (2009) has warned of the weakness of narrow approaches to data collection, and this is one of the great weaknesses of research in our discipline.

Faced with complex information behaviour, the task of exploring its development in relation to digital resources, its deviation from established norms and the extent of the change is not a simple practice. Adopting a multifaceted approach to collecting and analysing appropriate data is vital, and it involves the use of a mixture of qualitative and quantitative methods. The theoretical battle over the supremacy of quantitative and qualitative methods that occurred in the past is now less relevant, and most researchers now recognise the benefits of combining qualitative and quantitative methods. The methodological debate received a great deal of attention in the social sciences, and the historical rivalry between positivism and interpretivism was closely followed by LIS scholars. Positivism seeks to "take the rules and practices of the natural sciences of physics, astronomy and chemistry and apply the same investigative techniques to social theory and human theory" (Pickard, 2007). It emerged in the nineteenth century, when it was devised as a means of examining social phenomena as an empirical science. The concept has undergone a series of refinements since its creation, but it fundamentally favours the use of quantitative methods to analyse social phenomena in the belief that knowledge can only be based on objective observation and reporting. Interpretivism, as it initially emerged, provides a fundamentally different approach, proposing that reality is not objective, rather it is grounded in individual contexts and experiences. As a method, it replaces the concept of an empirically derived "universal truth", with the production of meaning through interpretation of the actions of participants in a particular occurrence. Dey notes that "from this perspective, meaning depends upon context, and the interpretation of action or opinion must take account of the setting in which it is produced" (1993). For this reason, interpretivism is most closely associated with qualitative research. These definitions are extremely relevant to the production of knowledge in LIS, precisely because they have influenced a positivist approach in previous decades. Indeed, there is still a strong empirical focus in LIS research. Gorman and Clayton have insightfully linked this methodological trend to the nature of information work:

> For decades in the past, information work was viewed as a profession in the positivist tradition, and libraries as "laboratories" in which quantitative survey techniques were the best, and often the only, way to collect data for (primarily statistical) analysis.
>
> (2005)

While this positivist tradition has facilitated research into emerging areas, there have been claims that it provides little value in improving library services in reality. Its empirical emphasis tends to prioritise objective measures of technological impact over qualitative approaches to the roles of newspapers. Yet, in the tradition of Ranganathan, librarians have posited service as a core library value and thus implicitly placed information work within the framework of user experience. If we are to support the idea that a key role for libraries is to support intellectual freedom and development, then empirical methods in isolation can side-line the experience of these key beneficiaries of LIS innovations.

The interaction of humans and technology relies on tacit knowledge and external contexts over the particular characteristics of a technology. By contrast, the technocentrism of the discourse around large-scale digitisation has often limited our understanding of this relationship by overemphasising the importance of the technology in defining user behaviour. The desire to distance user studies from the postmodernist rhetoric of disruptive technologies is therefore a key motivating factor in adopting mixed methods approaches to the impact of digital resources. While the framing of the "human-as-instrument" (Maykut and Morehouse, 1994) is important, the reality of working with online users is that a solely qualitative approach also leaves many questions unanswered. As the Berkeley study demonstrated, a group of motivated respondents to a survey or focus group call is unlikely to be representative of the whole user community of a library, let alone the distributed network of users of digital resources. It is therefore necessary to approach user studies with two key concepts in mind: a certain methodological flexibility, and a theoretical pragmatism towards the idea of subsuming methods to the research question. The necessary pragmatism of mixed methods research has become increasingly accepted, allowing qualitative and quantitative methods to be used in combination to mitigate for weaknesses or gaps. In this way, the strengths of each method can be used to account for the weaknesses of others, and to facilitate a deeper consideration of the problem, as Thelwall explains:

> Whereas qualitative techniques alone risk missing the big picture due to their necessary small-scale nature, quantitative techniques risk being superficial or misleading if they are not complemented by supporting qualitative analysis.
>
> (2009)

This can be seen in the influence of theoretical pragmatism for defining which approaches to use for specific case studies. Pragmatism works on the basis that the method should remain secondary to the research question. The term "methodological triangulation" is used to describe the combination of qualitative and quantitative methods in order to study a particular phenomenon. Gorman and Clayton describe the benefits of triangulation:

By triangulating data collection methods, especially by using a quantitative method in conjunction with a qualitative method, the
researcher is able to draw on the unique strengths of each – thus providing both macro- and micro-level perspectives in a single project.

(2005)

Or, as Punch (1998) more simply states: "Sometimes quantitative methods
and data will be required to answer the questions we have asked; sometimes qualitative methods and data will be required; sometimes both will
be required".

In response, this chapter is based on the argument that combining the
case study approach with an inductive mixed methodology is the most
fruitful in assessing the impact of large-scale digitisation. The inductive
approach, unlike in the past, is now common in LIS studies, in which
many researchers begin with an open-ended question which drives their
approach. It demands a long-term engagement with research datasets to
derive maximum value from the analysis, as data may not provide significant insights into emerging trends without adequate longitudinal scope.
Such an in-depth, multifaceted approach to user studies is a necessary and
direct response to the theoretical milieu that surrounds new technologies.
I would position it as a conscious rejection of the hypothesis-driven discourse which can occur when understanding lags behind adoption.
Indeed, while the most noteworthy examples of hyperbole are often those
which are negative, there is also a need to guard against research which
presupposes the positive impact of a particular phenomenon and then
builds an approach based on proving this presumption. The methodology
for case study work in LIS should therefore emphasise flexibility in data
collection and analysis but also a willingness to refine research questions
in response to emerging areas of analysis:

Flexibility in any approach to problem-solving permits information
professionals to understand complex organizational and social phenomena more clearly. Indeed, this is a particular strength of the qualitative approach, which, with its interpretive focus, permits a more
flexible understanding of complex and evolving social constructs.

(Gorman and Clayton, 2005)

With this in mind, the rest of the chapter will engage with some of the
major methods that can be considered in online user studies, with an
honest appraisal of both their strengths and their weaknesses.

Quantitative methods

Web analytics

The concept of web analytics is defined by the Digital Analytics Association as the "measurement, collection, analysis and reporting of internet data for the purpose of understanding and optimizing web usage" (2012). Its use in academic research emerged from the field of infometrics in the 1990s, when it was roughly defined as "the research of all network-based communications using infometric or other quantitative methods" (Almind and Ingwersen, 1997). Since then it has become an increasingly common tool for analysing web usage in the cultural heritage sector. The most obvious application is to support research into web phenomena, where other methods may prove inadequate due to remote, poorly defined user populations. Although some early webometric techniques necessitated specific expertise in quantitative data analysis, the launch of Google Analytics (GA) provided an efficient web-based tool to gather usage and engagement metrics for any website, implemented by the simple addition of a segment of code to each web page. This has significantly lowered the technical bar for undertaking webometric analysis and has facilitated an increase in the number of LIS researchers who now use GA to evaluate the effectiveness of online services. Particularly appealing is the fact that it provides data in aggregated, anonymised form, albeit in a way that doesn't address whether users expect or want to be tracked in their use of cultural heritage resources. In addition to tracking user location, aggregated engagement metrics, technology usage and page-level data, GA offers features which assist with other webometric techniques such as referrer analysis. The service automatically excludes simple web crawler traffic, increasing the accuracy of its dataset. Additionally, the process is unobtrusive to users: a small piece of JavaScript code runs on the webpage, which gathers extensive user data without, importantly, manifestly changing the user experience in any way. It is therefore an effective way to track real user behaviour without bias being introduced by the presence of a researcher, by specific interview questions or even by an awareness that the user's behaviour is under observation. As Nicholas *et al.* (2004) describe, GA and other webometric techniques are successful in providing "a direct and immediately available record of what people have done: not what they say they might, or would, do; not what they were prompted to say; not what they thought they did".

However, one of the notable problems with GA in LIS research is its narrow methodological scope and its disregard for other contextual contributors to user behaviour. Studies which rely solely on webometrics inevitably understand user behaviour in terms of the website infrastructure, rather than as a mediated relationship between user and content. Webometric analysis can only reveal how a website is used and not the motivating factors which encourage a user to return or leave without engaging. In this respect, the existing literature can provide a superficial understanding of LIS-related web usage, treating webometric analysis as a tool to iterate functionality, or to demonstrate empirical measures of impact, without the requisite contextualisation that is required to understand the user behaviour that is discovered. Instead, the key research projects to date have all used web log analysis rather than GA. Although there are difficulties in gathering and analysing web logs, they provide notable benefits because they record use by all users of a system. The technique relies on the collection and analysis of those web logs that are automatically produced by a website server each time a user accesses a website. Servers record basic information about each user, including unique identifiers, date and time of interaction, and the type of content viewed. This allows deep analysis of user behaviour, including tracing individuals throughout their visit by isolating unique user identifiers. Because web logs are directly under the control of the researcher and provide unfiltered data, they offer many possibilities that are absent from Google Analytics.

There are, though, a number of problems with web log analysis. Web servers include data from automatic web crawlers, commonly known as bots, which are computer applications designed to do automated tasks. Major search engines use bots to automatically and systematically browse the web, most commonly for the purpose of web indexing. These results are tracked indiscriminately by web servers, and introduce noise into the logs which must be cleaned of automatic traffic before usable results can be obtained. Because each log entry only tracks the start of an interaction with a web page and not the end, web logs are also unable to return an accurate measure for when users leave a website. Additionally, user identification can be unreliable: web logs often provide an IP number to identify individual users, but this number can only be traced, at best, back to a machine rather than an individual. The use of proxy servers, which allow computers to act as intermediaries between a client and host computer, and Point-to-Point Protocol connections, which allow data communication between two different entities on a network, also mean that the IP address cannot be assumed to relate to a specific user on a specific machine. One IP address might represent a group of users, making the tracking of return users difficult. When combined with the data-intensive task of analysing a large dataset of web logs, this technique is more time-consuming and intricate than GA. It is also increasingly common to find that organisations either turn web log collection off at the server side, or delete logs regularly due to their large size. The main barrier to their collection is the need for an organisational strategy for storage and analysis, whereas GA can be set up to run in the background and be analysed via a convenient web platform. As a result, GA has become increasingly popular as a web analytics platform, despite providing many challenges for in-depth research. Google, for its part, clearly phrases GA's utility in terms of business outcomes:

Google Analytics not only lets you measure sales and conversions, but also gives you fresh insights into how visitors use your site, how they arrive on your site, and how you can keep them coming back.

(2012)

It is therefore a powerful platform for gathering aggregated business data, but when using it for research into user behaviour there are two major problems to consider: redundancy of features and problems caused by its data collection and reporting methods. The business analysis tools are largely redundant for most LIS research questions, which focus primarily on user behaviour and website optimisation. Conversions are not a useful way of conceptualising user behaviour with digital resources, given that many positive user outcomes cannot be neatly summarised in terms of financial gain for the website host. There is a concurrent absence of advanced analytics suitable for academic users, which leaves gaps in understanding that require the use of alternate methodologies. There are also larger flaws in GA which demonstrate it should not be treated as a uniquely authoritative platform for user behaviour analysis.

First, the limited data banding applied to GA datasets can be problematic for researchers investigating digital resources with extremely high levels of engagement by website standards. For instance, the banding for the metric for average page views per visit are listed from 0–19 pages, with a final category covering all visits with more than 20 page views. For content-heavy websites with high levels of user engagement, this obscures fascinating data relating to the most engaged users. As a result, for this and other metrics, nuance is lost in the section of the dataset which contains the most evidence relating to deep engagement. This is exacerbated because there is no way to export raw GA data to undertake manual analysis which is more closely tailored to a specific research question. This final point is vital for academic users. The lack of raw data means that GA results remain opaque to a large extent, in that as a research tool it lacks the key features of transparency and reproducibility. This opacity is particularly problematic when dealing with sampled data. GA utilises the complete dataset where possible but, when over 500,000 sessions are recorded, it presents the data in sampled form. By default, this sample is approximately 250,000 sessions, but the user is able to specify a sample size to a maximum of 500,000 sessions. Because the sample is automatically processed using an inaccessible dataset and undisclosed algorithms, the user must rely on Google to provide a representative and reproducible sample. My experience has been that samples vary marginally between sessions – a small margin of error, but one that introduces inaccuracy to the findings without any means to address it. The lack of raw, exportable data is largely responsible for this limitation. While there are extensive data exporting options available, these all limit the user to pre-processed datasets. Google hides the raw data for valid reasons, not least to preserve user privacy but, as a result, the data from which results are calculated remains unavailable.

Overall, GA provides an adequate replacement for web log analysis in a number of areas: for referral analysis, gathering usage and engagement statistics, tracking social media visits, and recording technical and demographic data. However, it provides a weaker source for deep analysis of user behaviour with digital resources, with additional implications for the transparency and reproducibility of academic research. The major benefit of GA for academic research is that it provides metrics which can be repurposed to support other kinds of user analysis.

Referrer analysis

Referrer analysis is one such technique that uses data gathered through webometric datasets. In the context of web analytics, referrer analysis provides an important source of information about the users of a particular web resource. A web referral occurs when any hyperlink is clicked that leads a user to a new page or file in any website, with the originating site being the referrer. It provides a meaningful way for researchers to identify patterns in where web traffic arrives from. GA provides a powerful suite of tools for undertaking this work, as it automatically gathers referral data and additionally gathers usage data which allows analysis of the levels of engagement among different types of user. The same information is present in web logs, but the limitations around identifying individual users mean that GA offers an easier way to identify and track user behaviour at aggregate level. For impact analysis, referrer analysis is useful on two levels: first, for telling us more about how users navigate to the resource and what broad communities they derive from; and second, for providing insights into user behaviour based on broad categorisation of referral locations. The categorisation of referring websites is important to the success of this technique. Researchers can pull a list of referring websites together and categorise them depending on the type of referrer. For digitised newspapers, categories are likely to include national libraries, public libraries, online educational resources, educational institutions, social media and blogging platforms. With GA, researchers can then analyse user behaviour and engagement by category, which can provide important insights into the differences in use between various categories of user. There is still an element of manual data analysis, as it is often necessary to follow hyperlinks to identify the type of website they represent. The real power of this kind of analysis is that it breaks down users into groups which can be more usefully explored through qualitative analysis. On its own, it provides information on the types of users of a resource and their aggregate behaviour, but not why specific groups may be interested in the resource.

Citation analysis

Citation analysis provides a technique for looking at how academic users ultimately make use of materials discovered in digital resources. It relies on the examination of the frequency and patterns of citation in scholarly works. Part of the wider field of bibliometrics, citation analysis has been used to judge the impact of journal articles and, more recently, web resources. Citations are widely considered to be indicative of how frequently a particular document or resource is used, and thus provide an empirical data source for usage in academic scholarship. The insights that citation analysis provides are founded on the assumption that there is a strong positive correlation between the number of citations that a resource or article receives and the quality of that output – an assumption that has found support in a number of studies into citation of scientific papers, journals and scholars (Smith, 1980). Citation analysis appears to have been inspired by the publication of the Science Citation Index in 1961, which allowed researchers to search accurately for later articles based on which articles or authors they had cited and to discover which papers had been cited most frequently (MacRoberts and MacRoberts, 1989). Traditional citation analysis is therefore a well-established bibliometric technique and, with the introduction of increasingly comprehensive online databases of scholarly works, it is now easier than ever to track the number of citations in articles. Full text searching makes it simpler, too, to discover citations which include hyperlinks and thus aids the discovery of web resources within citations.

Citation analysis is useful for assessing the influence of particular authors or papers, but this influence works differently when considering digital resources. Previous research can be considered influential if it has in some way shaped the direction of future research in its field and beyond. Citations act as a proxy measure of this influence, where it is considered that the mention of another's work, either directly or through secondary sources, is a sign of validation. If we are to use citation analysis to track usage of digital resources, though, the idea of influence is less applicable. The resource may well have influenced the creation of a work by making a particular source available, but it is less certain that the digital resource itself has any direct intellectual influence represented in that citation. An LIS researcher may cite a resource that has influenced her thinking in relation to digital resource creation, whereas a historian may cite it only as the originating source of their material. As the LAIRAH study points out, scholars are willing to use digital resources if they perceive them to contain valuable material, so citations cannot be reliably linked to the quality of the resource. Instead, frequent citation of a particular resource can be linked either to its quality or to the importance or quality of the material contained therein. Citation analysis of digital resources is therefore a stronger indicator of the value of a resource to its community, through the material it makes available, than its influence on researchers. There are several reasons to treat citation data with caution. It concentrates largely on published research outputs as an information source and, although Google Scholar covers some grey literature, materials such as teaching resources and papers published via non-traditional routes are poorly tracked by citation databases. Citation analysis is, furthermore, only effective when applied to mature digital resources. There is a significant lag between the beginning of an academic research project and the publication of its results, meaning that citation analysis cannot track short-term usage but should instead be considered a long-term indicator of scholarly impact. We may find that a digital resource with high value for teaching has received few citations and thus its value is hidden. Similarly, usage outside the academic community is deemed irrelevant if we focus too heavily on citations as a measure of value.

The assumed effectiveness of citation analysis also relies on the idea that citation practices are universally understood, and followed, by academics. In reality, researchers are often unsure how to cite digital materials due to a widespread lack of clear guidance on how to cite from databases or digitised resources. In 1980, Smith noted that there were a number of reasons that academics did not cite a particular document, including lack of relevance to their work, lack of awareness of a source, inability to obtain a document or inability to read a foreign language. For digitised collections, we should add to this list a lack of awareness of how to cite digital resources and a certain unwillingness to include them in the first place. As Meyer *et al.* note:

> Citation habits in many fields favour citing the original paper version of a document, even if the only version consulted was electronic.
>
> (2009)

Digitised collections still suffer from a perceived lack of academic authority in comparison to the printed text for some academics. In her study into practices for referencing electronic sources in academic publications, Sukovic found that many authors were unwilling to cite an electronic version of a text because they felt their academic credibility could be undermined:

> The lack of credibility or unclear trustworthiness of many primary materials in electronic form made these e-texts less useful for scholarly argument ... Even when digitized materials were established as trustworthy sources, hard copies were often cited because they provide final evidence and were considered as more authoritative.
>
> (Sukovic, 2009)

Moreover, the reasons for citing physical versions over digital texts can include aesthetic considerations, with some academics disliking the way that a hyperlink looks when written in full on the page. Citation practices reflect individual value judgements, norms within particular fields and the degree to which researchers understand and adhere to these norms. They are also indicative of the instability of web resources. Stable URLs are vital for academic researchers, as they allow readers to reliably discover cited texts, but there remain too many examples of digital resources either failing to provide stable URLs for individual items within a collection or changing the resource URL after its launch. As a result, they do not provide a precise record of citation levels of a digital resource. These factors will work to artificially lower the number of citations discovered, and citations for a particular digital resource can therefore be considered to be a minimum baseline for their use in academic publications. Extensive citation databases have been available in print and digital forms for many years and provide an unobtrusive and readily available source of usage data which does not require the cooperation of respondents. Above all, citation analysis provides an effective way to judge the use of a particular digital resource. Given that a poor collection with popular content will garner more citations than an excellent collection with niche texts, the impact of a digital resource can only be partly ascertained through this approach.

Link analysis

Link analysis is a common method in LIS for evaluating the impact of digital resources and websites. Thelwall explains its role:

> A key feature of the web is the ability for pages to interlink. Link analysis is performed in very diverse subjects, from computer science and theoretical physics to information science, communication studies and sociology.
>
> (2006)

Links are typically designed as a navigation aid for web users to move quickly between pages, but they also contain implicit information: a hyperlink can be taken as an endorsement of a target page, much in the manner of a citation. It has therefore been argued that the number of web pages linking to a given web page may be a reasonable indicator of the importance of the document or the resource it contains. A number of studies of hyperlinks have demonstrated this connection, showing that link counts typically correlate with a tangible positive aspect of the linked resource, such as productivity or citation levels. The premise for link analysis is therefore that counting the links to a web page or digital resource provides an indicator of its significance or impact. However, my experience of link analysis has been that it brings up a number of practical issues. First, the idea that links are endorsements of target content can be misleading.

In common with citation analysis, there are various reasons for linking to a particular web resource: it could be controversial, or the link could be used in the context of a disagreement with the target page, or the link could have gained notoriety through social media. The number of links will likely indicate that a particular page is of interest to users, but this does not necessarily indicate that it is of high quality. Additionally, internal changes to URLs can cause empirical measures of impact to be lost or increase the difficulty of tracking them across time. Content which is hidden behind paywalls also provides a challenge when gathering data for link analysis. Like Eccles *et al.* (2012), I found it impossible to collect accurate link data for digital resources which operate behind an institutional paywall. British Library Nineteenth Century Newspapers (BNCN) is a prominent resource which has been available through the majority of HE and FE institutions for many years, but none of these institutional links are discoverable using automated link harvesting. Manual link analysis is too time-consuming to be systematically undertaken, so resources which defeat link harvesting tools are almost impossible to accurately track. Similarly, link analysis is reasonably ineffective for new resources or for comparison between two resources which were created at different times.

Largely, quantitative methods share a major weakness when exploring user behaviour: they are unable to track what happens to downloaded material when a user goes offline. While the number and format of downloads can be tracked, there is no way to track the myriad uses which occur when a user stores a file locally on their computer. Users may, for instance, view large amounts of textual material offline; they may bookmark relevant articles locally for future visits; they may download PDFs of scanned pages and store them on their hard drive; they may download citations that allow them to reference material in future; or they may print material and store, use and annotate printed copies in multiple ways. None of these uses can be tracked by the methods noted above. There is then an artificial divide between what can be characterised as user behaviour (that which relates to the use of a digital resource online) and information behaviour (that which relates to the wider context of how humans relate to, and use, information), due to the limitations outlined in this chapter. For this, among many other reasons, it is vital for qualitative approaches to fill the gaps that webometric analysis inevitably leaves – in essence, to "place" webometric data through triangulation with qualitative methods.

Qualitative methods

Qualitative methods provide the human context that, combined with empirical measures of use and impact, can vastly increase the significance of user studies. They allow research to involve users directly in the research process, whereas quantitative methods often bypass the user entirely. The following section outlines some of the major qualitative methods that can be used in evaluating the impact of digital resources. The chapter points to several resources which give a more thorough description of implementing these methods, and I can recommend them as sources for those who are interested in using them. I will focus here upon their particular utility in user studies.

Interviews

Interviews are used frequently in qualitative studies, and within LIS they are useful for a number of reasons: they allow complex discussions of issues that arise from direct interaction between interviewer and interviewee; they facilitate the collection of a large quantity of rich data in a short time; they allow interviewers to ask consistent questions to support comparison of different answers; and they allow interviewers to confirm opinions across multiple stakeholders in a particular community. When undertaken face-to-face, points of confusion can be addressed with participants immediately. The credibility of data is enhanced if it can be confirmed via several sources, albeit while taking into account the possibility of bias being introduced by the fact that interviewees have agreed to be interviewed and will therefore be likely to have a particular existing viewpoint on the subject in question. Interviews enable a researcher to explore *why* individuals or organisations behave in a certain manner, allowing them to understand the intrinsic motivations or structural factors that lead to the development of particular approaches to a problem or resource.

Surveys

This note of caution applies to the other methods under discussion here too. Surveys, for instance, have proven themselves to be a valuable way of gathering information from large populations and are a common technique in LIS research. They provide many advantages, allowing researchers to gather quantitative and qualitative data by using a variety of carefully designed questions. For digitised collections, surveys can be used to gather demographic data which can be compared to similar datasets from GA or web log analysis. Users appreciate the opportunity to address particular areas of concern, and the information that they provide can be both surprising and hugely valuable. Online surveys are common to the point of saturation and provide further benefits over traditional survey methods. This maximises global reach, flexibility, speed, convenience and low administration costs. They can also yield high response rates when placed on websites with high traffic volumes and ensure that participants are drawn from the user community by placing a survey link on the resource in question. In the case of digital resources, this is a particularly valuable way of making sure that only those with experience of a resource are involved, although this does raise important questions about how representative the findings can be. Self-selection bias is a major problem for online surveys: in addition to the potentially skewed attributes of internet users compared to the general population, there is the additional possibility that those who complete an online survey are a self-selecting minority of an already potentially unrepresentative group.

This last point is problematic when we consider that the benefits of digital resources are unevenly spread throughout society. As a result of data collection techniques, most studies are unable to include voices from excluded communities. Considering the benefits of digitisation purely through the voices of those who use them and are therefore the most likely to have benefited has negative connotations for our ability to address social exclusion online. Formulating a data collection strategy that guarantees the representativeness of a survey sample is therefore problematic. While one of the major theoretical benefits of online digitised collections is increased access, the possibility of identifying the demographic constitution of the whole user community is low: records are often incomplete beyond basic usage statistics; there can be multiple access routes which distort usage; and resource providers are understandably uncomfortable with releasing subscriber lists to researchers when these are available. There is therefore little evidence available to build a representative sample for surveys, and this particular problem is exacerbated by the poor response rates that several studies have managed to achieve – hundreds of users, or fewer, in comparison to a user community of many thousands.

Summary

The methods considered above are by no means an exhaustive guide to undertaking impact evaluation. My hope is that the information provided will act as a springboard to other resources which have engaged more thoroughly with methodology (Gorman and Clayton, 2005; Pickard, 2007) and, indeed, entire books are necessary to do the topic justice. Instead, the methods discussed in this chapter are presented in the course of its key argument, that quantitative and qualitative methods can be fruitfully combined for studying the impact of large-scale digitised collections. It is necessary to carefully consider how each dataset supports the formulation of deeper insights which are driven by carefully gathered data rather than theoretical speculation. Data triangulation is key as, without combining several methods, we can be left with too little evidence which can be generalised beyond a specific instance of a digital resource. The preceding chapters have shown the huge disconnect between the work undertaken by LIS researchers and the wider social discourse. The two bear little relation in tone, and it is striking that the most significant LIS studies have drawn on a wide evidence base to draw their conclusions, whereas rhetoricians have driven the hyperbolic discourse. Digitised newspaper collections fit the criteria established in the introduction for LSDC. As Toobin

(2007) writes, they are also the most often used, and most important archival source for historians. Despite the problems that I described with microfilm, it has provided great benefits to the accessibility of the newspaper archive, and digitised newspapers stand to facilitate further benefits. For this reason, the following chapters will return to the narrower context of large-scale digitised newspaper collections, presenting information that has been gathered from two case studies. They draw largely upon my own work with two major national library digitised newspaper collections.

The first collection, British Library Nineteenth Century Newspapers, is managed by Gale Cengage and contains around 70 UK and Irish national and local titles, with over three million pages of searchable digitised content. The project was undertaken in two phases. The first phase, which was completed in 2007, digitised roughly two million pages of BL newspaper content, made available for free to UK Further Education and Higher Education institutions via an agreement with JISC. On its launch in 2007, it was available through institutional subscription and via a second site which gave access to individuals for an annual subscription charge. This second site was closed in 2012, leaving the institutional website as the only available version. A second phase of the project was completed in 2010, which successfully digitised a further one million pages of BL newspaper content. In addition to UK educational institutions, public libraries and international audiences are able to subscribe to the resource for an annual fee. The closure of the public website came around the time that the BL launched an alternative newspaper site. Released in 2010 in partnership with Brightsolid, the new resource was called the British Newspaper Archive and began a programme to digitise more newspapers and make them available via subscription to members of the public. This study will focus on BNCN, but the launch of this rival newspaper collection has had an impact upon the BL's digital newspaper offering and will therefore be discussed.

The second collection which I consider at length is Welsh Newspapers Online (WNO), a free resource which aims to make over one million pages of newspapers available from the collections of the NLW. The resource is partly funded by the Strategic Capital Investment Fund[1] and the European Regional Development Fund[2] through the Welsh government. The newspaper collection was scanned at the NLW (2013), following investment in a digitisation suite, specialist scanning equipment and workflow management software. The online resource was launched in 2013 to widespread media publicity. It was positively greeted by academics due to its open approach and site functionality (Mussell, 2013; Tanner, 2013). The open principles adopted by the project are the major difference between the two resources. The NLW did not claim ownership of copyright in digital copies of items in its collections. Library staff have made it clear that they consider this an important attribute for all their digital collections and that they expect it to lead to novel uses of their digitised newspapers in the future. The collections offer several points of differ-ence. BNCN is a well-established collection, with an existing user base, while WNO was launched in early 2013; the resources therefore represent how technological and presentational norms have changed since the launch of BNCN. Their funding models also bear closer scrutiny. BNCN was funded in part by a £2 million grant from JISC, which provided for the digitisation of up to two million pages of newspaper content for access within UK educational institutions. WNO was partly financed by public funding of roughly £2 million from the Welsh Assembly, with the aim to "digitise all of the National Library's paper holdings of out-of-copyright newspapers and journals – generally those published in Wales up to 1911" (National Library of Wales, 2012). The scope of each project is different, so a direct financial comparison is slightly misleading; but what is certain is that, despite the input of similar levels of public grant, each institution adopted a very different access model, with the BL relying on commercial partnership, while the NLW produced the resource independently. The following chapters will therefore consider the impact that these different approaches have had upon access to, and usage of, these important large-scale digitised collections. While the focus is upon the UK, I will argue that these subscription models and the impact that each resource has had can tell us a lot about how to conceive and create large-scale digitised collec-tions for the benefit of the greatest number of users globally.

The remainder of the book is split into chapters which will introduce the key aspects of the impact that digitised newspaper collections have had upon library users. Chapter 4 will explore the ways in which large-scale digitisation has had a major impact on the way that institutions in the cul-tural heritage sector work and how this has affected their role in society. It does so through the lens of the large-scale digitised newspapers collections that many libraries have produced in recent years and the ways in which these projects have changed their relationship with their users, with their collections, and with the publishing industry. Libraries have become increasingly involved in the production of resources as a result of digitisa-tion, spanning the line between sources of information and publishers in a way that fundamentally influences what services their users expect to be provided. Chapter 5 moves on to this user context, examining how user behaviour has been affected by the introduction of large-scale digitised collections. We have seen the value of digitised resources in improving access to collections, in allowing new audiences to engage with libraries and in allowing libraries to deliver their resources beyond the confines of their buildings. But I will argue that the impact of this has been to high-light the problems with existing models for disseminating information. Whereas digitisation supports the theoretical possibility to democratise access, to facilitate global use of library collections and to allow for innov-ative research to occur, the reality is that users have been limited by the way that digitisation has been implemented in the real world. The shift towards the interface as an intermediary between researcher and artefact has produced a certain type of user behaviour which largely resembles an accelerated version of existing practices, with an increased focus on efficient keyword search and retrieval within a web interface. But this falls some way short of the utopian vision outlined by some critics, and Chapter 6 explores how this has occurred. It uses the example of two high profile paywalled newspaper collections to demonstrate that the benefits of digitised collections are often limited primarily to those in information-rich environments. Indeed, the divide between those with widespread access to large-scale digitised resources and those without resembles existing divides to a worrying degree. While I recognise the important benefits of digitised resources, I will argue that large-scale digitisation has a long way to go before achieving the noble aims outlined in libraries' strategic documents. The modern library is built on the twin pillars of access and service, but I will show that the reality of digitisation falls short of this. Existing social structures shape the way that users experience digitised collections and constrain the potential for truly disruptive impact to emerge. Chapter 7 will therefore conclude by outlining the ways in which LSDC could be more successful in creating deeper impact, by moving away from the close remediation of existing media, behaviours and social constructs towards a space where this intellectually distinct medium begins to exert its own artefactual identity as one part of a wider digital information age.

Notes

1 This fund is managed and administered by the Welsh government. It was established in 2008 to take decisions on investment proposals within Wales and oversee the delivery of capital investment programmes.
2 The European Regional Development Fund aims to correct imbalances between its regions through strategic investment, in order to strengthen economic and social cohesion in the European Union.

Bibliography

Almind, T. C. and Ingwersen, P. (1997) 'Infometric analyses on the World Wide Web: methodological approaches to "webometrics"', *Journal of Documentation*, **53**(4).

Bawden, D. and Robinson, L. (2013) 'No such thing as society? On the individuality of information behaviour', *Journal of the American Society for Information Science and Technology*, **64**(123), pp. 2587–2590.

British Library (2008) 'Digitisation strategy 2008–2011, British Library – about us'. Retrieved from: www.bl.uk/aboutus/stratpolprog/digi/digitisation/digistrategy/.

Darke, K. and Shanks, G. (2002) 'Case study research', in Williamson, K. (Ed.) *Research Methods for Students, Academics and Professionals: Information Management and Systems* (2nd edn). Wagga Wagga: Centre for Information Studies, Charles Sturt University (Topics in Australasian Library and Information Studies, 20), pp. 111–123.

Dey, I. (1993) *Qualitative Data Analysis: A User-Friendly Guide for Social Scientists.* London: Routledge.

Digital Analytics Association (2012) 'Digital Analytics Association: About'. Retrieved from: www.digitalanalyticsassociation.org/?page=about.

Eccles, K., Thelwall, M. and Meyer, E. T. (2012) 'Measuring the web impact of digitised scholarly resources', *Journal of Documentation,* **68**(4).

Glaser, B. G. and Strauss, A. L. (1967) *The Discovery of Grounded Theory: Strategies for Qualitative Research.* New York: Aldine de Gruyter.

Google (2012) 'Gain insights that matter, Google Analytics features'. Retrieved from: www.google.com/analytics/features/index.html.

Gorman, G. E. and Clayton, P. (2005) *Qualitative Research for the Information Professional* (2nd edn). London: Library Association Publishing.

MacRoberts, M. H. and MacRoberts, B. R. (1989) 'Problems of citation analysis: a critical review', *Journal of the American Society for Information Science,* **40**(5), pp. 342–349.

Maykut, P. and Morehouse, R. (1994) *Beginning Qualitative Research: A Philosophic and Practical Guide.* London: Farmer Press.

Meyer, E. T., Eccles, K., Thelwall, M. and Madsen, C. (2009) 'Usage and impact study of JISC-funded phase 1 digitisation projects & the Toolkit for the Impact of Digitised Scholarly Resources (TIDSR)'. Oxford: Oxford Internet Institute, University of Oxford. Retrieved from: http://microsites.oii.ox.ac.uk/tidsr/sites/microsites.oii.ox.ac.uk.tidsr/files/TIDSR_FinalReport_20July2009.pdf.

Mussell, J. (2013) 'Welsh Newspapers Online launch event', blog post, 13 March 2013, Parsing Passing Events. Retrieved from: http://jimmussell.com/2013/03/13/parsing-passing-events/.

National Library of Wales (2015) 'Welsh Newspapers Online: digitisation projects'. Retrieved from: www.llgc.org.uk/index.php?id=4723

Nicholas, D., Huntington, P., Williams, P. and Dobrowolski, T. (2004) 'Reappraising information seeking behaviour in a digital environment: bouncers, checkers, returnees and the like', *Journal of Documentation,* **60**(1), pp. 24–39.

Pickard, A. J. (2007) *Research Methods in Information.* London: Facet Publishing.

Punch, K. F. (1998) *Introduction to Social Research: Quantitative and Qualitative Approaches.* Thousand Oaks, California: SAGE Publications Ltd.

Smith, L. (1980) 'Citation analysis', *Library Trends,* **30**, pp. 83–106.

Sukovic, S. (2009) 'References to e-texts in academic publications', *Journal of Documentation,* **65**(6), pp. 997–1015. doi: 10.1108/00220410910998960.

Tanner, S. (2013) 'The value of Welsh Newspapers Online', blog post, 28 March 2013, *When the data hits the fan! The blog of Simon Tanner.* Retrieved from: http://simon-tanner.blogspot.co.uk/2013/03/the-value-of-welsh-newspapers-online.html.

Thelwall, M. (2006) 'Interpreting social science link analysis research: a theoretical framework', *Journal of the American Society for Information Science and Technology,* **57**(1), pp. 60–68.

Thelwall, M. (2009) *Introduction to Webometrics: Quantitative Research for the Social Sciences.* Morgan and Claypool Publishers (Synthesis Lectures on Information Concepts, Retrieval, and Services). Retrieved from: www.morganclaypool.com/doi/pdf/10.2200/S00176ED1V01Y200903ICR004.

Toobin, J. (2007) 'Google's moon shot: the quest for the universal library', *The New Yorker,* 5 February 2007. Retrieved from: www.newyorker.com/reporting/2007/02/05/070205fa_fact_toobin?currentPage=all.

4 Institutional impact of large-scale digitised collections

The contemporary library is a centre of learning, engaged in a two-way process to simultaneously provide digital resources and learn about how their users engage with them. As Niggeman *et al.* explain, memory institutions are adapting to large-scale digitisation in meaningful ways:

> For centuries, libraries, archives and museums from across Europe have been the custodians of our rich and diverse cultural heritage ... culture is following the digital path and "memory institutions" are adapting the way in which they communicate with their public.
>
> (2011)

Institutions the world over are engaged in wide-reaching digitisation programmes, but the resultant change varies across institutional and national barriers. This chapter focuses on how these changes have manifested themselves at an institutional level for the library sector in the United Kingdom. It will draw on evidence from my work with two major libraries: the National Library of Wales and the British Library. These institutions have seen the way they provide users, define staff roles and do their day to day work change as a result of creating the large-scale digitised collections that they now provide to their users. However, the chapter also draws on the wider literature to understand these impacts. While the evidence comes from specific institutional contexts, the challenges that emerge are more widely applicable. The chapters are supported by a series of highlighted case studies that address the methodologies discussed in Chapter 3 and provide more detail on how I implemented specific methods in the course of my own research. They also present aspects of the empirical findings, in order to provide evidence to enrich the arguments that I will make in these chapters and, I hope, give further insights into ways of undertaking impact evaluation.

This chapter is split into three sections. The first explores the extent of change as it relates to libraries as institutions and whether this has led to a change in how they provide library services to users. Digital delivery of library collections has seen the role of libraries change in recent years, as they become increasingly involved in providing resources which reach beyond their traditional boundaries. As a result, I will argue that library roles are changing to adapt. National libraries are adopting a more pro-active approach to user engagement, creating specific digital research teams, which engage directly with users of digitised resources. This supports libraries in working with diffuse and anonymous user communities by ensuring an open dialogue between users. In conjunction, libraries are providing training opportunities to their staff to ensure that they are prepared to support users in new research methodologies and to provide remote support to users who may never enter the library premises in person.

The second section explores the ways in which user support is changing, arguing that libraries are moving towards a model where support will be provided remotely via the internet and phones. It argues that users increasingly expect to access information resources on their own terms, rather than through tightly controlled proprietary platforms, and it explores ways in which libraries are reaching out to platforms such as Flickr and Wikimedia to engage with new user communities.

The final section will argue that the current trend of removing materials from the public domain, through licensing digitised scans as distinct creative works, is damaging to the proactive approach to engagement that libraries have taken. It makes the case that libraries have a key role to play in the digital age, but that this role will largely be defined by their ability to relinquish their traditional gatekeeper role and reach audiences on diverse platforms. In an age of information overload, libraries have a powerful role to play in making information available to users in ways that allow them to utilise the strengths of digitised content for transformative activities. However, in some cases, this potential impact is limited by a combination of licensing conditions which prevent users from reusing content freely, web interfaces which constrain the nature of their inter-actions, and funding models which limit access at a more fundamental level. In the digital age, libraries face the challenge of providing access to huge quantities of materials online, while balancing resource sustainability with their goal to widen access. Indeed, access is the key theme for librarianship in the digital age: with the diversification of information providers, libraries are no longer the default information provider. Instead, they must address barriers to access to ensure that their work reaches an online audience, which is crying out for high quality cultural materials.

Institutional impact

Line and Line identify four conceptual roles that national libraries fulfil, noting that:

> [National libraries] may be national in the sense that they contain the literary production of the nation; or in the sense that they are the nation's book museum, containing a high concentration of the

nation's treasures; or in the sense that they are leaders, perhaps co-ordinators of the nation's libraries; or in the sense that they offer a national service (to the nation's libraries or population).

(1979)

In fact, national libraries simultaneously fulfil more than one of these roles. In the United Kingdom, where our focus lies, the legal deposit libraries balance all of these dimensions, providing collections for heritage purposes, interlibrary lending and national library infrastructure, and a reference library service to members of the public with a specific research need. Digitised newspapers are therefore relevant to many library activities, and the impact of digitisation at institutional level is felt by two key communities: first, the library as an organism, a public institution with collections which are accessible in physical and/or digital form; and second, the library staff who are directly or indirectly affected by large-scale digitisation. The impacts can include changes in professional practice, job titles and training, professional redundancy or new types of job. There is a general agreement that the cultural and heritage sector will need to adapt in meaningful ways as a result of large-scale digitisation.

For centuries, libraries, archives and museums from across Europe have been the custodians of our rich and diverse cultural heritage … culture is following the digital path and "memory institutions" are adapting the way in which they communicate with the public.

(Niggeman *et al.*, 2011)

The digital path to which they refer is being walked by institutions across the world, but the extent and nature of change is defined by the local context, at institutional and national level. While this is true, there are lessons that can be taken from this snapshot of two major UK institutions that are more widely applicable. This chapter will therefore explore many of the impacts that have been manifested in recent years, including the impact of digitisation on library funding and skills, issues of resource sustainability, and the ways in which staff and institutional practices are adapting in order to meet the demands placed upon them by the large-scale digitisation of their collections.

The demands that have been placed upon institutions to digitise their collections in such large quantities are summed up well by Tanner:

Frankly, managing content and context in digital repositories is a large and unfunded mandate that has been forced upon the LIS community because of perceived user demand and the short timeframe in which action must be taken.

(2009)

Case study: using interviews to identify institutional impacts

It is important to consider both the user and institutional perspectives when investigating the impact of large-scale digitisation. For my research, I undertook a series of studies with staff from the case study institutions in order to identify the self-reported impact of digitisation on their working environment, professional practices, and interactions with collections and users. When dealing with representatives of an institution, there is a risk that participants will give a sanitised version of their opinions, but this can be mitigated by ensuring their anonymity and making clear the personal nature of any opinions expressed. My interview selections met the definition of a purposive sample; in other words, participants were chosen to include "representatives from within the population being studied who have a range of characteristics relevant to the research project" (Gorman and Clayton, 2005). This allowed for a multiplicity of voices and meant that the opinions gathered represented the range of roles within the institution. I therefore undertook interviews with those involved in the planning, creation and administration of the digitised newspaper collections (including representatives from senior management), rights and copyright officers, digitisation project managers, reader services librarians and marketing officers.

Because interviewees were chosen for their expertise and relevance to the project, the interviews were considered to pose no major ethical considerations. With this in mind, appropriate ethical procedures were followed. Participants were told about the project, the purpose of the interview and the intention to record it. They were also given a consent form which explained how their responses would be used in the research and were presented with the opportunity to either sign the form to indicate their agreement or withdraw from the interview at any point. This form included assurances that interview data would be anonymised as far as possible, that interviewees would have the right to check the accuracy of any quotes attributed to them in the study and that they could request that any information they wanted to remain private would not be published. I decided that a semi-structured interview was the most effective approach, as it allowed the interviews to remain informal and adaptive, while also ensuring that all major themes were covered in-depth. An interview guide was therefore used to ensure that topics were covered, but the wording of the questions was spontaneous and enabled the interview to feel more natural to participants. Interviews were recorded and later transcribed, with notes taken only as prompts on the day. These transcriptions were then further analysed by coding the data in order to bring out important information and themes and to allow comparison between interviewees. This approach to transcription and coding of interview data is conducive to inductive analysis: by allowing the data analysis to determine coding systems, issues were allowed to emerge from the data (Mansourian, 2006). This chapter draws on these interviews with experts to explore the impact of large-scale digitised collections at an institutional level, and all responses are reported with an institutional identifier (e.g. BL1) and interview number in line with the ethical information above.

External pressures have influenced the pace and nature of change that has occurred alongside large-scale digitisation. Users have now come to expect extensive digital resources: when asked what improvement libraries could make to digitised collections, their most common answer is to provide more digitised content to be made available online. But core funding has not been increased to meet this demand; the opposite is largely true in the United Kingdom, as libraries struggle even to maintain existing services in the face of severe austerity. Institutional approaches to digitisation have arisen from this pressure, relying on external funding to create the digitised resources which users now demand as standard, while trying to also meet their aims to open their collections up to new audiences online. Librarians have needed to respond to these developments quickly, and best practice in creating LSDC has largely been created through first-hand experience, rather than in response to specific research needs. As a result, library staff have no clear sense of how digital research might develop in the coming years, although they expect it to become increasingly important and to expand beyond textual analysis:

> People can do analysis of text pretty well, just starting to be able to do analysis of images, very nascent with sound and hardly at all with moving image. So we're going to see that line shift over the next decade: what is today easy to do with text, in five years will be easy to do with audio.
>
> (BL1)

The overall experience of large-scale digitisation for libraries and their staff is one of learning: due to the difficulty of predicting emerging trends in digital research, the sector must continually engage with researchers and the public to ensure that it can adapt its practices in response. The approach of the two UK institutions I will consider here, the BL and the NLW, has been extremely proactive. Both have responded to trends in the sector by creating dedicated teams with responsibility for ensuring that digital services adapt in line with the needs of their users. This proactive role, I will argue, is one that libraries will need to adopt in order to stay current in the digital age.

The British Library has embraced digital scholarship by creating a specific team of digital curators with responsibility for training, development and outreach in digital research and skills. This team is part of the digital scholarship section, which has three main roles: direct responsibility for several collection areas with a strong digital practice focus; digital skills training and dissemination within the BL; and knowledge exchange with digitally engaged researchers. The digital scholarship team has been involved in a number of initiatives, of which two will be discussed here. The first is an extensive, structured training programme to increase familiarity with digital research methods for BL employees. The programme aims to ensure that "staff across all collection areas are familiar and conversant with the foundational concepts, methods and tools of digital scholarship" (McGregor and Farquhar, 2013). The training programme, initially delivered only to the BL's curatorial staff, subsequently expanded to include other staff when space allowed, and it plays an important role in ensuring that staff skills keep pace with technological developments and changing user requirements. In scoping their training activities, the team actively sought out scholars working with computing and scholarship and consulted the proceedings of major digital humanities conferences to identify emerging trends in research. The finished curriculum was forward-thinking, incorporating everything from the basics of digital scholarship through to specific research methods and metadata standards. This approach is indicative of an emerging culture of proactivity towards engagement with users of the BL's digital collections in recent years.

The second initiative which has been central to this is British Library Labs. Funded by the Andrew W. Mellon Foundation, the initiative invites researchers and developers to work with the BL and its digital collections to answer important research questions. It also hosts an annual competition to showcase the best of digital scholarship using BL digital collections, with the results made available to the public when possible. These activities have a dual role: they actively assist in widely disseminating the BL's digitised collections, drawing attention to materials and making staff aware of the innovative research being done using digitised collections; and they allow vital bidirectional knowledge exchange between researchers and the library sector:

> It's to initiate a discussion for people to start presenting us with ideas, and the purpose of doing this is so that we can learn what things we need to do better to support digital scholarship, what tools and services we need to develop.
>
> (BL3)

This relatively recent strategy for actively engaging with users of digital collections and supporting digital scholarship is extremely positive. BL Labs has started the difficult process of working through rights and licence agreements to make digital collections available, and the creation of a specific team with expertise in digital scholarship provides a point of contact for researchers working in this area. This constitutes a positive response to the challenges of large-scale digitisation and a realistic solution for ensuring that greater use is made of all aspects of digital curation in the future.

To achieve this, the BL has had to adapt its previous curatorial model; they have moved from having curators with responsibility for specific collection areas towards having them grouped thematically. This has helped to create a core of expertise within the library, ensuring that digital research is more appropriately supported. Above all, it suggests that the library is eager to see its collections used to their full potential. The digital scholarship team provides a point of contact in an institution which, like many large organisations, is sometimes characterised as monolithic and fragmented. This has meant that, until now, there has been no coherent strategy for identifying reuse in digital collections:

> One of the things, I think, is to find out what digital content there is. There have been a number of initiatives in the library to do that, but it's quite fragmented ... the British Library doesn't necessarily know what can be used.
>
> (BL3)

The benefits to staff and users in identifying what can be reused are immense, allowing research to be done more effectively without having to individually negotiate access to collections. The digital scholarship team is therefore playing an important role in assessing the extent of BL digital collections and working with staff and researchers to ensure that they are used to their full potential.

The National Library of Wales has adopted a different approach to digitising its newspaper collections. Rather than rely on external funding and commercial partnerships, the majority of NLW projects have been undertaken in-house with contractors appointed to bring specific expertise at strategic phases. Digitisation is now considered a core library function, with the library using their annual grant in aid to fund an ongoing digitisation programme. This means that WNO was produced in-house by the library's digitisation and web design teams. Creating full text searchable records was outsourced due to the complexities of digitising bilingual materials:

> The bilingualism, I think, was an added challenge. The OCR had to be outsourced: we did have software to undertake OCR internally for most print materials but not for this aged material from several centuries ago.
>
> (NLW4)

Employing an internal digitisation team has both drawbacks and benefits. It means that collections are digitised on an ongoing basis, with downtime between major projects allowing other collections to be scanned. It also ensures that all metadata and content remain unequivocally in the library's control, retaining the ability to use the library's collections more flexibly than commercial partnerships might allow. However, in-house digitisation brings additional overheads associated with retaining staff and equipment between larger projects. The NLW has therefore taken on board these extra costs in exchange for the flexibility to respond to future institutional needs. This greater control of processes and content means the library can adapt its delivery of digital collections more efficiently, without renegotiating licences.

This has happened concurrently with a push to ensure that staff gain the skills necessary to provide digitisation services and to support users of digital collections. As one interviewee notes, large-scale digitisation has had a positive impact on staff skill levels:

> It's definitely upskilled our staff. It's probably created a new breed of staff in that the team are semi-technical – they are more like digital curators than operatives, so I think we've created a new breed of professionals, and the skills they've built are being shared with others.
>
> (NLW4)

In addition, the NLW has created an internal research development team, which was initially led by Professor Lorna Hughes with close links to the nearby University of Aberystwyth. As one interviewee noted, this approach is extremely novel and has opened up new opportunities for the library:

> When Lorna was appointed, we think that was the only Chair in Digital Collections in a National Library in the world ... It's definitely improved the library and what it has to offer and opened up new doors for ourselves as a library, but also for users.
>
> (NLW4)

The digital research team retains a small group of researchers, who provide core expertise and knowledge exchange in a similar way to the BL's digital scholarship team. This allows the NLW to undertake its own research and to improve its collections through internal activities and external engagement. This, combined with extensive participation in relevant professional groups, has laid the groundwork for developing the internal expertise necessary to track and respond to technical shifts.

The development of specific teams to work with digital collections shows a clear strategic focus on skills development for library staff and on knowledge exchange with the library and academic sectors. These activities are important for developing appropriate strategies for maximising the potential of library digital collections and represent a shift in policy that has occurred within the last decade. I noted in my introduction that libraries had initially approached digitisation conscious of the pressure to make their collections available online but without a sense of how the materials they were producing would be used by researchers. These activities are a clear indication that the sector is beginning to redress the balance. Existing licences (and previous mistakes) may not be easily corrected, but the proactive approach described here could allow the sector to avoid similar problems in future and to address the role of large-scale digitisation in supporting users in the coming years. The importance of this focus on users cannot be overstated: it is my argument that the particular representational decisions that are made with digitised content, and the platforms on which this content is hosted, are responsible for shaping the long-term meaning of that content as well as the ways in which users can interact and reuse it. As Dahlstrom *et al.* note:

> The library that digitizes selections of its collections not only makes existing cultural heritage accessible, but also actively shapes, re-shapes and creates such a heritage. The user who enters a digitised library collection faces material that is, to varying degrees, already encoded and interpreted.
>
> (2012)

Libraries were slow to come to terms with their role in shaping the meaning and reuse of heritage materials in the early years of digitisation. The more critical approach to digital scholarship that has been adopted in recent years will allow them to engage in discussions with the community to understand the impact that this has had. I will argue that the library has become a producer, and a codifier, of heritage materials at large scale. It influences the presentation and meaning of materials in a way that, while having echoes of the remediation of physical library collections via binding, microfilming and format transfer, is being done at a larger scale and with a greater focus on the library as a producer of material than has previously been the case.

Implications for user support

We will see in Chapter 6 that large-scale digitisation affects how users interact with library collections; institutional paywalls, for example, have implications for accessibility and the way in which material is presented. Content licensing models not only have the potential to severely limit the types of people who can access digitised newspapers, but they can fundamentally define the interfaces that are produced to interact with materials online. We can address this problem by adopting an open approach to reuse of digitised content. The NLW, for instance, has implemented an open access strategy for its digital resources, which one interviewee argues allows them to better serve their users' needs:

> It's one thing to say there are no rights restrictions, but you can still be restricting use by the very way in which you're representing the

material to the user. I think that is something we're trying to look at … trying to open that up.

(NLW1)

This approach recognises that users are not and should not be limited by libraries in the uses that they can put public domain content to. In fact, the European Commission has addressed this directly, noting that more work needs to be done to ensure that digitisation does not limit the ability of users to take full advantage of the public domain:

> Digitised public domain content is an area of concern. Frequently, accessibility to these resources is jeopardized by intrusive watermarking, low resolution or visual protection measures, and its re-use limited by the prohibition of reproduction or use of such materials for other than non-commercial purposes.
>
> (2014)

The drawbacks of allowing institutions and commercial partners to remove materials from the public domain by the process of digitisation are clear. On the other hand, there are an increasing number of high profile examples which show the benefits of a more open approach. The BL, for instance, gave away over one million public domain images in December 2013. The images were taken from seventeenth, eighteenth and nineteenth century books digitised by Microsoft and donated to the British Library, who uploaded them to Flickr under a Creative Commons licence. The impact of this image giveaway has profoundly proven the power of free content. The British Library Flickr photostream was accessed over 260 million times by June 2015 and even helped to inspire an art installation created by David Normal for display at the Burning Man festival (Durham, 2015). These uses show the transformative potential of digitised materials when institutions trust users to remix and reuse their collections. One BL interviewee, for instance, noted that increasing access via non-library web platforms can extend access and make library content visible to new audiences:

> I'm very, very interested in how moving content to another place will increase access. I'm very interested in the stuff that was done with a small collection of Canadian photos which were put onto Wikimedia … It's content that was BL-owned, and it's been put under a CC0 licence and it's just been made available through Wikimedia and it's just increased the access.
>
> (BL3)

The NLW has also experimented with uploading library content to alternative platforms, noting that their Flickr stream of around 1,500 images had been viewed over one million times in four years. As one interviewee noted, "That's more than would ever, ever, in all eternity see the collection in person" (NLW2). A strong case can be made for making library content available on other websites, if libraries can ensure their role in providing the content is clear. It considerably widens participation, allowing users who might be unaware of library collections to discover them on their own terms. Releasing content in this way also increases the audience that may discover it, and properly attributed content can help to increase awareness of the host library. This hints at the increased proactivity of librarians, who are beginning to explore opportunities for reaching new users through online platforms. Such an approach fits the idea of libraries as institutions both providing stewardship for users and operating in the interests of these users. By ensuring that barriers are removed, libraries can support users nationally and globally in using large-scale digitised collections in creative and innovative ways. The diverse, diffuse and largely anonymous nature of the web means that it has become increasingly hard for libraries to engage directly with these new user communities, but this response is a powerful resource for the new problem of user engagement for libraries.

Profiling the user community of web resources is extremely difficult, and libraries are therefore having to adapt in how they support their users. Users who respond to online surveys about digitised resources generally possess a high level of competence in discovering and using large-scale digitised collections; it would be dangerous to assume that the most engaged users are representative of the whole community. Those users with lower levels of digital literacy may struggle with digitised collections but never set foot in a library where trained staff can help them. Libraries must therefore make arrangements to ensure that those with lower levels of digital literacy are supported in their research. Library staff already provide services to users, but the distributed nature of the web requires a shift in how this service is delivered. One NLW interviewee summed this up by noting that, as information behaviour moved online, there would be a decreased demand for face-to-face user support in libraries, but that this would likely be mirrored by an increase in the need for remote customer service teams trained in using digital collections to support users via the web and telephone. This is likely to affect how libraries provide enquiry services and the type of support that will be necessary:

> I've heard our team go through it step by step: "Click on this, now go to this", and they will talk them [users] through ... There's a shift in the way our enquiries are being handled, from the physical to the remote, through telephone lines and Question Point.[1]

> (NLW4)

This represents a fundamental shift in how library support services are understood. Both academic and national libraries receive large numbers of physical visitors every year, but the nature of what they do in this space is changing. Now, the provision of comfortable seating, Wi-Fi connections and digital resources is just as important to users as access to physical collections. In this respect, the shifting nature of user support will affect the library's relationship with users: as digitisation has partially removed the geographical boundaries of library collections, so too does it require a re-appraisal of the face-to-face support model. We can expect to see an increase in the number of libraries which provide remote user support in coming years. This trend has already begun, with many libraries now offering "ask a librarian" services via their library catalogue.

Activities of this kind provide a route map for supporting remote users who, as I will note in Chapter 5, are using LSDC for types of research which will be largely familiar to library staff. The growth of digital research methods will provide a different set of challenges and demand skill sets which many librarians do not currently possess. Digital research methods need mastery at disciplinary level but also an understanding of the tools which are required to undertake meaningful work. As one interviewee pointed out, many researchers, who may be comfortable with using digital resources for information discovery and reading, may not have the skills to undertake digital methods such as corpus analysis:

> They don't have the background, they don't have the [knowledge of] statistics, they don't have simple-to-use visualisation tools that they're taught about, starting as undergraduates.
>
> (BL1)

This puts pressure on libraries to adopt solutions that non-expert users can manage. Yet this approach will limit the types of research that are being undertaken. Google Ngrams, for instance, has been immensely influential in lowering the technical knowledge required to effectively data mine literary corpora. Its release was closely linked to the quantitative work of Michel and Shen (2010), whose work fits into a longer tradition of quantitative literary analysis. However, as Brake (2012) notes for digitised newspapers, it is common for the most easily available resources to assume a higher profile than would be warranted otherwise. In the case of Google Ngrams, this has led to an uncritical approach in research. Barbosa's (2013) widely publicised "Books of Cities Infographic" is one such example. It uses the English language Ngrams dataset to visualise the number of mentions of a variety of world cities in books, purporting to give an overall idea of the amount of literature produced in the twentieth century for each city. The concept is visually arresting but flawed, for the simple reason that its author fails to take into account the evolution of city names, attributing significance to the growth in mentions of Mumbai and Beijing without recognising that the end of British colonialism in the East brought with it name changes that gradually gained wide adoption. The infographic therefore provides an inadvertent warning of the dangers of relying on datasets without the appropriate field-specific knowledge to interpret the findings successfully.

This example foregrounds the risk of adopting one problematic tool as the de facto solution for research on the basis of its simplicity, accessibility or high profile. In reality, researchers require a range of tools, depending on their own expertise and requirements:

> If everybody had agreed that the Google Ngram viewer is the be all and end all of research tools and that's all you needed, then we would buy it, lease it or build it and away you go. But that's not how it is: a lot of people use all sorts of linguistic analysis packages in any language you might care to use.
>
> (BL1)

Thus the lack of universal standards in corpus analysis, like many digital research methods, demands the existence of open library collections which are flexible enough to serve diverse requirements. Rather than providing specific tools, librarians must consider how to create a technical infrastructure for digitised collections into which users can bring their preferred tools. As one interviewee describes:

> We want to ensure that people can use it [British Library Nineteenth Century Newspapers] with the tool they want. So if you use Mathematica, you're a power user of it, that's the tool you should be using because it's your research tool. So we're trying to figure out infrastructurally how to set that up.
>
> (BL1)

Adapting library infrastructures is a long-term task, and standards remain unclear. More fundamental steps can be taken in the creation of large-scale digitised collections that address the need described above to facilitate digital research methods. These steps must focus on making digitised content open access. Open Application Programming Interfaces (APIs), open metadata, Creative Commons licensing of scanned images and the availability of full text corpora would all allow appropriately skilled users to adapt collections for their own tools, while developing flexible collections that can be used to facilitate emerging methods. The emphasis for libraries should be on facilitating research rather than shaping it. The interface and the tools which are provided to users play a key role in defining how digitised collections will be used. While there is a valid argument that some users require library support in selecting and using research tools, there is a risk in selecting tools on behalf of users. As Baker correctly identifies:

Bolting, for example, a georeferencer onto an interface for OCR'd newspapers is shaping rather than enabling research – it is promoting one method over another.

(2013)

I would go further than this, though, in noting that the search interface which is so often the default is similarly not a neutral influence upon researcher behaviour. Every decision regarding interface and functionality is an editorial decision which will promote one form of interpretation over another. Mussell and Brake both argue that search functionality impacts upon the user experience, separating researchers from the context of the information they discover, and presenting digital surrogates as decontextualised snippets rather than part of a wider whole. In addition, the search interface demands a particular kind of behaviour on the part of the user, mediated through the web browsing experience where the aim is often to process large quantities of information through searching, browsing and skim reading pages. I will argue in Chapter 5 that the behaviour of users of large-scale digitised collections is deep and sustained, but it is certainly influenced by the norms of the internet and the reliance on a search interface for defining form and meaning. The danger of providing digitised collections with search as the dominant behavioural model is therefore clear: by doing so the library promotes a particular kind of behaviour. Tanner comments that "the public want content – where they are, when they want it and are agnostic about the source" (2013). I would endorse this but with one added facet: the public also want content to be open, in the sense that it can be accessed freely, and in the sense that it can be reused in their desired manner. If we provide the researcher with a tightly constrained interface that contains content with limited reuse rights, we already shape rather than enable research, even before the question of tools arises. Unless resource creators support other approaches, through open licences and the provision of suitable tools, the impact of digitised content will already have been constrained.

This will require careful consideration on the part of libraries, starting with how they conceive of licensing conditions and resource design and infrastructure. We can look to the NLW's approach to copyright for inspiration: their decision to provide all scanned pages under CC0 licences, with open metadata and access to full text, will make the entire resource far more supportive of future reuses. This is important because it makes fewer assumptions about the intended use of the collection. Another way in which user requirements can be met is the provision of what Whitelaw calls "generous interfaces":

As an interface, search fails to match the ample abundance of our digital collections and the generous ethos of the institutions that hold them. A more generous interface would do more to represent the scale and richness of its collection. It would open the doors, tear down the drab lobby; instead of demanding a query it would offer multiple ways in, and support exploration as well as the focused enquiry where search excels. In revealing the complexity of digital collections, a generous interface would also enrich interpretation by revealing relationships and structures within a collection.

(Whitelaw, 2015)

The features of generosity are open data, flexible interfaces and additional services which improve on basic search functionality. We can see a gradual shift in focus from supplying basic interfaces towards one where researchers and developers will have more freedom to produce novel interfaces and applications. Large-scale digitisation has the potential to remove the gatekeeper role of memory institutions, moving them towards a model built upon facilitation; we can encourage users not only to access library materials online but to build tools to undertake transformative research and to create new modes of interaction. In this sense, our thinking should reflect the idea that, by separating content from its physical form, we can facilitate sharing and reuse. This is one of the biggest strengths of digital content, yet the opportunities for widening participation and interactions have not yet been fully realised. Two reasons loom large: the first being the commercial and regulatory framework within which large-scale digitisation is situated, and the second being an ongoing fear over how this generosity will have an impact on the relevance of libraries in a digital age.

Licensing and copyright: dual barriers to impact

In October 2015, Wikimedia announced that the Reiss Engelhorn Museum in Germany filed a lawsuit concerning copyright claims over 17 images from the museum's public domain works of art which were uploaded to Wikimedia Commons. Although the images are in the public domain, and therefore exist for people to freely reuse, the museum argued that the skill and effort of the photographer who was hired to photograph these items ensured that a new copyright term began. The case emphasises a particular tension which lies at the heart of how copyright has been viewed in the digital age. I have argued in this chapter for the benefits that cultural heritage institutions can realise from working with other platforms, and yet one of the main barriers to reuse of cultural collections is the renewal of copyright based on the transformation of public domain images into a new format. The argument echoes that which underscored the Google Books court case: the extent to which digitisation can be considered to be transformative is fundamental to whether new images can be considered to be a distinct intellectual output. There is a tension, then, between the idea of digitised media as a distinct medium and the call for digitised materials to be made freely available online. Yet these two ideas are not as oppositional as they seem at first: although digitisation redefines the meaning of an object by changing its format and materiality, the intention of copyright has always been to protect the rights of people engaged in original creative production. The change to a digital format demands new modes of understanding from the user, but it does not necessarily represent a distinct intellectual contribution from the image creator. The ability of commercial companies to monetise digitised content is entirely predicated on the assumption that the mere act of digitising represents a creative or intellectual contribution in itself.

Copyright and commercial licensing agreements play a big role in defining access and user engagement with digital resources, meaning that some collections can remain relatively inaccessible in the medium term. Despite this, there are ways in which the impact of strict licensing could be minimised, including returning to existing collections and investigating opportunities to extend access and renegotiate the terms of reuse:

> Maybe there needs to be a re-engagement with the original publishers, for example in the terms of the licenses that were agreed because that was twenty years ago or whenever it was, and you know technology's moved on.
>
> (BL3)

The agenda for open access to digitised content is intellectually tied to ongoing efforts to provide open access to publicly funded research. Niggeman *et al.* (2011) have called for institutions in the European Union to adopt digitisation practices which ensure widespread access and interoperability, suggesting the following: the removal of digital watermarks; efforts to make material digitised with public funding as widely available as possible; the harmonisation of rights statuses for digitised materials across EU member states; the expectation that cultural institutions take greater responsibility for digitising European cultural heritage; and the provision of freely and widely available metadata. Many institutions have already taken steps to fulfil these responsibilities. The National Library of Australia (NLA), through Trove, makes its collections freely available and engages with users to crowdsource OCR improvements. The NLW has also rejected the idea of reasserting copyright on digitised public domain content, with one interviewee noting that this seemed the only logical option:

> I couldn't see a valid or robust argument in favour of claiming copyright on a digital reproduction of a scanned image of something that was out of copyright ... essentially it was a decision made on principle.
>
> (NLW2)

The interviewee acknowledges the role of personal conscience in deciding how to license content. My position is that libraries, and particularly national libraries, are custodians of content and not owners. It is therefore incumbent upon them to ensure the widest and most diverse access to their collections that is possible. The extent of access to digitised collections is theoretically boundless and means that libraries are entering new territory in the scale of their user base, yet they are at greater risk of irrelevance if their collections are inaccessible than if they are freely and widely available.

I asked interviewees what they expected to happen to commercially licensed digitised newspapers once the term of any agreement had expired. They were keen for the material to be openly accessible once its commercial value had been realised by the commercial partner. While the BL has embraced commercial partnerships, there was a sense that this was only due to a dearth of alternate funding: the choice was between commercial collections or no collections, not between paywalls and open access. As one interviewee notes, the BL is not ideologically wedded to the idea of commercial partnerships for large-scale digitisation projects:

> There was the sugar daddy need there … We're simply not currently resourced, and I wouldn't expect for the next five years for that situation to change, which means that we are a little bit at the whim of commercial interests.
>
> (BL1)

This position represents a difficult balancing act between users' desire for digitised content, the need to develop digital collections with long-term viability, and the lack of funding available for these activities. Many decisions regarding open access are influenced by short-term barriers, which profoundly limit the potential of digital collections in the medium to long-term. The political and cultural context within which individual institutions operate plays a role; it was clear from NLW staff, for instance, that there was governmental support for their digitisation programme:

> We always intended to make the items freely available and accessible to all; we definitely decided against the model that the British Library had, and we were supported in that by government. So I think that's an important point to make – the fact that government supported the model we went for.
>
> (NLW4)

Hunter and Brown have written of the phenomenon of "small, smart countries" which have a desire to demonstrate their own cultural identity to a global audience.

> Such countries are politically, educationally, socially and technologically advanced, however they are relatively small on the world stage …

These small countries may have cultural identities under threat from globalisation, yet their very size might enable them to respond rapidly to changing circumstances.

(Hunter and Brown, 2010)

Small, in this context, is by no means derogatory; it merely refers to nations with smaller populations than those served by the largest institutions. As a result, these smaller national libraries have a slightly different remit. In the United Kingdom, the BL has responsibility for preserving the British cultural record, whereas the NLW has a stated aim to preserve and make accessible the cultural record as it relates to Wales. This means their collections are smaller, which provides benefits to the scalability of their digitisation programmes. They can feasibly digitise complete collections, which is almost unachievable for the largest national libraries where collection size numbers in the hundreds of millions. As Hunter and Brown point out, smaller nations can respond more quickly to change, meaning they can benefit from identifying and tackling common issues and undertaking knowledge exchange to build a community of expertise with similar nations. They can also focus on less obvious materials or collections which specifically showcase the nation's cultural importance. This brings with it the added benefit of allowing smaller nations to ensure their culture is represented in the digital domain and thus address the risk of homogenisation.

The position of commercial providers complicates the cultural and social mission of national libraries and has an impact on the way that search is viewed. In collections where content is protected by a paywall, search is often provided freely to showcase the wealth of information in the resource. Users are allowed to undertake searches and view the complete results, but when they attempt to click through to newspaper content they are redirected to information on purchasing subscriptions. This is reminiscent of the model adopted by Google Books, which allows searching of copyrighted material but redirects users to online sources for purchasing the book. Its stark transactional nature makes more sense for materials protected by copyright, where a searchable database of books allows for improved discoverability. Sergey Brin (2009) argues that this represents an overall benefit to users, given that the majority of physical books are not accessible for users either, but in fact commercial digitisation has failed to address this problem: the vast majority of books are still inaccessible online, and the accessibility of even public domain works is undermined by the act of claiming renewed copyright through scanning. We can therefore expect collections such as BNCN to remain relatively inaccessible in the short to medium term. At the moment, interviewees are unclear about exactly what will happen once existing agreements expire:

That's very much a commercial decision because I think ... unless things change from the path we're on ... then I can see that means more content coming along, but maybe a longer duration that news-paper is under this sort of embargo situation ... On the other side, if that commercial value is all expended, then there is still great benefit because then we have the resource and can presumably then be open data.

(BL2)

Many interviewees expect to see further change in the next ten years. One suggestion is that multiple formats will be combined to create a digital multimedia workspace:

One of the challenges for the library ... is to create basically digital editing tools, a suite of editing tools that could be downloadable potentially from the library's website, which would allow people to embed video, to cut and crop images, and to put those into that multi-media thesis environment ... And I think that will be normal; I think that's what we would expect people to be doing.

(BL4)

The potential is certainly there for news media to move beyond early textual materials and incorporate audio-visual content and images from radio, television, and web-based sources. Such advances will only be pos-sible, though, if libraries can either renegotiate existing licences or move towards more open models for the end user. This leaves a sense that short-term sacrifices are considered necessary to fulfil long-term commitments to collection development and preservation. A sense of long-term respons-ibility is emphasised by Hunter and Brown, who explain:

National Libraries, by their nature, take a long-term view. They need an awareness of the past and they need to anticipate the needs of future generations. They need to consider not only current needs and demands, but must also bear in mind how the publications of today will form part of the cultural heritage of the nation in future.

(Hunter and Brown, 2010)

In this respect, the caution surrounding contemporary materials is understandable; on the other hand, the logic of the public domain for published works is that future generations will have the ability to benefit from works when their commercial value to the originator has expired. Allowing corporate interests to assert ownership of public domain materials denies this right. The DPLA in the US provides a compelling vision for building digitised collections for the public good. The UK has been extremely successful in digitising its heritage collections, but the local context has failed to support our institutions in constructing a similarly visionary model for allowing the public to benefit from the rich opportunities afforded by the confluence of public domain materials and digital technologies.

What role do libraries have in an age of large-scale digitisation?

One area where libraries still have a key role to play is in addressing the "black hole" of copyrighted materials in digital collections. The majority of LSDC are based upon public domain materials because copyright continues to play a vital role in defending the intellectual property rights of authors of contemporary works. Extending digitisation to copyrighted works is therefore fraught with problems surrounding the ability of living creators to profit from their work. The relevance of library collections is bolstered by this dearth of contemporary material available online. Libraries have been risk-averse in deciding which materials to digitise, with an NLW representative outlining their approach for newspaper digitisation:

> Some degree of due diligence would be undertaken for material from around 1868 originally because that was a date that had been used by the British Library and Google, but we kind of rounded softly around 1870, so 140 years.
>
> (NLW2)

Copyright law ensures that there is a roughly one-hundred-year period during which very little material is freely available online. Libraries will continue to play a vital role in ensuring some level of access to these materials, however: journals and books, both physical and electronic; archival materials; born digital content such as websites and software; images; and audio-visual materials. This emphasises the dual role of libraries, which have a responsibility to provide access now, while simultaneously ensuring the preservation of these materials for the future. The challenge exists in expressing this role to users, many of whom have bought into the media narrative that everything of importance is available online. This is certainly not the case: for instance, a recent survey found that, on average, European cultural institutions had digitised only 4 per cent of their collections, with a target of increasing this proportion to 62 per cent. For newspapers, only 17 per cent of the total had been digitised, with 54 per cent catalogued using digital metadata standards (Stroeker and Vogels, 2012). The scale of investment required to digitise libraries at this scale is also huge; Poole (2010) estimates that the cost of digitising the complete cultural record of the European Union is roughly €100 billion. We are a long distance, and many billions of pounds, away from even being close to achieving a universal digital library.

There should be no great concern about the relevance of libraries, but there should be concern with the fact that they are so often considered irrelevant despite their role in providing both digital and physical materials. The challenge for libraries is to make sure that their contribution is recognised among the myriad information sources which compete for our attention. Some users do not make the link between the library as a physical institution and the online resources which it provides. Libraries must therefore consider how to disseminate their collections widely, while ensuring that their role in producing these collections remains evident. They can do so through sector-specific engagement, public outreach and presentations at conferences for appropriate audiences. Representatives of the BL, for instance, presented a paper on their Digital Scholarship Training Programme at Digital Humanities 2013 (McGregor and Farquhar, 2013). The National Library of the Netherlands presented a poster at Digital Humanities 2015: as a result, they noted anecdotally the huge increase in librarians present among conference delegates (Wilms, 2015). The NLW is also actively engaging with user communities:

> We have a post who is responsible for our research services and what she does is interact with groups from university. We've made headway this year and got in touch with groups that we wouldn't have known before because one talks to another and they get in touch so it goes from one to the other. And we've got a summer school next year.
>
> (NLW4)

These approaches ensure that national libraries are deeply engaged with the research community. Libraries are subtly shifting their position in the information ecology, putting them into the same space as publishers and content producers. Their shift towards content creation has already put them into conflict with commercial publishers. For instance, James Murdoch directly attacked the impact of cultural institutions using digital materials to expand online audiences:

> Like the search business, but motivated by different concerns, the public sector interest is to distribute content for near-zero costs – harming the market in doing so, and then justifying increased subsidies to make up for the damage it has inflicted.
>
> (Wray, 2010)

Murdoch's argument is weak, insofar as it assumes that the market is the most suitable method for distributing public domain materials online, but it does address a change in the role of libraries as a result of digitisation: instead of acting as repositories, libraries are increasingly engaged in content creation and, by extension, content provision. While Niggeman *et al.* (2011) have made a strong argument for the public good in making digitised collections available online, the involvement of commercial partners places libraries in a complex position. In some respects, it undermines the national library's public service remit and represents a partial paradigm shift from library users as patrons to library users as customers.

With this in mind, it is evident that the UK's public service remit for digitisation is more limited than that of nations such as the USA. This is most clearly summed up by articles published within a few weeks of each other by Robert Darnton and Roly Keating in 2013, describing their respective visions for digitisation at the national level. Darnton (2013), a founding board member of the Digital Public Library of America (DPLA), used visionary language to describe its launch. He outlined a number of concepts which contribute to a vision of the DPLA as a platform for effectively supporting user-focused, large-scale digitisation: interoperability, distributed networks and accessibility. The DPLA was conceived as an open platform, offering great potential for its future development. Tanner has described the opportunities created by open source thus:

> Open source offers new opportunities for collaboration and technical sophistication with interesting new total cost of ownership models. The Open Access movement provides a similar revolution to the financing of content to populate the digital library.
>
> (2009)

Keating (2013), the CEO of the British Library, described a far more modest vision than Darnton, talking instead about the ways in which digitisation allowed users to search content. In doing so, he implicitly positions front-end discovery platforms as an end of digitisation in themselves, rather than one of a potential suite of tools for engaging with digitised content. His words reflect the subtle shift towards positioning the library as a more commercially orientated publisher. As a result, there is now a tension at the heart of national library services, which is represented by the way that the commercial digitisation model has limited the impact of library collections.

The British Library has received criticism for this approach. Torkington, for instance, stridently argued that their strategy was deeply flawed:

> The British Library had a company digitise, and then got limited access and rights to the digitised content ... You can see the mistake they made. They focused on collecting digital assets and digitising their physical ones, probably even convened conferences on digital metadata. And then they hid their fabulous collections out of sight. It's like they WANT [author's emphasis] to be irrelevant.
>
> (2011)

There are no easy answers for libraries. Users are desperate for digital content, and institutions face immense pressure to provide it. But at the same time, sacrificing rights to digitised materials in the short to medium term, in exchange for huge progress in obtaining these materials, will have a profound impact on the ability of libraries to serve their users in the coming years.

Summary: online access and the future of libraries

I have argued in this chapter that libraries have seen their role change in several important ways. First, the way that they serve their users has shifted away from face-to-face contact with a clearly defined community and towards networked communication platforms where the audience is not immediately identifiable. Libraries are beginning to redefine their support services to take account of this change, having staff trained in using digital collections to provide support to users. A key component of this change is the creation of specific teams of library staff who are tasked with pro-actively engaging with communities undertaking digital research. This represents a second important shift for libraries, which are in the process of identifying the most suitable platforms for delivering digital content to their users. The search interface which many rely upon for this is often inadequate for providing the services which some digital researchers require, and there is a need to reconsider the library's gatekeeper role in relation to digitised content. This role has been forced upon libraries, who have had to face increased demand for digitised content without appropriate funding. There is no specific appetite among library staff for creating closed resources in partnership with commercial partners; instead, they view this as a solution which helps them meet user expectations. Yet the licensing conditions which arise from these agreements, and the library sector's encroachment into producing information at a large scale, has led to tension between existing laws and the needs of users. It has also led to conflict with commercial providers. But access is key to ensuring the relevance of libraries in the digital age. Torkington's angry comments about the BL's digitisation programme came from a longer speech to the National and State Librarians of Australasia, in which he directly addressed this issue of relevance. This deliberately confrontational speech contains some key concerns about the impact of digitisation upon libraries. In particular, Torkington identifies providing access to collections as the most important library activity:

> You can argue until you're blue in the face about the intrinsic value of collections, but as your research monopoly has been destroyed, you need to start delivering some other value. Access to those collections is it. Collections, discovery, distribution.
>
> (2011)

Access, quality and usability define digitised collections for users and have a huge influence on how library services on the web are perceived. The attention of the user, who as we will see in Chapter 5 is agnostic in their attitude to information sources, can no longer be guaranteed if those sources do not serve their needs. Lankes (2011) argues that access is a service that varies by the community that publishes the material. We assume that the commercial sector will limit our access to their content because we assume that they want to profit from its existence. The same assumption does not apply to libraries: Lankes argues that the library is a facilitator for knowledge creation through providing access, creating participatory environments and supporting participation. These are all key roles for libraries, and the existing framework of copyright enforcement and commercial partnerships, while not sinister in itself, severely limits the ways in which those values are expressed through large-scale digitised collections. Andrew Green, the former head librarian of the National Library of Wales, offers a visionary description of how libraries can avoid the trap of irrelevance which Torkington warns against, suggesting that:

> An alternative is to view both the creation and provision of digitised knowledge as a public good. Public libraries were established and still flourish as a means of ensuring that all members of society, irrespective of their circumstances, could have access to all published knowledge ... The 21st Century equivalent is surely to offer citizens free access, where possible online.
>
> (Green, 2009)

To fulfil the public service aspect of their remit, libraries should therefore focus on providing content to users in the location and format that they require, wherever possible. This has two benefits: it reasserts the user as the key beneficiary of library activities; and it ensures that library digital collections will have the widest possible impact, thus demonstrating their undoubted continued relevance in the midst of a boom in the available of digitised materials.

This chapter has explored the impact of large-scale digitisation upon libraries, using evidence from case studies focusing on digitised newspaper collections, interviews with staff members and reference to the related literature. It has made the case for how library services have changed as a result of digitisation. Libraries have experienced large-scale digitisation as a learning process, and the developments I have highlighted in training, user engagement and digital scholarship offer models for how libraries can adapt to the lessons they have learned. They must continue to develop expertise in the technical aspects of digitisation, and they must also learn how to facilitate varied use of their digital collections. Restrictive rights have damaged the ability of some institutions to fully realise the potential of their materials, even though there are still major benefits to be derived despite the limitations placed upon their reuse. To realise greater benefits from digitisation, it is vital that collections are developed to be as open and interoperable as possible in order to allow institutions greater flexibility in providing services to their users in the future. They can achieve this by opening content up through using non-library platforms for dissemination and by facilitating both novel and traditional usage of research materials through generous interfaces and less restrictive licensing arrangements. The opening of collections is one way of ensuring the relevance of libraries as information providers in the twenty-first century. Through an open dialogue with users of their digitised collections, libraries can more thoroughly address the important role that they will be required to play in cutting through some of the rhetoric of the digital age. In combating the mistaken belief that everything is available online and by providing high quality resources in print and digital form, libraries will play a key role in supporting users as both parties adapt to changes in how our knowledge is produced and received online.

Note

1 Question Point is the NLW's online user support platform: it allows users to type their enquiry into a pop-up window and receive immediate support from a member of the enquiry team through their web browser.

Bibliography

Baker, J. (2013) 'Digital research in the wild', *British Library Digital Scholarship Blog*, 19 November 2013. Retrieved from: http://britishlibrary.typepad.co.uk/digital-scholarship/2013/11/digital-research-in-the-wild.html?utm_content=buffer 2d359&utm_source=buffer&utm_medium=twitter&utm_campaign=Buffer.

Barbosa, E. (2013) 'Books of cities infographic', *Behance.* Retrieved from: www.behance.net/gallery/Books-of-Cities-Infographic/9188073.

Brake, L. 'Half full and half empty'. *Journal of Victorian Culture* 17(2), pp. 222–229.

Brin, S. (2009) 'A tale of 10,000,000 books', *The Official Google Blog*, 9 October 2009. Retrieved from: http://googleblog.blogspot.com/2009/10/tale-of-10000 000-books.html.

Dahlstrom, M., Hansson, J. and Kjellman, U. (2012) '"As we may digitize" – institutions and documents reconfigured', *LIBER Quarterly*, **21**(3/4), pp. 455–474.

Darnton, R. (2013) 'The national Digital Public Library is launched!', *The New York Review of Books*, 25 April 2013. Retrieved from: www.nybooks.com/articles/archives/2013/apr/25/national-digital-public-library-launched/?utm_medium=email&utm_campaign=April+2+2013&utm_content=April+2+2013+CID _187e091a0341e73a378dd51cd52deedf&utm_source=Email%20marketing%20 software&utm_term=The%20National%20Digital%20Public%20Library%20 Is%20Launched.

Durham, W. (2015) 'Crossroads of curiosity: 6 days to go!', *Digital Scholarship Blog.* Retrieved from: http://britishlibrary.typepad.co.uk/digital-scholarship/2015/06/crossroads-of-curiosity-6-days-to-go.html.

European Commission (2014) 'Cultural heritage: digitisation, online accessibility and digital preservation – report on the implementation of Commission

Recommendation 2011/711/EU'. European Commission. Retrieved from: www.den.nl/art/uploads/files/Publicaties/Report_on_Digitsation_online_accessibility_and_digital_preservation_of_cultural_material_Europese_Commisie 2014.pdf

Gorman, G. E. and Clayton, P. (2005) *Qualitative Research for the Information Professional* (2nd edn). London: Library Association Publishing.

Green, A. (2009) 'Big digitisation: where next?', in *Digital Resources for the Humanities and Arts Conference*. Belfast. Retrieved from: www.llgc.org.uk/fileadmin/documents/pdf/darlith_big_digitisation_where_next.pdf.

Hunter, D. and Brown, K. (2010) *Thriving or Surviving: National Library of Scotland in 2030*. National Library of Scotland. Retrieved from: www.nls.uk/media/808985/future-national-libraries.pdf.

Keating, R. (2013) 'How the British Library is breathing life into old books', *Guardian*, 30 March 2010. Retrieved from: www.guardian.co.uk/commentisfree/2013/mar/30/digital-british-library-life-old-books?CMP=twt_gu.

Lankes, R. D. (2011) *The Atlas of New Librarianship*. Cambridge, Mass.: The MIT Press.

Line, M. B. and Line, J. (1979) 'Concluding notes', in Line, M. B. and Line, J. (Eds) *National Libraries*. London: ASLIB.

Mansourian, Y. (2006) 'Adoption of grounded theory in LIS research', *New Library World*, **107**(1228/1229), pp. 386–402.

McGregor, N. and Farquhar, A. (2013) 'The Digital Scholarship Training Programme at British Library', in *Digital Humanities, 18 July 2013*, University of Nebraska-Lincoln. Retrieved from: http://dh2013.unl.edu/abstracts/ab-264.html.

Michel, J.-B. and Shen, Y. K. (2010) 'Quantitative analysis of culture using millions of digitized books', *Science Magazine*, **331**(6014), pp. 176–182.

Mussell, J. (2012) *The Nineteenth-Century Press in the Digital Age*. Basingstoke: Palgrave MacMillan.

Niggemann, E., De Decker, J. and Levy, M. (2011) *The new Renaissance: report of the 'Comité des Sages' reflection group on bringing Europe's cultural heritage online*. Brussels. Retrieved from: www.eurosfaire.prd.fr/7pc/doc/1302102400_kk7911109enc_002.pdf.

Poole, N. (2010) 'The cost of digitising Europe's cultural heritage: a report for the Comité des Sages of the European Commission'. The Collections Trust. Retrieved from: http://nickpoole.org.uk/wp-content/uploads/2011/12/digiti_report.

Stroeker, N. and Vogels, R. (2012) 'Survey report on digitisation in European cultural heritage institutions 2012', ENUMERATE Thematic Network, May 2012. Retrieved from: www.enumerate.eu/fileadmin/ENUMERATE/documents/ENUMERATE-Digitisation-Survey-2012.pdf.

Tanner, S. (2009) *Technological Trends and Developments and Their Future Influence on Digital National Libraries*. King's College London. Retrieved from: www.nls.uk/media/808985/future-national-libraries.pdf.

Tanner, S. (2013) 'The value of Welsh Newspapers Online', *When the data hits the fan! The blog of Simon Tanner*, 28 March 2013. Retrieved from: http://simon-tanner.blogspot.co.uk/2013/03/the-value-of-welsh-newspapers-online.html.

Torkington, N. (2011) 'Libraries: where it all went wrong', 23 November 2011. Retrieved from: http://nathan.torkington.com/blog/2011/11/23/libraries-where-it-all-went-wrong/.

Whitelaw, M. (2015) 'Generous interfaces for digital cultural collections', *Digital Humanities Quarterly*, **9**(1). Retrieved from: www.digitalhumanities.org/dhq/vol/9/1/000205/000205.html.

Wilms, L. (2015) 'DH2015 – Researchers, librarians and a lot of information', *KB Research: Research at the National Library of the Netherlands*. Retrieved from: http://blog.kbresearch.nl/2015/07/13/dh2015/.

Wray, R. (2010) 'James Murdoch attacks British Library for digitising newspapers', *Guardian*, 21 May 2010. Retrieved from: www.guardian.co.uk/media/2010/may/21/james-murdoch-attacks-british-library.

5 The impact of large-scale digitisation on users

One of the major challenges for user studies in the digital age is connecting with online users. We are able to wield a range of quantitative methods which provide us with insights into what users do online but, as I argued in Chapter 3, these findings are at their most useful when combined with qualitative insights from users themselves. Libraries and archives have invested heavily in large-scale digitisation, and with good reason: there is no doubt about the demand for access to digitised materials online. What we have often lacked is an understanding of why users are so eager for digitised materials. Chapter 4 noted that libraries are becoming proactive in engaging with users in order to better shape collections to meet their needs. User studies have an important role in this respect: by undertaking empirically driven research into how large-scale digitised collections have been received and used, we can better understand how to develop them in the future to avoid creating barriers to reuse. To date, large-scale digitisation has often come at the expense of universal access, as the realities of contemporary social and political structures work to shape and constrain the impact of digitised collections.

This chapter explores two of the key impacts of mass digitisation on users. First, I will argue that LSDC have been positive for users. Drawing on survey data and a citation analysis of British Library Nineteenth Century Newspapers, I will argue that users benefit immensely from online access to resources. They are extremely positive about this impact, and this positivity is reflected in a growing number of citations for key resources. However, there is less certainty over how these benefits are truly transformative. It is certainly the case that remote access to digitised collections is, in itself, a hugely beneficial development for users. But there is no clear sense of how this has actually changed what users are doing. I will argue that, other than a few innovative projects, which use digitised newspapers in ways which are uniquely facilitated by the media specificity of computers, the majority of users are really engaged in accelerated versions of their existing research behaviours. In the second section, I will present findings from a web log analysis of Welsh Newspapers Online. This will show that users are still deeply engaged with collections online, often spending significant periods of time on a resource, but that their behaviour does indeed more closely resemble what we would expect from a networked web interface rather than a physical archive. In doing so, I will reflect on the theoretical shift from "reader" to "user" that has been proposed by Brake (2012). Although there is evidence that this abstraction has indeed occurred, I will argue that, in fact, it represents a logical reaction on the part of users to the problem of information overload. Users are provided with huge quantities of digitised content and very specific web interfaces, which support a limited range of interactions, and the behaviour they exhibit reflects this fact. If there is genuine concern about the negative impacts of digital media upon users, then the imperative is not to build a case for the intellectual diminishment of these users. We must instead address the inadequacies of the interfaces which foster this kind of behaviour. Interface design plays a key role in confining users to specific types of interaction, and we must therefore address ways in which better interfaces can be created which allow users to transcend the current dominance of the search paradigm in library digitised collections.

Users of large-scale digitisation

LIS researchers are extremely positive about the impact of large-scale digitisation, and this enthusiasm is shared by the majority of users. LSDC have helped to mitigate the negative impact of physical distance between archives and researchers and, for users who live and work a long distance from relevant archival materials, there are huge benefits to being able to access digitised materials online. The separation of artefacts from their specific material location is therefore an unequivocal positive for researchers, with a commensurate improvement in working conditions. I noted previously that researchers have not moved straight from physical archive sources to web-based surrogates but from physical remediations such as microfilm, which have been heavily criticised by those who work with them. Even in physical archives, the average researcher is unlikely to be able to access all the resources they require in the original format, and microfilmed newspapers are particularly inadequate from the perspective of users. Brake talks of "managing microfilm" (2012), and the phrase is revealing: rather than working with materials, it suggests that users are instead forced to cope with format-specific difficulties. This contrasts vividly with the overall positivity towards digitised collections, which save travel time for researchers and allow them to work at their own schedule and from their own devices. Digitised newspapers understandably seem to be widening the kinds of scholarly activity which make use of them as sources. Newspaper sources fill a gap for content that is not found elsewhere, and their increasing accessibility has been very effective in increasing their use in academic research. Using citation analysis, we can get a better sense of the extent of this growth in use and identify which disciplines are making use of digitised newspapers as a resource.

Case study: citation analysis of BNCN

Citation analysis is a long-term method for evaluating scholarly impact. It involves identifying the citations referring to a particular article, resource or website in order to evaluate how frequently it is used as a source in academic outputs. The prolonged period between writing and publication for academic articles means that it can take many years until a new digital resource is commonly found in citations. British Library Nineteenth Century Newspapers is now a mature collection, having been launched in 2007, but when Meyer *et al.* (2009) undertook a citation analysis of the resource two years after its launch, they found just four related papers. I decided to repeat this analysis, gathering data for the number of citations of BNCN from launch until 2012. I used the methodology from the previous study but adopted a more thorough search strategy to ensure that fewer citations were missed. Scholarly citation of digitised resources is inconsistent, and it is therefore necessary to use a wide range of search terms which include current and historical URLs, all the names that the digital resource has adopted and keyword searching. Without this, we run the risk of missing relative papers, and indeed I found eight relevant citations which were published before 2009. There are three main sources of bibliometric data on the web: Scopus (www.scopus.com), Google Scholar (http://scholar.google.com) and ISI Web of Knowledge (www.isiknowledge.com). All three have their own particular strengths and weaknesses, so it is necessary to search across them to achieve the best results. Google Scholar is freely available and immediately familiar to users. It allows users to search full text and citations in addition to abstracts and article titles. It also has the most extensive coverage of grey literature. It does, however, demand greater effort from the researcher because it combines a huge breadth of material with a relatively imprecise search. Scopus and ISI Web of Knowledge are both commonly subscribed commercial databases. The former includes full text and citation searching, while the latter allows users to directly query citations, but they have a more limited range of materials than Google Scholar. All three databases were queried for a period from the BNCN's launch in 2007 until the end of 2012.

Within this period, I found 75 unique papers which had directly cited BNCN. This included a number of papers in the time period covered by Meyer *et al.*'s study, which can be attributed to additions to online databases and a more thorough search strategy during data collection. The two most commonly represented disciplines within these citations included Library and Information Science and Victorian studies, but literary studies, minority studies and the history of science were also found to have cited material from the resource. The remaining citations all referred to histories of particular disciplines, but the range of information available through historical newspapers was very much in evidence: politics; the history of accounting; architectural history; European history; the history of tourism; and geography. LIS citations differed from others because they referred to the resource as an entity for discussion rather than the source of materials. This analysis showed that Victorian Studies scholars are a core audience for digitised newspapers, but increased access to the resource allowed for a "long tail" of citations in other disciplines. I would therefore suggest that the presence of historical newspapers has been beneficial to historians of disciplines across academia and even beyond the core arts and humanities subjects that we would expect.

In addition to the increase in citations, large-scale data-driven analyses of newspapers are becoming more numerous, with users describing their work in tracing history and usage patterns of words and phrases. These methods show a desire to use digitised newspapers in innovative ways and emphasise the importance of libraries working to improve access not only to materials but to the data which underpins large-scale digitised collections. Access to the datasets and full text of digitised newspapers is becoming important for researchers. The importance of these surrogate materials is revealed by the way that many users of online collections qualify their criticisms with praise. When criticising navigation within BNCN, for instance, researchers are still eager to emphasise how vital a tool it is. They couch their criticisms in a pre-emptive explanation that the resource is still highly valuable despite the problems they face. It is worth emphasising that academics, librarians and users all value digitised newspaper collections highly and use these collections extensively. The criticisms in this chapter should not undermine the vital importance that digitised content now has in the hybrid library. Yet there are certainly issues which need addressing. One is the impact of limiting online access, a factor in the digital divide which is emerging as a concern. While the idea of a global digital divide describes the disparity in access to the internet and digital devices, and the resultant loss of opportunity, the term is also used to refer to inequalities between households, individuals and other demographics. For large-scale digitised materials, inequality manifests itself in a divide between different academic institutions and residents of different regions. Subscriptions are charged at either individual or institutional level, but the cost of subscribing to LSDC can be prohibitive for individuals and institutions alike. Smaller institutions, or those with less funding, are unable to provide their members with the levels of access that are necessary to be competitive on a global or even national scale. This is particularly damaging for those scholars without the necessary resources to undertake competitive research, who then suffer as the proliferation of digitised content raises expectations for the breadth of research undertaken in their field. In this respect, the supposedly democratising effect of digitised resources can become a detrimental myth for those who are left behind. Access to appropriate materials has always been a problem for researchers, but it is an ongoing reality that the rhetoric of universal online access has ignored. The theoretical benefits of a "post-scarcity world" (Aguilar-Millan *et al.*, 2010), in which digital technologies would remove all barriers to access, therefore deleteriously contradict the contemporary balancing act that occurs between the desire to widen access and the need for commercial companies to see a return on their investment in digitisation activities.

This concern about access is exacerbated by confusion over the differing models adopted by otherwise ostensibly similar LSDC. For the end user, there appears to be little difference between the content provided by open access resources such as Australian Newspapers Online and those which charge a subscription fee. It is difficult for users to understand why some resources are not free, and little information is provided within resources to clarify the situation. UK citizens, for instance, may struggle to understand why they cannot access British newspapers for free through their public library when they can access Australian newspapers from home. The value of digitised newspapers becomes virtually irrelevant if the user is priced out. LSDC are just one part of a large information infrastructure, and research tasks require users to engage with multiple resources for, in some cases, just a few hours at a time. We will see that use of digitised newspapers is deep but intermittent and wide-ranging, meaning that users may not extract maximum value from a subscription model built around sustained access to just one resource.

Case study: online survey of users of digitised newspapers

Surveys are useful for developing awareness of how users perceive digital resources and gaining information on how researchers perceive their own interactions with digitised content online. In order to apply this to digitised newspaper collections, I formulated an online survey which called for respondents drawn from the user communities of BNCN and WNO. Two surveys were created, each containing a series of questions on use of and attitudes towards digitised newspaper collections. The Likert Scale was adopted for some questions: this uses a series of statements which elicit answers on a five-point scale from "strongly agree" to "strongly disagree", which allows a numeric agreement level to be indicated for the whole sample, from one for strong disagreement to five for strong agreement. The survey was designed using a web-based survey design application, before being piloted with colleagues and presented to the partner organisations for feedback. The surveys used different methods of dissemination: for BNCN, I sought responses through social media, academic mailing lists, relevant web forums and other online sources that were likely to reach users of digitised newspaper collections. The WNO survey differed in two key ways. First, because the National Library of Wales works bilingually, the survey was produced in English and then translated into Welsh by in-house translators. Structurally, however, the survey was identical to the English language version. Second, the survey was placed in a prominent position on the collection's homepage. This approach conferred some benefits: it showed clear support from the NLW, which was strengthened by the web team's efforts to format the survey to match the site's overall appearance. This gave a stronger sense of institutional support for the study and meant that all users who visited WNO were exposed to the link: I could therefore be more confident that respondents had recently visited the site, and mounting it directly on the home page avoided user frustration with pop-up windows. Both approaches were unable to guarantee a representative sample considering the diffuse and anonymous user community. Effectively, the study was forced to adopt a sample of convenience,[1] and thus we must bear in mind that there may be specific biases reflected in the feedback or data. The primary bias in our sample was the overrepresentation of academic users in comparison to the overall proportion of academic users of the websites.

The idea that LSDC have changed the way that users undertake research is one shared by critics and users alike. The majority of researchers who were surveyed agreed that large-scale digitised collections had changed their research methods. For instance, in my survey, users of WNO were in almost universal agreement with the phrase "large-scale collections of digitised newspapers have changed the way I undertake research". The extent of this change, though, is less clear. We can certainly point to novel uses of digitised collections which would be almost impossible to achieve using physical materials. The most high profile projects have been undertaken using book corpora, but there have been attempts to use digitised newspapers for quantitative analysis (e.g. Liddle, 2012; Nicholson, 2012). There is little evidence, however, that the majority of users are using digitised newspapers for anything other than information discovery, browsing and research – all activities that could be done before online access, albeit more slowly and within the confines of the archive. That researchers value the shift to digital so highly indicates the widespread benefits of digitising historic materials. Instead of creating whole new ways of working, the most common benefits of large-scale digitisation are, in fact, the major improvements in efficiency and working conditions for those researchers lucky enough to have access. The importance of this shift is great, although it seems modest in comparison to the hyperbolic claims of disruptive technological changes.

In line with this incremental but highly valuable impact, researchers report that LSDC have not had a major impact on their use of physical collections. Researchers now rely on physical archives slightly less, but there is no sense they have abandoned them entirely. One reason for this is that digitised newspaper collections do not provide researchers with everything they are looking for. Most users are acutely aware that the historic record online is by no means complete. As a result, digitised collections are viewed as a useful but not disruptive technology. They still work in a hybrid environment where digitised materials are becoming increasingly vital. Researchers have readily adopted digitised resources which provide notable benefits or new ways of working, relying on physical resources whenever the benefits are less clear. It is worth noting, for example, that many researchers still report storing content by printing out and filing copies of materials they discover, while others indicate that they keep notes by hand and file them manually. Digitised collections are a vital research resource, but only in the context of a wider information ecology which encompasses physical and digital content. The increasingly central position of digitised collections for researchers is reflected in the afore-mentioned growth of citations to BNCN. However, if we accept that the majority of users are not applying quantitative methods to digitised news-papers, we can characterise the majority of behaviour as using digitised collections to make existing research tasks easier and more efficient.

Large-scale digitised collections currently lend themselves to research tasks where searching for information is important, and this searching takes place across multiple resources. A researcher may, for example, search in a digitised newspaper collection for the names of ships carrying British passengers to the colonies and then search online passenger lists using the ship's name and date of sailing. They mention commonly using Welsh Newspapers Online, British Library Nineteenth Century News-papers, the British Newspaper Archive, Trove Australian Newspapers, Library of Congress Newspapers and the Times Digital Archive, as well as more general collections such as Google Books and HathiTrust. In addi-tion, complementary resources for cross-referencing information are extremely valuable. This type of behaviour is extremely common among users, who see digitised collections as part of a wider network of resources: they are essentially agnostic about the resource, caring more about the ways in which the information can be usefully discovered, combined and analysed than about which resource it comes from. This, as Chapter 6 will demonstrate, is particularly troublesome when considered in light of the dominant model of subscription to a solitary resource.

This begs the question of whether the online behaviour outlined here in fact differs from the reality of physical information behaviour rather than the idealised perception of reading I have previously referred to. Information seeking in online newspaper collections does bear many similarities to research in physical archives. In both, users are largely reliant upon and appreciative of finding aids such as indexes or keyword searching. Additionally, research in physical archives already incorporates prolonged periods in which deep reading does not occur. Instead, researchers take advantage of these time-saving resources and use multiple physical sources concurrently. These are all actions that digitised collec-tions can facilitate superbly, which suggests that traditional archival research methods can be mapped onto certain features of digitised resources. There are two particular areas of research where users can, theoretically, benefit from digitised collections. First, researchers frequently scan archival materials for keywords, rather than reading them in their entirety, and use this information to diversify their search. Second, researchers engage in multiple activities concurrently, instead of approaching research as a sequence of discrete stages. This, too, closely resembles the model demonstrated through web log analysis, where users of digitised newspapers engage with search and browsing in the same session as they actually read digitised content. This understanding is enriched by qualitative methods which give a broader understanding of their information behaviour, and we can therefore conclude that digitised newspapers enable an acceleration of existing practices, allowing users to scan material more quickly, to access sources more easily and to separate themselves from the considerable time and financial costs associated with archival research. As I will argue in the rest of this chapter, the model of the user is extremely relevant here, but it represents desirable traits designed to cope with information overload rather than an erosion of the importance of the reader. Reliance on the web interface entails a corresponding move away from the physical object and towards a representational norm built around digital media practices.

Changing models of user behaviour

Digitisation has significantly changed how researchers experience newspapers. The way in which newspapers are represented online varies subtly from collection to collection and, although there are recommended standards for best practice in digitisation, it remains the case that each project must engage with the textuality of the printed form which they hope to remediate. Thus, there is an editorial process involved in digitisation of all printed materials. Printed newspapers pose significant problems in this regard: their mix of visual and written content; the importance of typeface, layout and graphic design to their representation and meaning; their ephemerality; and their representation of varied viewpoints and multiple editions. Certain modes of representation demand a certain type of interaction from the user: digitised collections frequently privilege text-based searching and article-level viewing over the rich textual and historical context of the original material. This distancing of the material from its original context is manifested in an increasing indifference among users to the source of the information. Some researchers are not just platform agnostic but source agnostic: their primary concern is to access information, and the ability to consider the reliability of sources is impaired by the sheer volume of material under consideration. While Edwards (2013) goes too far in suggesting that "a willingness to trust surrogates is a willingness to abandon scholarly responsibility", it is true that web interfaces make it easier to access physically or textually demanding materials without engaging with a scholarly interpretive framework. This is not inevitable, however, and is merely a side effect of successfully opening up archival materials to a wider audience: as Benjamin (2007) argues, the process of widening access through reproduction also breaks down the aura of the original artefact. I view this as an opportunity for new interactions to be undertaken and new knowledge to be discovered. However, there should be further consideration of how digitised collections support researchers in taking account of new technologies in their practices.

Case study: web log analysis of Welsh Newspapers Online

The NLW provided me with two datasets for WNO: Google Analytics, gathered and analysed through the GA web platform, and anonymised web logs covering the period from 12 March to 30 June 2013. Google Analytics was used to provide overall usage and engagement metrics, while I relied on web logs to provide more in-depth insights into user behaviour. The GA data was harvested from the WNO analytics account. This process was complicated by the fact that the resource is actually split between two structurally identical websites, one published in English and one in Welsh. Both accounts were collated in Excel to facilitate analysis. A variety of metrics were gathered, including: visitor numbers; user engagement by page visit and visit duration; bounce rate; and mobile and social media usage.

The provided web logs specifically recorded information about user behaviour on the site which involved discovering and using material. The logs therefore tracked the following: searches undertaken by users on the website (henceforth referred to as search queries); instances where users browsed, filtered or otherwise interacted with search results (search result queries); and instances where users viewed content (content queries). The web logs recorded each of these interactions as a single line of plain code text in a file held on the website servers. The following is an example of a content query from the logs:

2013–06–02T12:26:50+01:00   51a5c97c3c8d3   llgc-id:3036868   llgc-id:3039814 llgc-id:3037695 Aberystwyth Observer 21 September 1872 [2] ART40

The elements, in order, are: date and time of interaction; unique user ID; server ID numbers for website content; title of newspaper viewed; date of newspaper edition; page number viewed; article number on the viewed page. Search queries contained an additional field for user search terms, and search results queries included a field recording the interaction with search results. This rich data source allowed several metrics relating to user behaviour to be assessed, including: most viewed newspaper titles; most viewed decades; most commonly viewed page numbers in newspapers; average number of page views per visit; and average number of page views involving each query category outlined above.

Briefly considering the GA results, I found that both websites had received a reasonably high volume or traffic since the resource's launch. Visits to WNO were dominated by UK visitors, and Wales was overrepresented in comparison to its population size, accounting for 37.21 per cent of UK users and 30.98 per cent of all visits, compared to just 4.8 per cent of the UK population. Users exhibited a reasonably deep level of engagement, which separated their use of the resource from that exhibited in general web browsing. The bounce rate, for instance, was low in comparison to reported figures for the general web, despite the open access nature of the resource allowing for short, curiosity-driven visits. The significant investment of time and effort, which went well beyond that associated with many websites, suggested that digital resource usage is deeper and more sustained than for general web traffic. The web results gave further insights into exactly how this user behaviour manifested itself at an aggregate level. Two findings were particularly significant. The web logs demonstrated that users view the title page more than any other by a large margin. Although there was an average of 6.4 pages per edition across the corpus, and the highest page number of any individual edition was 8, it was evident that users viewed each page after the title page with decreasing regularity. This is likely to reflect the way that the formal significance of the front page has been reinforced by the browsing interface: users accessing editions by browsing, for instance, will be taken to the title page by default, with no guarantee that they will browse further pages in the edition. Figure 5.1 illustrates the second finding: how information seeking takes place in WNO, tracking the proportion of users engaged in search, search result or content queries at any page view in their visit to WNO, with the page view number ascertained by access times for each unique user ID:

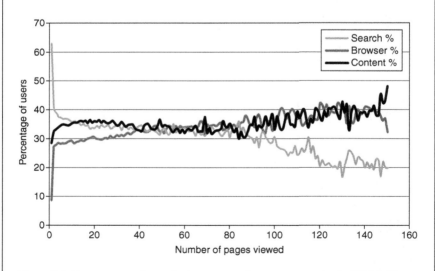

Figure 5.1 Percentage of search, browser and content queries in Welsh Newspapers Online, by length of time on website.

The chart shows that content queries remain an important element of user activity regardless of visit duration. In fact, once a visit incorporates over 100 page views, users view increasingly large amounts of newspaper content. By contrast, the longer a user spends on the website, the less likely they are to be engaged in searching. Instead, search result queries replace search queries, indicating that the average user moves away from searching during their visit, either moving towards browsing search results or viewing content. Content queries remain a vital component of user interactions with the resource, but despite this over 50 per cent of page views are engaged with either search or search result queries at any point: thus over half of all page views are dedicated to interacting with the web interface rather than the historical sources. This leads to two important observations: that users interact with WNO extensively while engaging with large amounts of content, in a manner reminiscent of the multifaceted information seeking behaviour in archives; and that, while this engagement is deep, it occurs primarily with the web interface and secondarily with the material. Thus, whereas after discovery users of physical resources must engage directly with the textual object for filtering, users of online resources rely primarily on automated processes facilitated by the web interface.

One of the most revealing findings from the web log analysis indicated the most commonly viewed pages in WNO by the number of content page views. With page one as the title page, readers viewed some of or all those up to page 8, which was the highest number viewed by users, despite the presence of newspapers up to 16 pages long. I found that users view the title page more than any other, with almost double the page views (over 50,000) compared to any other single page. This shows that the web interface lends itself to users accessing the title page more readily. For instance, users browsing by specific edition will be taken to the title page first, without necessarily continuing to browse further pages. It also reflects the fact that many historical newspapers contained fewer than eight pages. I found that the average number of pages per edition in Welsh Newspapers Online was 6.3, which may explain why so few users had viewed seven or eight pages. This tells us something extremely important: users are not browsing through editions; instead, they appear to be using search to find what they need and then are moving on. The browsing that is undertaken with digitised newspapers is therefore more closely analogous to web browsing than reading: users arrive on the title page by browsing or searching using the web interface but go no deeper in most cases.

This shift in textual focus has been expressed in Brake's distinction between the concepts of "reader" and "user". Her language is echoed by Mussell, who comments that "whereas 'reading' implies an engagement with the text, the term 'user' suggests that those interacting with digital resources must also 'do' something" (2012). His distinction is particularly strong because it comes without the implicit value judgement of Brake's argument. The idea of loss is common in theoretical accounts of digitisation, dating back to Benjamin's account of the loss of aura in mechanical reproductions and encompassing Baudrillard's radical scepticism towards the digital form. Yet, whereas Baudrillard presents the hyperreal as inevitably unreal and thereby inferior to the physical, Mussell's comment recognises that a potential loss of engagement with the text can instead be replaced by a different kind of behaviour. The findings of the web log analysis could be taken to confirm some of the fears of the erosion of deep reading caused by digital media, but I would warn against this interpretation. It is more representative of the automation of scholarly behaviour in physical archives: instead of manually searching through editions of newspapers, researchers are relying on search technology to automate aspects of their work. The impact of digitisation can only be interpreted as a loss if we assume that the digital medium holds no benefits over physical artefacts, which is certainly not the case. Conway's (2013) argument that digitised texts are new artefacts imbued with their own unique characteristics offers a more positive focus for innovation in digitisation because it addresses the new modes of understanding that emerge.

It should also be emphasised that digitised resources are part of a hybrid environment where users continue to find value in both physical and digital artefacts. There is only a minor shift away from using physical texts and libraries. LSDC are additive to research rather than disruptive. It has been propagated that the shallow bouncing behaviour of users online is a sign that readers are unable to engage with content online. Instead, if we refer to the theoretical framework of Chapter 1, it is in fact evident that online users engage *differently*. The fact that they do not browse historical newspapers in no way corroborates the claim that they are incapable of reading deeply in physical texts, not least because information discovery and reading are more clearly delineated with material texts than online resources, which act as a locus for search, discovery and reading. This is important because it addresses a shift away from engagement with the textual artefact. Users are unlikely to browse through consecutive editions of a newspaper online, and the majority of page views are dedicated to navigating the web interface. This does not suggest a limitation of the digital form but instead demonstrates where the transformative aspect of digitisation lies: users are engaging increasingly with web interfaces to filter the flood of information that is available. While the stereotype of deep reading is just one part of a multifaceted information behaviour, it is certainly true that digitised newspaper collections make the web interface central to the user's experience. This interface defines and shapes the user's behaviour, increasing their reliance on automated search and OCR, and demanding increased digital information literacy. In doing this, digitisation places an increasing demand upon resource creators to ensure these functions meet the requirements of their users, who effectively entrust discovery to search algorithms, metadata workflows and digitisation technologies. This is exemplified by the fact that the majority of users of digital resources rely on the interface of their chosen resource for information discovery: users of WNO, for instance, most commonly used either search tools in the resource interface or browsed via the provided options.

The behaviours that Deutsch (1961) attributes to inhabitants of the city are also evident in the use of digitised newspaper collections – using multiple resources simultaneously, extended searching and filtering behaviour, and increased exposure to a multitude of different interactions. We can thus return to the twentieth century city as a corollary for online information behaviour, and criticisms about the shift from "reader" to "user" must therefore engage with this point: in order to cope with the increased volume of information that is available online, research must necessarily adopt filtering techniques. In keeping with the idea of the freedom of city inhabitants to choose, I would suggest that modern researchers are in fact making a conscious choice to visit these resources and behave in this manner and, in doing so, accept that they are unable to process all inputs from their information environment due to the proliferation of available inputs. The pattern of prolonged information seeking, combined simultaneously with viewing fragments of original text, is therefore a deliberate approach to the problem of information overload in digitised newspaper collections. It is certainly true that we have lost some engagement with the textual artefact, now replaced by a different form of engagement with the web interface: the user's focus has shifted from the textual artefact as a carrier of information to the web platform as a carrier of much larger quantities of information. Technological developments have rarely led to the negative effects that have been proposed, and there is no reason to think that digitisation necessitates an overall diminishment of scholarship compared to previous innovations.

The surprise is perhaps that engagement has not been lost; instead, it has shifted focus. Nicholas *et al.* (2004) use the term "promiscuous" to characterise web users who are reading diversely, bouncing horizontally between sources and spending less time on each. Indeed, other studies into online behaviour have found that users are unwilling to search deeply. What we see with digitised newspapers is different, though: users do not engage with websites for short periods but view multiple websites while spending substantial time on each. They also expend considerable effort engaging with search tools, gradually refining and exploring results in a way that is often absent with other websites. Digitised newspaper collections therefore support users in discovering new sources quickly and efficiently. These newspapers, though, are taken away from the material in which their context is defined by their specific textual conditions and towards the paratextual where they exist as part of a much larger network of written words. Conway's argument that digitised materials are not inadequate remediations of physical materials, but important artefacts in their own right, is particularly apposite.

Because digitised newspapers provide distinct benefits and drawbacks to users, it is likely that physical newspaper archives will continue to retain value precisely due to the differing contexts of otherwise similar materials. As Brake (2012) points out, "the dialogic properties of digitised papers will be silenced if we deploy digital material alone and if the printed archive does not remain accessible and consulted". In this specific sense, Baker (2001) was correct: the remediation of newspapers in digital form does not remove the need for the physical artefact. It does, however, make it easier to undertake certain important research activities. For biblio-graphic research, and for maintaining the material context of archival materials among other things, the physical newspaper will remain vital. Digitised newspapers need to be viewed in terms of what they allow that other forms do not, namely: supporting comparative work; providing new perspectives on previously inaccessible material; freeing users from manu-ally searching newspapers by allowing them to query millions of pages simultaneously; facilitating computationally intensive research methods; and providing widespread access to historical sources.

However, the theory and practice do seem to match more closely in their interpretation of information seeking. While it is clear that users are engaging with content online, there is still evidence that they primarily undertake legacy online activities such as searching, browsing search results and assessing content to determine its relevance. It will therefore remain the case that digitisation projects must engage with the textuality of the printed form to determine the most effective modes of online representation. The shift in emphasis from the textual artefact to web-based platforms and article-level viewing has caused a theoretical separa-tion between the physical newspaper and the textual information contained within. For some users, digital surrogates are used as a confirm-atory source, scanning pages to check that search results are relevant and favouring specific information discovery over the wider context within which newspapers exist. It is thus a great concern that search functionality is found to be lacking by so many users. One effect of digitisation is that there are two layers of trust: the first refers to the authority and prov-enance of the content itself; the second refers to the functionality, reli-ability and trustworthiness of the web resource. A growing collection of digitised content must be carefully managed to ensure it is authoritative and directly addresses the needs of its audience. Whereas books have evolved and become codified in ways that are widely understood, the prov-enance of digitised resources can create problems for researchers: who created the collection? What algorithms determine the order of search results, and do these remain stable? What decisions did the creators make about presentation? Do permanent URLs allow others to access the same content through identical links? These are all important questions which will play a role in deciding how reliable and authoritative users consider LSDC to be, and many digitised collections fail to address these concerns.

Engagement with users of large-scale digitised collections

Given the way in which user behaviour has evolved as a result of digitised collections, the decisions that institutions take to support their users have repercussions in defining the extent of impact. Resource creators face ongoing difficulties in identifying and approaching suitable user groups for impact assessment. In cases where there is little user engagement and where individual demographic data is not gathered, it is difficult to even define trends within the overall user group: we can merely gain a sampled snapshot of users. Many resources now engage directly with their users via social media channels, mailing lists or community-driven collection improvement activities. When institutions do not keep informal contact with users, it becomes difficult to harness their expertise for improving collections. The result is that impact studies have to find creative ways of reaching out to potential users, without truly being able to judge how representative those participants are. Consideration must therefore be given to how user engagement will continue beyond the consultation phase of a digitised resource's development.

This is underlined when we consider different referral sources. Although social and mobile traffic tend to demonstrate lower engagement than direct referrals, this may be down to the specific characteristics of these mediums, with users effectively bouncing between different sources in a horizontal manner to follow links of interest. Social media and mobile users are more likely to be following links of interest and reading new content such as blog posts, events and interesting items from digitised collections. As such, they now constitute an important subset of website users, for whom the aims of a given visit differ from the stereotypical researcher. The absence of a social media presence for resources such as BNCN therefore means it is difficult to reach these users. Some resources have been extremely successful in publicising their work: the British Library Sound Archive tweets a mix of collection links and stories relevant to its collections, and the British Newspaper Archive tweets links to interesting or topical articles to an audience of over 12,000 followers. BNA also maintains a Facebook page where they respond directly to queries and comments from users. Perhaps this is indicative of the more commercial focus of the BNA but non-commercial resources also engage with their users in this manner. The lack of equivalent social media engagement from the creators of BNCN is indicative of wider problems with its usability, and yet we can see that the resource exhibits strong levels of user engagement. Therefore, it is evident that BNCN is a trusted resource for in-depth research, with users overlooking inadequacies in exchange for the benefits they gain.

While social media engagement allows resource creators to talk to their most loyal users and provides a possible route to identifying participants, social media does not appear to be a priority for the academic users who contributed to my case studies. When asked directly which features they would like to see, these users seemed indifferent to "added value" features such as multimedia or social media, instead prioritising website usability or increased amounts of digitised materials. We can only speculate as to the reasons, but this indifference was strong for users of BNCN and WNO; our survey results demonstrated almost no desire for social media integration, despite around 10 per cent of visits originating from social media sources. As such, it seems likely that academic users see little need for social media integration, whereas the importance of social media as a route for discovery suggests that there is value for engaging with other potential users. The role of social media in supporting interactions with digitised collections therefore warrants further consideration elsewhere.

There is also a need to support users in proper citation practices for digitised collections. This study strongly endorses the suggestion that digitised resources should provide prominently located guidance on how to cite materials; there are a number of ways this could be achieved, including a prominent FAQ, or a generated citation found on the page of each collection item (Meyer *et al.*, 2009). Citation analysis provides plenty of examples where citation practices are not followed: papers reference incorrect URLs, for instance, or cite their institutional login page rather than a collection-level URL. This may be due to unfamiliarity with the difference between URLs which contain unique login identifiers and unique URLs. In the case of BNCN, this problem is particularly acute. The collection has undergone a number of changes in its lifetime, including URL and name changes. There is therefore little consistency for users to draw upon, and a lack of stable URLs for collection items. The provision of stable URLs must be a basic minimum to allow for deep linking in scholarly resources, whether this is achieved through the use of semantic URLS or through allocating each item a DOI[2] number as an identifier. Without consistent guidance for users and consideration of a researcher's need for stable, rediscoverable content online, citation practices will remain variable.

Indeed, there is evidence that researchers are not recording their own use of digitised collections properly. Meyer *et al.* cover the issues faced by users in some depth:

> We have found in doing this study, for instance, that of the scholars who published results based on materials in the five collections, over one-third only cited the physical item represented in the digitised collection and made no reference to the digitised collection at all. Nearly half cited the original article, but also included the URL, and less than one in five cited the online version only.
>
> (Meyer *et al.*, 2009)

Researchers can certainly point to the lack of guidance as a contributing factor, but there is still a preference in some fields for citing the original paper version of a document, even when the author only consulted the electronic version. Sukovic's (2009) research into citation practices shows that e-texts are firmly embedded in the research practices of many scholars. She notes though, that the "multifarious nature of scholars' use of e-texts" is not reflected in their citation practices. Sukovic goes on to identify a number of reasons for the resistance to citing electronic sources: these are discussed in Chapter 3, but include traditions of a particular field (where citation of physical sources is expected) and a perceived lack of credibility or authority in digital texts. Despite the strong evidence for use of digitised collections in research, the acceptance of their authority in academic circles lags behind their adoption.

Summary: where we're going, we'll still need readers

Overall, users are extremely satisfied with the impact of large-scale digitisation on their research. They use them extensively, in a hybrid environment where they still see a role for physical library collections and printed materials. One of the most vital developments facilitated by large-scale digitisation is that geographical barriers are overcome: this is one of the great strengths of digital media. But there is still a question of the extent to which user behaviour has truly changed. For the majority of users, there is little sign that the way they work is fundamentally different as a result of digitisation. What has occurred, though, is the textual shift that I noted in Chapter 1. Digitised information is a pure manifestation of the networked intertext, in that its meaning can only be translated through the use of computational tools. Meaning, therefore, resides in enormous corpora of searchable words stripped of material context, and the user must adopt information seeking approaches which work most effectively within this paradigm. In order to make sense of digital remediations, users must adopt tools which allow them to reincorporate materials and which allow them to discover relevant content at scale. Given this, it is understandable that researchers engage in methods which resemble online user behaviour more generally, although it is clear that digitised newspapers demand a higher level of engagement. In common with other social experiences of information overload, though, the bouncing behaviour of users of online resources is a necessary reaction to an increase in the range of stimuli to which they are exposed. Large-scale digitisation has significantly increased the number of inputs which users must process, and we can address certain characteristics within this context: the allocation of less time to each piece of information, the use of filtering devices, and the creation of external platforms to externalise the processing of these inputs. With digital media, which are reliant on computers for substantiation, the locus of these behaviours is the web interface. Discovery, reading and analysis are all mediated by the interface which we provide to users and as a result shape their behaviour in fundamental ways. Any critique of user behaviour

online must therefore also begin with a consideration of how the interfaces which we provide feed into defining and constraining this behaviour
in undesirable ways.

These findings back up users' reports of the importance of digitised
newspapers to their research. My citation analysis of BNCN shows its
growth as a scholarly resource in the last few years, increasing from just a
few papers when analysed in 2009 to over 70 papers just three years later.
There is also evidence that researchers are eager to apply quantitative
methods to digitised newspapers. However, this behaviour is not widespread. We can characterise the majority of research with digitised newspapers as "using digitised collections to make existing research tasks easier
and more efficient". In particular, LSDC currently lend themselves to
research tasks where searching for information is key. One respondent to
my study describes a typical visit where resources were combined to gather
information thus: "Searching in Welsh Newspapers Online for names of
ships carrying Welsh emigrants to Patagonia and then searching online
ship passenger lists using the ship's name and date of sailing".

Users commonly access Welsh Newspapers Online, British Library Nineteenth Century Newspapers, the British Newspaper Archive, Trove Australian Newspapers, Library of Congress Newspapers and the Times Digital
Archive, as well as more general collections such as Google Books and
HathiTrust. In addition, they mention complementary resources where
names can be cross-referenced and information collated. Names can be
discovered via newspapers, then cross-referenced inline in contemporary
will indexes, census data and ship passenger lists. This type of behaviour
appears common among users and demonstrates that, while digitised
newspapers have become vital, they constitute just one of an interlinked
series of resources that aid research and discovery.

There are two points of comparison for user behaviour in digitised collections: first, we must consider whether it matches the stereotypes that
pervade the work of critics such as Birkets regarding physical reading;
second, we must compare it to models of researcher behaviour in physical
archives. I have argued that there are several stereotypes which define how
the popular discourse views physical reading: it is commonly assumed, for
instance, to be deeper and more engaged than reading online. Indeed, we
can see that browsing through specific newspapers in large-scale digitised
collections is rare, with search results acting as a proxy browsing mechanism instead. It still remains the case that two-thirds of a user's page views
are spent not engaging with the digitised artefact but instead undertaking
searches and filtering search results. In this respect, my findings indicate
that digitised resources impose a new kind of reading behaviour upon
users, in comparison to reading printed texts. This is not surprising, given
that digital collections combine reading and information seeking, whereas
the fetishised accounts of reading conveniently ignore discovery as an
aspect of information behaviour. In addition, many users have a specific

purpose for accessing newspapers online, which cannot be easily mapped onto the model of deep reading but still represent a sustained intellectual engagement with the material. Instead, researchers take advantage of web functionality to find the content they require quickly and efficiently, before dipping directly into the relevant article. The marginalisation of content browsing does make serendipitous discovery less likely and means that search functionality, OCR quality and website design are vitally important in aiding discoverability. Existing interfaces for remediating newspapers are therefore more likely to support patterns of information discovery which resemble online user behaviour than the reading behaviour attributed to adherents of the physical text.

The next question is whether the online behaviour I have outlined in fact differs from the reality of researcher behaviour, rather than the idealised perception of reading. My earlier review of the relevant literature demonstrates that information seeking in online newspaper collections does bear many similarities to research in the physical archive. In both scenarios, users are largely reliant upon (and appreciative of) finding aids such as indexes or keyword searching (Duff and Johnson, 2002). Additionally, research in physical archives does not always involve deep reading of historical sources for prolonged periods. Instead, we can see that researchers take advantage of time-saving resources, use multiple physical sources and engage in scanning behaviour to identify particular keywords in the text (Dalton and Charnigo, 2004). These are all actions that digitised collections support superbly, which suggests that traditional archival research can benefit from the efficient, accelerated filtering and search of digitised collections without fundamentally changing the underlying behaviour of researchers. The idea of the physical text as a source of deep reading, in comparison to bouncing through online resources, should also be put to rest in all but specific types of research tasks. Here, the literature suggests two things for information seeking in physical archives. First, researchers frequently scan archival materials for keywords, rather than reading them in their entirety, and use this information to diversify their search. Second, historians traditionally engage in multiple activities throughout their studies, instead of approaching research as a sequence of discrete stages (Uva, 1977; Case, 1991; Sinn and Soares, 2014). Both of these behaviours closely resemble aspects of the model demonstrated in my findings, which show that researchers undertake search and browsing in the same session as they actually read digitised content. Large-scale digitised collections consequently represent an acceleration of existing information behaviour, allowing researchers to scan materials more quickly, to access sources more easily and to separate themselves from the considerable time and financial costs associated with archival research. But this comes with the subtle shift towards Brake's "matrix" of textual information (2012). I have argued here that there is a theoretical shift in textual focus that has been expressed as a distinction between "reader" and "user" by Brake, who argues that digital representations of nineteenth century newspapers cause a fundamental transformation in the nature of the user. Where I have pushed back against this characterisation, though, is in the idea that there is a process of denaturalisation that occurs as a result of this remediation process. While the matrix-embedded user operates at a layer of abstraction from the original newspapers, understood through the lens of the web interface, this does not bring a corresponding shift away from Unsworth's (2000) scholarly primitives. While the theoretical implications of the shift towards web-interface mediated interactions are an essential consideration for resource creators, a differently remediated experience is not necessarily any less rich.

In this respect, Ranganathan's (1931) conception of the term "reader" as a user of library collections, rather than an individual engaged in the act of reading, remains relevant: he situates this reader as an individual with the need for library services and emphasises the importance of meeting user needs, regardless of how we perceive the value of those needs. This reinforces the idea of the library as a service, at a time when library user communities are increasingly diffuse and anonymous. It is the job of digital resource creators to facilitate varied uses, so that the particular strengths of search are supported by other digital interactions which shift the attention away from the web interface. Our sector's concern over digital media is partly predicated on the dominance of search in information seeking, but there is no reason that this dominance has to continue: the library sector can lead the way in supporting more diverse options for users of digitised materials. Users have not abandoned the physical but have augmented it through the adoption of digitised collections which contain material that they find valuable. The evidence for a shift in our intellectual paradigms does not therefore lie in the way that users interact with *digital* media: each medium requires different forms of engagement, regardless of its materiality. Instead, any such evidence would be expressed in changes to the ways that users interact with physical media. If the erosion of our intellectual faculties is presumed to be true, then we could safely expect user behaviour in physical archives to change in response to newly formed norms which would transfer from the digital medium. Instead, what we see is the norms of the physical medium being reproduced online. The transformative aspects of large-scale digitisation lie with how users interact with them online, and this behaviour is defined by a complex interaction between the interface of digitised collections, the way in which digital media are presented online, the needs and input of the user, and the social and regulatory constructs which enforce particular modes of interaction upon the user.

At this point, I would like to explore the impact of digitised collections on society as a whole. This book has so far focused largely upon academic researchers: they are an important beneficiary of large-scale digitisation, and they are beneficiaries of the proactivity of libraries. But the following chapter will show that the subscription-based model of digitisation severely undermines claims for universal access and instead reinforces existing divides between information-rich and information-poor communities. As Chapter 4 made clear, the value proposition of libraries in the digital age relies upon their ability to provide access to their materials to a wide and demographically diverse audience. I will argue that digitised collections reinforce and reflect existing divides and that paywalled digitised collections risk creating a "digital divide", between those with access to digitised materials in large quantities and those without, along demographic lines which reflect and reinforce existing models. Libraries have made it clear that they intend to expand access to their collections via web-based materials, and this opens the door to a potential audience which is not solely academic. Researchers include family historians, local historians, genealogists and enthusiasts drawn from the general public. The potential audience for digitised newspapers is broad. Chapter 6 therefore moves the debate in this book away from the user and towards a systemic understanding of the place of LSDC in society. It directly addresses the barriers that exist to participation for users outside academia and relates their experience of access to large-scale digitised collections to the wider context of the digital divide.

Notes

1 A sample that is drawn from the section of the community who are close to hand or willing to participate.
2 DOI is short for Digital Object Identifier, which is a character string used to uniquely identify digital objects. It allows metadata about the object to be stored in association with the DOI name, including a URL location where the object can be found.

Bibliography

Aguilar-Millan, S., Feeney, A., Oberg, A. and Rudd, E. (2010) 'The post-scarcity world of 2050–2075', *The Futurist*, pp. 34–40.
Baker, N. (2001) *Double Fold: Libraries and the Assault on Paper.* New York: Random House.
Benjamin, W. (2007) 'The work of art in the age of mechanical reproduction', in *Illuminations.* New York: Schocken Books (Penguin Great Ideas).
Brake, L. (2012) 'Half full and half empty', *Journal of Victorian Culture*, **17**(2), pp. 222–229. doi: http://dx.doi.org/10.1080/13555502.2012.683151.
Case, D. O. (1991) 'The collection and use of information by some American historians: a study of motives and methods', *Library Quarterly*, **61**, pp. 61–82.
Conway, P. (2013) 'Preserving imperfection: assessing the incidence of digital imaging error in HathiTrust', *Digital Technology and Culture*, **42**(1), pp. 17–30.
Dalton, M. S. and Charnigo, L. (2004) 'Historians and their information sources', *College and Research Libraries*, **65**(5), pp. 400–425.
Deutsch, K. W. (1961) 'On social communication and the metropolis', *Daedalus*, **90**(1), pp. 99–110.

Duff, W. M. and Johnson, C. A. (2002) 'Accidentally found on purpose: information-seeking behavior of historians in archives', *The Library Quarterly*, **72**(4), pp. 472–496.

Edwards, A. S. G. (2013) 'Back to the real?', *The Times Literary Supplement*, 7 June 2013. Retrieved from: www.the-tls.co.uk/tls/public/article1269403.ece.

Liddle, D. (2012) 'Reflections on 20,000 Victorian newspapers: "Distant Reading" *The Times* using *The Times* Digital Archive', *Journal of Victorian Culture*, **17**(2), pp. 230–237. doi: http://dx.doi.org/10.1080/13555502.2012.683151.

Meyer, E. T., Eccles, K., Thelwall, M. and Madsen, C. (2009) *Usage and impact study of JISC-funded phase 1 digitisation projects & the Toolkit for the Impact of Digitised Scholarly Resources (TIDSR)*. Oxford: Oxford Internet Institute, University of Oxford. Retrieved from: http://microsites.oii.ox.ac.uk/tidsr/sites/microsites.oii.ox.ac.uk.tidsr/files/TIDSR_FinalReport_20July2009.pdf.

Mussell, J. (2012) *The Nineteenth-Century Press in the Digital Age*. Basingstoke: Palgrave MacMillan.

Nicholas, D., Huntington, P., Williams, P. and Dobrowolski, T. (2004) 'Reappraising information seeking behaviour in a digital environment: bouncers, checkers, returnees and the like', *Journal of Documentation*, 60(1), pp. 24–39.

Nicholson, B. (2012) 'Counting culture; or, how to read Victorian newspapers from a distance', *Journal of Victorian Culture*, 17(2), pp. 238–246. doi: 10.1080/13555502.2012.683331.

Ranganathan, S. R. (1931) *The Five Laws of Library Science*. Bombay: Asia Publishing House.

Sinn, D. and Soares, N. (2014) 'Historians' use of digital archival collections: the web, historical scholarship, and archival research', *Journal of the Association for Information Science and Technology*, Online First. Retrieved from: http://online library.wiley.com/doi/10.1002/asi.23091/abstract.

Sukovic, S. (2009) 'References to e-texts in academic publications', *Journal of Documentation*, **65**(6), pp. 997–1015. doi: 10.1108/00220410910998960.

Unsworth, J. (2000) 'Scholarly primitives: what methods do humanities researchers have in common, and how might our tools reflect this?', in *Humanities Computing: Formal Methods, Experimental Practice*, King's College London. Retrieved from: http://people.brandeis.edu/~unsworth/Kings.5-00/primitives.html.

Uva, P. A. (1977) *Information-gathering habits of academic historians: report of the pilot study*. ERIC ED 142 483. Syracuse: State University of New York, Upstate Medical Center.

6 "Unequally free"

Mapping public access to digitised collections

Who Do You Think You Are? is a British documentary that has been broadcast on the BBC since 2004. Calling it a phenomenon may be an exaggeration, but 12 series have been broadcast to date, the show regularly attracts a UK audience of more than six million viewers, and the format has been syndicated to more than ten countries including the USA, South Africa, Germany, Poland and Sweden. The show follows celebrities as they trace their family trees and discover more about their ancestors. The huge interest in the show is indicative of a wider public interest in historical sources for the purposes of genealogical research. Tens of millions of individuals worldwide are said to have an interest in researching their family history, and there is a claimed link between a growth in the use of consumer DNA tests and the desire of these researchers to discover their ancestors. The global market for digitised resources which feed into this enthusiasm is huge.

And it is certainly a market, in the capitalist sense of the word. Global Industry Analysts, Inc., in a report costing nearly $1,500 to buy, noted that genealogical enthusiasts in the United States spend between $1,000 and $1,800 a year to discover more about their roots. Libraries are now part of a global network of information providers, all involved in digitising content to support online research into family history through archival collections of all sorts: ship records, birth and marriage certificates, court proceedings and, of course, newspapers. I have spent a great deal of this book distinguishing between commercial providers and libraries, but the reality is that the line between the two is increasingly blurred. In this chapter I will argue that, whereas open access resources provide a clear public good and serve a global audience in a truly equal way, subscription-based digitised resources have been responsible for limiting the extent of participation among certain communities. In stark terms, this has led to the privatisation of large swathes of the public domain, with the most profitable materials from globally significant collections disappearing behind paywalls. The heavy financial cost of accessing digitised collections means that many users are excluded from the benefits of large-scale digitisation. In this chapter I will provide evidence for this divide, which represents a continuation of existing inequalities rather than the creation of a second-generation universal library which has so vividly captured the imagination of critics.

It is within this context that national and public libraries currently work. Public libraries, despite half a decade of steadily decreasing funding, still provide an important service. Whereas the media has characterised library users as stereotypically affluent and middle class, the Department of Culture, Media and Sport statistics show that library users are drawn reasonably equally from the range of socio-economic backgrounds. Around one-third of UK residents used their public library in person in 2014, but those in the most deprived decile were more likely to have visited than the overall average (Department for Culture, Media and Sport, 2015). At some point between collections being separated from the physical walls of the library and placed within the digital platforms which deliver heritage materials to the public, a layer of inequality is introduced which is not reflective of the overall demographic constitution of library users in the United Kingdom. Large-scale digitisation, in theory, tends towards universal provision of services and information. This chapter reflects on the reasons this is not the case. It begins by exploring the long-standing tension between the aim for universal access to cultural heritage and limits to access for specific groups that the commercial and institutional frameworks engender. It then introduces the findings of a demographic study of access to British Library Nineteenth Century Newspapers and the Times Digital Archive, which demonstrates that the benefits of large-scale digitised collections are focused primarily on the most information-rich demographic groups. I will argue that the institutional affiliation of a user is more important to their ability to access digitised resources than their physical location and I will demonstrate that major inequalities in access exist as a result.

Innovative technologies, longstanding tensions

Niggeman *et al.* neatly encapsulate the need to ensure access to cultural heritage for a mass audience:

> Giving access to the European works and productions must become the yardstick of all initiatives taken in this field. And the many questions that have arisen with digitisation should be analysed through this prism and solved with the objective of making our heritage increasingly available to all.
>
> (Niggeman *et al.*, 2011)

Here, I should state my bias up front: the argument in this chapter builds on the assumption that digital resources should be open wherever possible, in order to facilitate significant impact which extends beyond the ability to merely access newspapers and use them in research. Indeed, the examples we have seen, where digitised newspapers were placed in the public domain, have had a huge impact on a much wider community than would have been possible with paywalled resources. Furthermore, user behaviour can be constrained and defined by the type of resource being used. While it would be wrong to suggest that open resources provide a perfect model for user interaction, it is true that a model built around flexible, open access to digitised materials can facilitate innovative approaches using full text corpora, APIs, and user-generated content. In the case of subscription resources, this chapter will begin from the very first step, demonstrating that users of digitised newspapers are in fact normally drawn from information-rich institutions in nations with high internet penetration.

In light of this argument, it is worth considering briefly what is meant by access. In this case, I understand it to represent an individual's ability to use LSDC without barriers. I have already argued that to support rich and diverse practices with digitised collections there is a need to provide access to corpora and metadata, address the licensing of derivative scanned materials and mitigate the costs associated with accessing digitised collections. This chapter, however, considers a more basic definition of access, focusing on the ability of particular demographics to access digitised newspaper collections online. Open Access resources such as Australian Newspapers Online and Welsh Newspapers Online provide free global access to their collections. Others such as the British Newspaper Archive and the Times Digital Archive provide both individual access via personal subscriptions and institutional access where a library service meets the upfront subscription costs. I will refer specifically to the problems associated with resources which require institutional subscriptions; many users are unable to maintain individual subscriptions to the resources they require and must rely on their institutional affiliation to remove the cost barriers of access. As we will see, though, it is frequently those who are least able to pay for access themselves who are also disadvantaged by the demographic divide between information-rich and information-poor institutions.

The case studies in the chapter concentrate on inequalities between residents of English-speaking nations, but the problems that I will identify feed into a wider debate on international inequalities in access to research. Clearly, differences in the ability to access large-scale digitised newspaper collections exist between different user groups. I will show that these differences manifest themselves in ways that largely represent the ways in which inequality is constructed in society: those from deprived demographics, rural areas and lower ranked educational institutions are disadvantaged in comparison to their peers. This is undoubtedly a divide that needs addressing, but it becomes particularly damaging in the face of discourses which claim that everything is available online and that everybody can access it. Priego addresses the academic environment, noting that realising that there are distinct infrastructural differences between academic institutions "means understanding that in a globalised Higher Education market, some simple measures, involving digital literacy strategies, can be, for the time being, an initial step towards preventing a normalisation which often leaves many scholars out of the competition" (2012). I will argue in this chapter that the need for digitised newspapers extends well beyond academia and that we must therefore also turn our attention to the growing digital divides as they relate to the ability of society as a whole to make the most of online digitised content.

The stakes for access to digital materials are thus felt on a global scale. The presence of low-cost or free digital resources has wider significance for the globalised HE market, whereas this chapter addresses the specific institutional and individual. These findings still hold value for the contribution they make to evaluating the scale of inequality even in nations where digital inclusion is a priority. In the United Kingdom, as Lord Carter writes, digital inclusion encompasses:

> The best use of digital technology, either directly or indirectly to improve the lives and life chances of all citizens, particularly the most disadvantaged, and in the places in which they live.
>
> (2009)

But this proclamation seems at odds with the austerity-driven cuts to the public sector. Libraries have been hit particularly hard by these cuts. The Chartered Institute of Public Finance and Accountancy's (CIPFA) annual library survey showed that, in 2014, 49 libraries closed in the United Kingdom, while many more were de-professionalised through transfer to a volunteer workforce. Since the 2009–10 financial year, the UK has suffered a net loss of 337 public libraries, and total net expenditure is down year upon year. Because libraries are busy just "keeping the doors open", (CIPFA, 2014), the question of how libraries can support digital inclusion given their budgetary straits is largely unaddressed. Despite this, the public library sector still has a key role to play in providing access to digitised collections which are otherwise inaccessible. The agenda to increase access to digitised collections, and to bridge the digital divide more generally, have had lip service paid to them in government, but this has not been supported by corresponding funding. National libraries have suffered from these cuts too, and the need to look outside the sector for support for digitisation activities is driven by a lack of budget. Large-scale digitisation is therefore a largely unfunded mandate for cultural institutions. There has been little political will for public investment in the United Kingdom, and the adoption of commercial partnerships has largely been borne out of necessity. Commercial companies have driven investment in digitisation, and the public and private sectors have been working in partnership since at least the 1980s to create digitised resources. An early example of cross-sector collaboration was between Yale Library and the US National Gallery, with Melissa Terras noting the mutual benefits of this approach:

> Such projects were beneficial to both institution and industry: providing the culture and heritage industry with access to expensive, advanced technology, and providing the industrial partners with real life test cases for research and development, publicity, and often financial benefits.
>
> (Terras, 2011)

The technical expertise of the private sector has certainly accelerated the growth of digitised collections, to the extent that GBS successfully digitised tens of millions of books in less than a decade. Commercial partnerships have also sustained financial investment in a time of austerity. Poole (2010) estimates the cost of digitising the complete contents of Europe's libraries, archives, museums and cultural institutions at €105.31 billion. Such heavy investment is otherwise inconceivable when institutions are already redirecting core funding towards maintaining expensive subscriptions to digital resources:

> The brilliant constellation of databases that dazzles any user of a modern library homepage is a cost center as well as an asset, one that takes up something like a third of any library's budget.
>
> (Grafton, 2009)

I noted in Chapter 2 that the commercial sector has played an important role in ensuring the viability of large-scale digitisation in the UK and in other countries. However, whatever the practical implications of commercial involvement in digitisation, there is a fundamental tension between their involvement in the production of digitised content and the library sector's stated aim to expand access to new communities. James Murdoch approached self-parody in an interview where he portrayed open access as an evil perpetrated by a predatory public sector (Sabbagh, 2010), but his business-centric perspective embodies this tension. Libraries, by creating digitised resources, have entered into a negotiated relationship between the needs of businesses to secure profit on their investment and the desire to facilitate wide access to digitised collections.

Mapping the digitised divide

It is against this background that I will present a specific example where local conditions have led to a divide in access to digitised collections. The issue of access to digitised resources is inextricably linked to the extent of their impact. In the globalised information age, users are able to access resources from around the world, and their expectations are shaped by the providers with the most generous access conditions. The National Library of Australia, for instance, claims that commercial newspaper collections have driven traffic towards their own, open access resources (Tanner, 2013). If the ability of the individual user to access the resource they require is affected, and they are unwilling or unable to pay to circumvent this difficulty, it is likely that they will look elsewhere. Furthermore, when a resource switches from open access to closed access, the resultant user leakage can undermine its potential impact. Eccles *et al.*, for instance, undertook link analysis of BNCN, which showed that around a quarter of links to the resources came from outside the UK. They reported that the fact it was behind a paywall stopped this evident global interest from translating into usage and that as a result it garnered fewer links than a website for a solitary open access nineteenth century newspaper:

> Compared to a single open access digitised Nineteenth Century British Library newspaper, *The Penny Illustrated Paper,* our project site performed less well, with less than twice as many links, perhaps indicating the impact of restricted access to content on the number of pages linking to a resource.
>
> (2012)

Access therefore plays a key role in defining impact for digitised collections. Bearing in mind my argument that the majority of users are engaged in research practices which rely on the web interface, I have not considered whether users can access underlying metadata or datasets for digital humanities research, although this is an important scholarly need that some resources have addressed. The word "access" is variously used in the literature, but at a thematic level it refers to the ability of a user to gain direct access to the materials they want: this can be free to all, free at the point of access or paid for via individual subscription. All these models have been used for digitised newspaper collections. Open access resources such as Australian Newspapers Online and Welsh Newspapers Online provide free global access to their collections. Others, such as British Library Nineteenth Century Newspapers and the Times Digital Archive, provide institutional access where institutions meet subscription costs and users can access the resource through some form of online authentication. Finally, resources such as the British Newspaper Archive provide individual access through personal subscriptions, where the end user is entirely responsible for meeting the costs of accessing the resource. This chapter will refer specifically to access that is covered by institutional subscription and is thus free at the point of access for their users. Although this model means that institutions are responsible for financing subscriptions, largely from library budgets, individual users are not dependent upon their own financial position for access if they are appropriately affiliated.

Individuals do not view digitised resources in isolation: five or more different collections can be viewed in a single session, with researchers taking advantage of a variety of digitised collections depending on content, unique features, cost and perceived usability issues. In a digital world where access is frequently limited by paywalls, users can be left needing to pay for multiple resources in one session, and thus the cost of access for the unaffiliated user can be high. Yet even the most affluent universities can struggle to provide for all the information needs of their users, as digital subscriptions require an increasing proportion of library budgets. The cumulative price increase of digital journal subscriptions has, for instance, forced Harvard Library to undertake "serious cancellation efforts" for budgetary reasons (Suber, 2012). While interlibrary loan systems were created to address the inequality between library services by assisting in the lending of physical materials between institutions, digital content is often licensed for access to affiliated users only. This leads to a diminished ability to share resources between libraries and individuals. Public libraries in the United Kingdom do allow users from other boroughs to register and access digital collections under the same terms as locals, but this re-introduces an unnecessary time and travel cost that digitised collections should theoretically remove. Given these factors, there is a strong benefit to being allied to an information-rich institution; universities and some professional institutions can and do subscribe to a wider range of digital resources than public libraries, which in turn provide a more diverse range than most individuals can afford. Yet even within this hierarchy, there are differences in resource provision between universities and between public library authorities. The difference, as Suber points out, can be extreme:

> In 2008, Harvard subscribed to 98,000 serials and Yale to 73,900. The best-funded research library in India, at the Indian Institute of Science, subscribed to 10,600. Several sub-Saharan university libraries subscribed to zero, offering their patrons access to no conventional journals except those donated by publishers.
>
> (2012)

Given this imbalance, an interpretation of access to digitised collections that focuses on the individual's point of access can only partly illuminate the impact of these collections at a general demographic level. In particular, it is necessary to ask deeper questions about how institutional access can shape individual access to digital resources. For the remainder of this chapter, I will attempt to answer two of these questions, by looking at specific cases where the primary mode of access to digitised newspapers is through institutional subscriptions:

- Which institutions provide access to subscription-based digitised newspaper collections?
- What can we discover about the demographic makeup of users of these institutions, and does this tell us anything about equality of access to digitised newspapers?

This chapter draws upon my demographic analysis of the BNCN and TDA user communities through mapping the location of institutions with subscriptions to the collections. I adopted a method generally referred to as a Geographical Information System (GIS), for which Curry (1998) provides a useful working definition: "I take geographical information systems to be technological means for the collection, storage, analysis, and representation of geo-coded data." The increased availability of networked and mobile computing has massively increased public awareness of the value of mapping technologies. The creator of a GIS is able to represent information using techniques that would be impossible in a purely textual treatment of data, and thus geographical representations have become relevant to many fields in the humanities. As Bodenhamer *et al.* note: "Within a GIS, users can discover relationships that make a complex world more immediately understandable by visually detecting spatial patterns that remain hidden in text and tables" (2010). Although researchers have considered how libraries can support their users in using GIS technologies (Argentati, 1997; Dixon, 2006), there appears to have been little consideration of the value of using them to visualise the extent and impact of library services. As a method, it has been relatively underused in LIS, despite obvious value in a field where library services are delineated on geographical and institutional boundaries. This information is usefully available to researchers, whether through user records or, in this case, web analytics platforms. Google Analytics processes usage statistics to provide detailed analyses of user locations, derived from mapping IP addresses to geographical locations. Automated tools like GA, though, concentrate on the location of the individual at the point of access, meaning that they lack demographic insights beyond the geographic. Other approaches can tell us about the education levels, affluence and other demographic details of users of LSDC. This approach to geographical information is known as geodemographics and works on "the suggestion that *where* you are, says something about *who* you are; that knowing where someone lives provides useful information about how that person lives" (Harris *et al.*, 2005). We can trace the use of geodemographics back to the Descriptive Map of London Poverty; Booth (1889) shaded each street in London to indicate the general socio-economic condition of its residents, thus creating a detailed map of the relative poverty of the whole of London. The aim remains the same today: to represent complex socio-economic factors on maps, on the understanding that a certain population, whether a neighbourhood, educational institution, or business, shares certain demographic characteristics. This approach is more suitable for exploratory analysis than for hypothesis testing, making it extremely suitable for this task.

Case study: mapping the users of digitised newspaper collections

My study adopted the principle outlined by Harris *et al.* (2005): while the location of individual users gives us a superficial idea of where people are using a digitised collection, it tells us nothing about their socio-economic status. Instead, grouping users together based on their demographic status allows us to discover general information about that population to compare them to other distinct populations. As a result, I chose to look at two similar digitised newspaper collections: British Library Nineteenth Century Newspapers and the Times Digital Archive. Both are primarily available to users through an institutional subscription, so I based this approach on the observation that an individual's affiliation is the strongest single indicator of their ability to access the chosen collections. Therefore, mapping institutional access gives us two benefits over mapping individuals: it gives us a more accurate representation of which institutions people use to access digitised newspapers, and where they are based; and it allows us to gather detailed demographic information in order to discover whether there are demographic differences between institutions with access and those without.

In order to achieve this, I collated a list of subscribing institutions for both BNCN and TDA. For each resource, the main subscribers were global HE and FE education institutions, major national libraries and research libraries, and public libraries in the United Kingdom. I therefore focused my analysis on these three categories. I gathered the information from publicly available online subscriber lists by Gale Cengage, with other subscribers confirmed in email correspondence with a representative of the company. For public libraries, I gathered subscription data by visiting each local authority's library website and manually identifying whether the resource was available. To display the data geographically, I compiled a complete table of subscribing institutions in each category, with a corresponding longitude and latitude recorded in the table for education institutions and national libraries. Public libraries represent a geographic area, so I sourced polygon shapes that could accurately map the region covered by each authority.[1] I then compiled detailed demographic data. For HE and FE institutions, this included student population, library budget information in the public domain and university rankings. For public libraries, this included total regional population, total library spend per public authority, and relative deprivation ranking data from the UK government (Department for Communities and Local Government, 2011). Finally, I inserted the subscription data into a column that allocated a colour value based on access, green representing an institution or authority with access, and red for one without.

I chose to visualise this data using a web-based map using Google Fusion Tables. This is an experimental interface for creating custom maps using the Google Maps API and provides limited customisation options in its native interface. The maps can be further customised via the API and embedded in any website using a combination of JavaScript and HTML. While this option is less powerful than dedicated GIS software, it provides benefits derived from its open, flexible nature: the data that underpins each map can be made publicly available for reuse, re-appropriation and editing by any interested parties. The map contains two layers: the first shows, to the best of my knowledge, which FE and HE institutions around the world have access to BNCN, with each institution geographically represented by a pin[2] on the map. The second layer provides a complete indication of which English public library authorities had access when the study was undertaken, with each area represented by a polygon shape covering the relevant part of the map, and coloured green or red depending upon the access status. In addition to the mapping, I undertook a detailed analysis of the demographic data to learn more about the socio-economic status of institutions and local authorities with access in comparison to those without. The rest of this chapter will elaborate on the key findings of this method but, given its experimental nature, it is worth briefly critiquing it. First, this is not a method that can be applied to all collections: open collections still need to be considered in relation to wider issues of social inclusion, but for connected citizens they offer no barrier to access. Furthermore, mapping is only partially helpful in answering the research questions I have posed. It does allow the emergence of geographical patterns and successfully disregards the role of individual geographic mobility, which acts as an obscuring factor in assessing inclusion in digital media. But in some senses the map is limited: the true value of the method comes from collating publicly available demographic data to discover more about the differences between subscribing and non-subscribing communities. The patterns that emerge from this data, combined with reframing how we think about the nature of access to digitised resources, provide the real value of this approach.

When I collected the data in 2013, JISC provided free access to British Library Nineteenth Century Newspapers and this was limited to HE and FE institutions in the United Kingdom. UK national libraries, and some private institutional libraries, also provided access to their users. JISC's investment in access to digital resources has ensured a semblance of parity within the United Kingdom, at least for those resources which come under a group agreement. This is an important benefit for educational users in the United Kingdom. However, there is no evidence of widespread access elsewhere in the world, with only the United States, Canada and Germany representing large markets for the collection (see Figure 6.1).

This confirms that global interest in resources does not necessarily translate into sales or access. The geographically diverse position of individuals accessing the resource is therefore less relevant than their affiliation to a geographically homogenous group of institutions, which allow their users to access resources from any location. The internet and, by extension, large-scale digitisation are frequently viewed as an opportunity

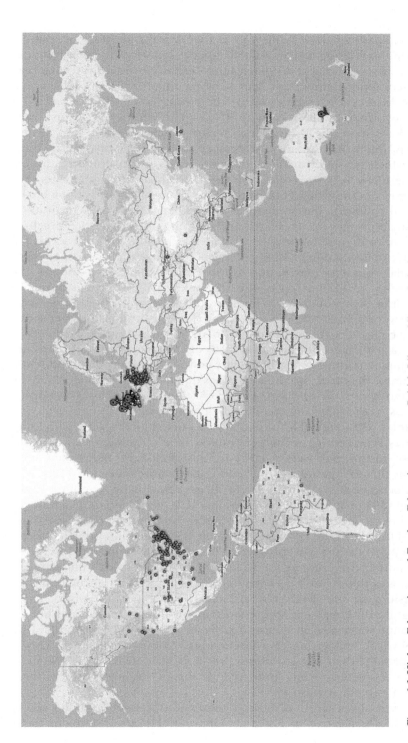

Figure 6.1 Higher Education and Further Education access to British Library Nineteenth Century Newspapers globally (January 2013).
An interactive version of this map is available at http://bit.ly/2beO9b5.

to widen participation. While this is theoretically accurate, it assumes that content is being made available equally, ignoring the important distinction between what technologies theoretically facilitate and what real-world conditions allow. The gap between theoretical universality and real-world access is emphasised by the strong correlation between US university rankings[3] and access to BNCN. The USA is one of just three countries where the educational sector widely subscribes to British Library Nineteenth Century Newspapers and is the only one of these three which has individually negotiated access for institutions; the UK and Germany rely on collectively negotiated access agreements. For universities in the United States, the decision to subscribe is not a binary one, and collection development priorities play a large role. Institutions without access may have research and teaching priorities which preclude the need for digitised newspapers; some may be able to afford access but have decided that other resources may better serve their needs; or usage of similar resources may be too low to justify expenditure. Indeed, the universities in the top ten of the US rankings illustrate this perfectly: Massachusetts Institute of Technology and California Institute of Technology were found to be the only top-ranking institutions without access to the collection. Their technical focus suggests that digitised newspapers are perhaps not a central facet of their teaching and illustrates the complex reasoning and budgetary control that individual library services must negotiate in their purchasing decisions. While this is an important point, the findings of my work still uncovered a striking divide in access, as the following section will demonstrate.

In total, 199 national universities were ranked by US News, with lower numbers representing a higher position in the rankings. The average rank of institutions with a current subscription to BNCN was 66.4, whereas the average rank of non-subscribing universities was 112.1. The divide between the 178 liberal arts colleges was equally pronounced: the average rank of subscribing colleges was 41.4, compared to 93.6 for non-subscribing colleges. If we consider the top and bottom of the rankings, we find that 14 of the 20 highest ranking US universities provided access to BNCN, while just 5 of the lowest ranked 20 universities had a current subscription: the presence of MIT and CIT in the top 20 illustrate the starkness of this division between information-rich and information-poor universities, in one of the most affluent HE systems in the world. There is a significant inequality, where more highly ranked universities benefit from superior access to educational resources, despite the removal of the physical limitations of contemporary library collections. This is unsurprising when put so bluntly, yet it is indicative of the extent to which the democratising potential of digital resources has suffered through implementation.

There is also a clear correlation between investment level and access. The ARL (Association of Research Libraries) Library Investment Index

Table 6.1 Comparison of American Higher Education institutional access to British
Library Nineteenth Century Newspapers (January 2013)

Access status	Average rank: total library investment	Average rank: total materials expenditure	Average materials expenditure
With access to BNCN	45.94	42.96	$14,350,155
Without access to BNCN	65.66	67.75	$10,422,917

ranks institutions numerically based on their library investment spend. It does so by using the metrics of total library investment and materials expenditure. As Table 6.1 shows, those institutions with higher overall budgets and higher materials budgets were more likely to subscribe to BNCN.

In addition to higher library investment, subscribing universities had an average of roughly 5,000 more students than non-subscribing universities, meaning that those institutions with higher student numbers, higher library investment and higher materials expenditure are more likely to subscribe to BNCN. While this should come as no surprise, it sounds an important note of caution against idealising digitisation as a universal technology. Instead, even when considering Western educational institutions which, considered globally, are among the most information-rich organisations, there are significant inequalities in access to resources.

Inequalities in access by English Public Library authority

This inequality is also evident when we consider the worrying divide between public library authorities in England and, by extension, their patrons. While a large number of libraries do subscribe to British Library Nineteenth Century Newspapers, socio-economic factors[4] point to regional inequalities in access. Leaving behind any further consideration of the damage wrought upon the United Kingdom's public library service by the ideologically driven cuts of recent years, this section explores the correlation between demographic and financial factors and a particular library's ability, or decision, to provide access to BNCN. The map in Figure 6.2 shows subscribing library authorities in light grey and non-subscribers in dark grey, as of January 2013.

The map suggests a north-south divide in access, which corresponds closely to the findings of the Social and Spatial Inequalities Group (SASI) at the University of Sheffield. SASI defined a rough boundary for the north-south divide based upon data relating to life outcomes throughout the United Kingdom. This line stretches from the Bristol Channel in the

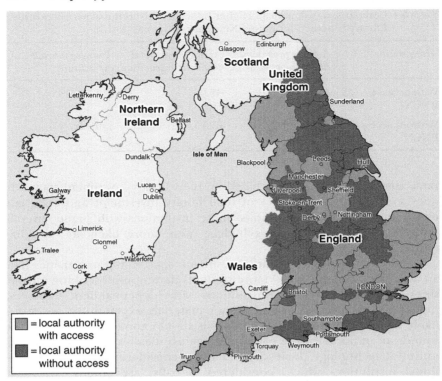

Figure 6.2 Map of access to British Library Nineteenth Century Newspapers by English Public Library authority (January 2013).

west of England to the Wash, between Kings Lynn and Lincoln in the east, and refers to the general observation that the south of England has demonstrably better outcomes in health, life expectancy, income and education than the north (Dorling, 2007). Access to digitised newspapers through public libraries is another example of a resource whose unequal distribution correlates strongly with this geographical divide, although there are notable exceptions. London provides the most notable, with virtually none of the inner-London authorities maintaining a subscription to British Library Nineteenth Century Newspapers. This contradicts received wisdom about the connectivity afforded to residents of large cities, but particular demographics of London may explain this; the inner-London boroughs are, to a large extent, more deprived than the outer boroughs. Translating this to our consideration of the digital divide, this means that residents in deprived inner-London boroughs are excluded from the opportunity to access digitised newspapers for free, while those in affluent boroughs find their more privileged social position reinforced by prevailing access models. Figure 6.3 shows this divide in stark terms:

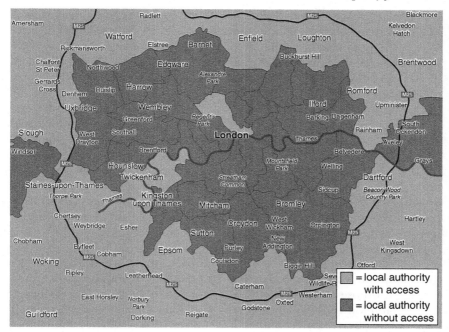

Figure 6.3 Map of access to British Library Nineteenth Century Newspapers in Greater London.

Nationally, meanwhile, the evidence for a divide is supported by comparing metrics for population, deprivation and library funding levels in England. The UK government defines deprivation as covering "a broad range of issues and refers to unmet needs caused by a lack of resources of all kinds, not just financial" (Department for Communities and Local Government, 2011). Regional deprivation levels in England are tracked, in order to provide a Relative Deprivation Index which ranks local authorities from the most deprived (1) to the least deprived (149). By using this numerical ranking, I was able to work out the relative levels of deprivation for library services which provided access to British Library Nineteenth Century Newspapers and the Times Digital Archive. For both resources, I found that a higher level of deprivation corresponded with a decreased likelihood that the local public library service maintained a subscription to either resource. In recent years, library users have been stereotyped in the media as increasingly affluent. In fact, the share of respondents that visited a public library in 2014 is relatively evenly split by level of deprivation, as a household survey by the Department of Culture, Media and Sport (2015) demonstrates. Whereas visits to public libraries are evenly balanced between demographic groups, these findings demonstrate that the benefits of digital library services are in fact focused on those in the least deprived communities.

I compared the 25 most deprived boroughs to the 25 least deprived. The most deprived boroughs accounted for 7,546,943 residents (14.21 per cent of the population), while the least deprived boroughs accounted for 11,379,000 (21.43 per cent). Figure 6.4 presents the portion of each of these populations with access to BNCN, TDA or both through their local public library service.

The findings show a strong correlation between deprivation and access to both resources. In the most deprived areas, 47 per cent of residents had access to neither collection, in comparison to 19 per cent in the least deprived. By contrast, 58 per cent of the population in the least deprived regions could access both collections, compared to just 10 per cent in the most deprived regions. If we expand the sample to cover the whole of England, the pattern continues. I calculated an average deprivation ranking for the whole dataset by taking the average numerical value for regions with and without subscriptions: a lower number represents a higher average level of deprivation. The average deprivation ranking for regions with access to BNCN is 87.78, compared to an average of 68.53 for those without. The same is true for TDA, where the average deprivation ranking for those with access is 84.01 compared to 65.29 for those without. Over 15 million residents have access to neither collection through their local public library service, a total of 29.52 per cent of the population and a number that is disproportionately drawn from residents of the most deprived areas.

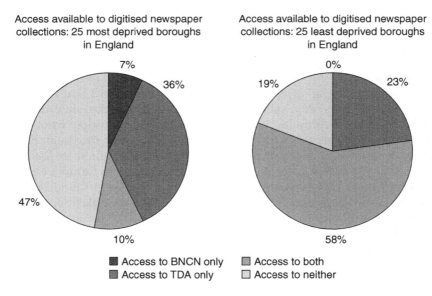

Access available to digitised newspaper collections: 25 most deprived boroughs in England

Access available to digitised newspaper collections: 25 least deprived boroughs in England

7%   36%   47%   10%

0%   19%   23%   58%

■ Access to BNCN only ▨ Access to both
■ Access to TDA only   ☐ Access to neither

Figure 6.4 Comparison of levels of access available to digitised newspaper collections of British Library Nineteenth Century Newspapers and Times Digital Archive: most and least deprived boroughs in England.

Additionally, spend per capita is less important than total spend in ensuring broad provision of digitised resources: effectively, a small but well-funded public library service will be unable to afford the same resources as a larger service with lower funding levels. Expenditure data was taken from the CIPFA reports into English public library authorities (2012).[5] The results (see Figure 6.5) show that there is little correlation between high spending per capita and access to BNCN.

However, there is a strong correlation between total expenditure and access, as seen in Figure 6.6, which suggests that the cost of digitised resources is too high for smaller public libraries to afford, due to their lower overall budget.

The importance of population size is confirmed when we consider this factor more closely. Areas with larger populations are able to maintain a wider selection of digitised materials for their residents, with Figure 6.7 comparing access in the 25 most populous regions to the 25 least populous regions.

These results show that nearly 61 per cent of residents in the most populous regions have access to both resources, compared to just 0.23 per cent in the least populous. Just over half of residents in the least populous regions have no access at all, compared to just 16.1 per cent in the most populous.

These results are concerning because they so strongly replicate existing divides between rural and urban areas, and affluent and deprived areas. In

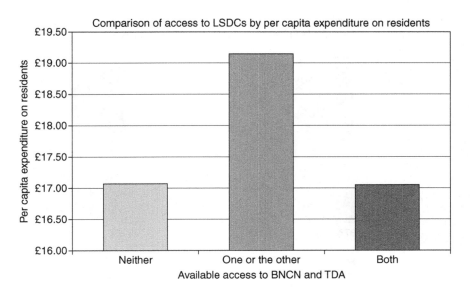

Figure 6.5 Comparison of access available to digitised collections of British Library Nineteenth Century Newspapers and Times Digital Archive: per capita expenditure on residents.

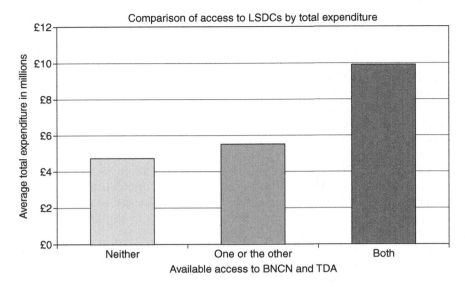

Figure 6.6 Comparison of access available to digitised newspaper collections of British Library Nineteenth Century Newspapers and Times Digital Archive: total library expenditure.

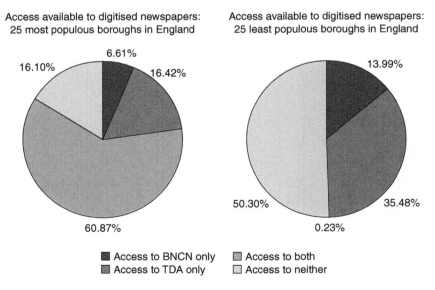

Figure 6.7 Comparison of access available to digitised newspaper collections of British Library Nineteenth Century Newspapers and Times Digital Archive: most and least populous boroughs in England.

HE, to which the majority of the discussion in this book has applied, there are genuine inequalities between the institutions with the highest reputations, budgets and student numbers, and those without. This inequality is also found in wider society where digitised newspaper resources are in high demand. Free access to digitised newspapers is more readily available to those areas which have more expansive life opportunities in general. I would therefore like to propose that digitised materials can be considered "unequally free"; that is, they are free only if you meet certain criteria such as membership of a specific organisation or residence in a particular location, while other people are refused access based on these criteria. The assumption of universality based on technical features of the digitisation process has created a hyperbolic sense of the democratising impact of large-scale digitisation when the reality, as I argued in relation to user behaviour, does not bear out the idea of a significant change in opportunity for audiences. Existing issues with inequality, copyright, revenue protection and intellectual property rights continue to dominate how access to digitised collections is defined, to the detriment of participation. The situation closely matches Castells' earlier description of the conditions of internet diffusion:

> Key urban centers, globalized activities, and the higher educated social groups are being included in the Internet-based global networks, while most regions and people are switched off.
>
> (2002)

Castells claims that key urban centres are generally included in online networks, but these findings suggest there are exceptions; while population is a key factor in predicting opportunities for access, the heavily populated central London public authorities provide a notable exception. Thus, patterns of inclusion are not always predictable and individuals can still be excluded due to social and economic barriers. My concern is that overstating the benefits of digitisation could cause problems for those who are excluded, in addition to their inability to access resources on the same terms as their peers. Expectations for online digitised collections have escalated in recent years, with declarations of the universal digital library frequently occurring in discussions of large-scale digitisation (Toobin, 2007; Simon, 2012). But this universal library is only likely if we are to ignore the evidence that, beyond disparities in access to the internet, there are further inequalities in access between individuals and user communities.

The problem of access to relevant resources has always existed for researchers, but in an era where the physical barriers have been theoretically removed, it is instead our information structures that reinforce existing problems rather than remove them. This has particular implications for users who may be based at smaller universities with little access to relevant resources and, indeed, for the increasing number of researchers who exist on precarious contracts. The large number of researchers who may be unaffiliated due to unstable employment or their place of residence can become isolated from the very tools that would allow them to remain competitive in the academic job market. In this sense their opportunities are concretely affected by their societal position, in line with Hargittai's observation:

> The societal position that users inhabit influences aspects of their digital media use such as the technical equipment to which they have access and the level of autonomy they possess when using the medium.
>
> (2008)

For these users, who cannot guarantee their long-term ability to maintain access to relevant resources, overstating the universality of web-based resources can become a damaging myth that raises expectations without equipping researchers with the tools to meet them. While digitisation has continued apace, the utopian vision of democratised access is undermined by the lack of individual autonomy for users. Instead, their access to digitised resources is subject to a series of technological, social and financial dependencies. Technological inequality does not necessarily disappear over time, influenced as it is by these factors which are external to the technology. Castells notes that "as one source of technological inequality seems to be diminishing, another one emerges" (2002). In academia, this inequality can be seen in the way that differing levels of access to digitised collections can further entrench the privileged positions of those institutions best-placed financially to capitalise. Exclusion from this group exists even in the relatively information-rich university system.

Beyond academia, there is a clear appetite for digitised newspapers. A thriving local and national history scene and widespread interest in genealogy both provide large audiences for digitised newspapers, yet subscription models spread these benefits unevenly. Whereas the concept of the digital divide was initially concerned with the unavailability of access to digital technologies, social exclusion is a more nuanced concept which encompasses other forms of exclusion, including "mental and physical disabilities, age, ethnicity, gender, class, occupation, sexuality, lifestyle, geographical location, political or religious affiliation, and family or legal circumstances" (Liew, 2012). Access to large-scale digitisation collections is an equality and participation issue that libraries must address. Liew neatly describes the feeling of many potential users:

> One gets the feeling that the current situation with digital initiatives appears to be that a *big digital information party* [author's emphasis] is

being planned but somehow, in the excitement, someone is being left out.

(Liew, 2012)

It is not my contention that commercial involvement in digitisation has been universally negative. I have discussed several positive aspects, not least the accelerated rate at which digitisation of library collections has been undertaken. The problem lies with access models that focus inadequately upon user needs, and which limit the impact of large-scale digitisation. The interface for digitised collections can define how they are used, to the detriment of user autonomy, and the model, by which they are funded and made accessible, can define who they are used by. As things stand, the educational sector has been the primary beneficiary of access to digitised newspapers. These benefits have not been felt evenly outside academia, though – those most benefitting being from affluent or heavily populated areas. This is disappointing when we consider the taxpayer contribution to BNCN which has allowed it to be free for educational users, without securing equal access for potential beneficiaries from other communities. The UK trend towards subscription-based resources contradicts the current emphasis in government and academia on opening up access to the products of publicly funded research. Darnton summarises the problem extremely well:

> To digitise collections and sell the product in ways that fail to guarantee wide access would be to repeat the mistake that was made when publishers exploited the market for scholarly journals ... it would turn the Internet into an instrument for privatizing knowledge that belongs in the public sphere.
>
> (2009)

I would suggest that, in cases where projects receive significant public funding to undertake digitisation projects, consideration should be given to the feasibility of securing truly equitable access for the public. The NLW has achieved this with its newspaper collection, with an ambitious, global open access resource that is widely accessible by all users with the appropriate web access. While open access is an admirable aim, with clear benefits over subscription resources, it is not necessarily feasible in the current financial climate. However, collective agreements could at the very least rationalise public library provision of subscription resources to provide a consistent offering at national level: in effect, a national digital public library. This should be combined with the removal of geographical limitations for national library users of public domain digitised materials to alleviate inequality within the UK. The BL is the only UK national library which cannot provide its users with remote access to BNCN. Forcing users to travel a great distance to access digital resources through a limited number of terminals is a very literal instantiation of a flawed gatekeeper culture in libraries. It should be a minimum requirement for libraries to provide remote access to their digitised collections for all registered users: this provides a middle ground that addresses the user's need to access material and allows for the marketing of digitised collections outside the country of origin. This, however, is just a starting point in addressing the global market for digitised collections. Here, as Priego points out, the focus is necessarily on "open access, interoperability when possible/desirable, affordable technologies and sustainability" (2012).

Summary: the digitised divide in action

These findings illuminate the difficult relationship between the democratising potential of digitisation and the reality of relying upon access models that are limited by economic, institutional and regulatory frameworks. The British Library 2020 Vision report states that:

> At the heart of our vision is a passionate belief that everyone who wants to do research should have access to the rich resource of content held by the British Library. The digital environment provides an immense opportunity to democratise access to content through removing physical barriers.
>
> (2010)

Yet this vision is irrelevant if the physical barriers are replaced by virtual barriers arising from the BL's role as a legal deposit library, combined with the lack of funding specifically for large-scale digitisation. Jean-Claude talked about the possibilities for digital libraries in 1998:

> Digitised birds are notoriously difficult to keep behind bars ... In effect, the technology no longer contributes to the strict control of scarcity that stands at the heart of any pricing system within a liberal economic scheme. With digital materials, the engineering of scarcity becomes tricky at best, impossible at worst.
>
> (1998)

He has sadly been proven wrong in the intervening decades: scarcity has been replicated and reinforced using web technologies, and libraries have been inadvertently complicit in the process of transferring control of large quantities of public domain into the hands of private companies. I have not previously referred to the national libraries as subscribers to digitised newspaper resources, but the way in which they access BNCN is illuminating. The BL, as a major stakeholder in the resource, has a licence agreement which allows its registered users to access BNCN for free only within the physical boundaries of its reading rooms. By contrast, both the NLW and the NLS provide free remote access to BNCN and a number of other collections to their registered users. Furthermore, both allow these users to register for access to e-resources using an online form. As they allow all residents of their respective nations to sign up, this effectively means that Scotland and Wales provide free remote access for any resident with the requisite technology and desire to access the resources. The BL, despite owning the physical materials, cannot provide the same. This is not purely a commercial decision, driven as it is partly by a cautious approach to the library's responsibilities in relation to managing and protecting its legal deposit collections. Yet it means that other national libraries that pay for subscriptions have more opportunity to serve their users remotely than an institution which supplied materials, finance, expertise and staffing to the project. The BL's role as legal deposit library has combined with its requirement to work with commercial partners to provide inferior access to users within England.

What Darnton described as the privatisation of knowledge has occurred through financial necessity, but it will have significant implications for the way in which digitised collections will be used for many years. We can look to the originator of the maxim "information wants to be free" for an explanation. While Brand's words have been selectively quoted to justify a utopian view of online access, his original quote refers to the contradictions between open access and information as a commodity:

> Information wants to be free. Information also wants to be expensive. Information wants to be free because it has become so cheap to distribute, copy, and recombine – too cheap to meter. It wants to be expensive because it can be immeasurably valuable to the recipient. That tension will not go away. It leads to endless wrenching debate about price, copyright, "intellectual property", the moral rightness of casual distribution, because each round of new devices makes the tension worse, not better.
>
> (1989)

This tension, as Brand predicted, persists because web technologies theoretically provide a platform to eradicate information scarcity. Unlike printed texts, the reproduction of scarcity online is entirely removed from the limitations of physical reproduction. The cost of digitisation and reliance on external investment require a value proposition to be presented and, where material lies in the public domain, financial value can only be manufactured by controlling access to replicate a sense of scarcity. This leads to two pressures which work against the goal of truly democratising access, first, because large-scale digitisation as conceived nationally in the United Kingdom requires a financial return on investment, and second (with the notable exception of Welsh Newspapers Online) because there are very few free alternatives which provide British newspapers for free.

This results in a digitised divide in access to digitised newspapers, which largely recreates and reinforces existing inequalities.

It should be noted, though, that this line of thinking could lead us to logically conclude that achieving open access to public domain materials is only possible if libraries control digitised resources. The extent of this shift varies between institutions and indeed between nations. The local context plays a huge role in defining access to web resources, both at the specific level of digitised cultural heritage and the wider level at which the digital divide is manifested. As Risam notes:

> The digital divides that exist in the world do so unevenly, the local contexts matter and are inflected by linguistic, cultural and social dimensions, each location – and even local communities within national contexts – uniquely constituted beyond binaries like east or west or humanities and sciences.
>
> (2015)

Risam's comments are directed at research in the digital humanities and identify that local contexts primarily define and codify how specific academic practices develop, but the point applies equally to local contexts for digitisation of cultural heritage. The divide in access that we have seen in relation to many resources created in the UK comes from the specific cultural climate within which the BL and other memory institutions must operate.

Notes

1 Specifically, I used polygon data from www.gadm.org, which licenses its content for all non-commercial use. This makes it a valuable academic resource.
2 The pin is technically known as a node.
3 Data for US university rankings was taken from the US News tables, which provide separate listings for university rankings (US News, 2012b) and liberal arts college rankings (US News, 2012a). Additional financial data was gathered from the Research Libraries Library Investment Index (Price, 2013), which ranks member libraries on their relative investment and materials expenditure levels.
4 Not least the agenda of cuts to public services in the United Kingdom, which have placed great pressure on library services and force inevitable difficult decisions regarding their spending priorities.
5 All figures are provided here as revenue expenditure before income is taken into account; in other words, the level of funding that each library service receives per 1,000 residents before profit-making activities are considered. The per capita spend was also multiplied by the number of residents to give a figure for total expenditure.

Bibliography

Argentati, C. D. (1997) 'Expanding horizons for GIS services in academic libraries', *The Journal of Academic Librarianship*, **23**(6), pp. 463–468.

Bodenhamer, D. J., Corrigan, J. and Harris, T. M. (Eds) (2010) *The Spatial Humanities: GIS and the Future of Humanities Scholarship.* Bloomington: Indiana University Press.

Booth, C. (1889) 'Descriptive map of London poverty', London, 1889. 27.120. Museum of London.

Brand, S. (1989) *The Media Lab: Inventing the Future at M.I.T.* New York: Penguin Books Ltd.

British Library (2010) *2020 Vision.* British Library. Retrieved from: www.bl.uk/aboutus/stratpolprog/2020vision/2020A3.pdf.

Carter, Patrick Robert (2009) 'Letter from Lord Carter to champion and task force members re: digital inclusion'. Retrieved from: www.berr.gov.uk/files/file51885.pdf.

Castells, M. (2002) *The Internet Galaxy: Reflections on the Internet, Business, and Society.* Oxford: Oxford University Press.

CIPFA Business Limited (2014) 'CIPFA library survey shows continuing decline in buildings, books and borrowers as cuts continue to bite', *Chartered Institute of Finance and Accountancy.* Retrieved from: www.cipfa.org/about-cipfa/press-office/archived-press-releases/2014-press-releases/cipfa-library-survey.

Curry, M. R. (1998) *Digital Places: Living with Geographic Information Technologies.* London and New York: Routledge.

Darnton, R. (2009) 'Google & the future of books', *The New York Review of Books,* 12 February 2009. Retrieved from: www.nybooks.com/articles/archives/2009/feb/12/google-the-future-of-books/.

Department for Communities and Local Government (2011) 'Statistics: English indices of deprivation 2010', Inside Government. Retrieved from: www.gov.uk/government/publications/english-indices-of-deprivation-2010.

Department for Culture, Media and Sport (2015) 'Taking part 2014/15, quarter 4: report'. London: Department of Culture, Media and Sport. Retrieved from: www.gov.uk/government/uploads/system/uploads/attachment_data/file/438442/Taking_Part_2014_15_Quarter_4_Report.pdf.

Dixon, J. B. (2006) 'GIS and the academic library', *Journal of Map & Geography Libraries: Advances in Geospatial Information, Collections & Archives,* **2**(2), pp. 5–20.

Dorling, D. (2007) 'The north-south divide – where is the line?', *Social and Spatial Inequalities: How Where We Live Matters.* Retrieved from: http://sasi.group.shef.ac.uk/maps/nsdivide/index.html.

Eccles, K., Thelwall, M. and Meyer, E. T. (2012) 'Measuring the Web impact of digitised scholarly resources', *Journal of Documentation,* **68**(4).

Grafton, A. (2009) 'Apocalypse in the stacks? The research library in the age of Google', *Daedalus,* **138**(1), pp. 87–98.

Guedo, J.-C. (1998) 'The virtual library: an oxymoron'. Retrieved from: www.mlanet.org/publications/old/leiter98.html.

Hargittai, E. (2008) 'The digital reproduction of inequality', in Grusky, D. (Ed.) *Social Stratification.* Boulder, CO: Westview Press.

Harris, R., Sleight, P. and Webber, R. (2005) *Geodemographics, GIS and Neighbourhood Targeting.* Chichester: John Wiley & Sons (Mastering GIS: Technology, Applications and Management).

Liew, C. L. (2012) 'Towards socially inclusive digital libraries', in *Digital Libraries and Information Access: Research Perspectives.* London: Facet.

Niggemann, E., De Decker, J. and Levy, M. (2011) *The new Renaissance: report of the 'Comité des Sages' reflection group on bringing Europe's cultural heritage online.* Brussels. Retrieved from: www.eurosfaire.prd.fr/7pc/doc/1302102400_kk7911109enc_002.pdf.

Poole, N. (2010) 'The cost of digitising Europe's cultural heritage: a report for the Comité des Sages of the European Commission'. The Collections Trust. Retrieved from: http://nickpoole.org.uk/wp-content/uploads/2011/12/digiti_report.p.

Price, G. (2013) 'Now available: Library Investment Index summarizes relative size of ARL university libraries for 2011–2012', 29 August 2013. Retrieved from: www.info-docket.com/2013/08/29/now-available-library-investment-index-summarizes-relative-size-of-arl-university-libraries-for-2011-12/.

Priego, E. (2012) 'Globalisation of digital humanities: an uneven promise', blog post, *University of Venus: GenX Women in Higher Ed, Writing from Across the Globe.* Retrieved from: www.insidehighered.com/blogs/globalisation-digital-humanities-uneven-promise.

Risam, R. (2015) 'Across two (imperial) cultures', in *HASTAC 2015*, Michigan. Retrieved from: http://roopikarisam.com/uncategorized/across-two-imperial-cultures-2/.

Sabbagh, D. (2010) 'James Murdoch v the British Library', *Guardian*, 7 June 2010. Retrieved from: www.guardian.co.uk/media/2010/jun/07/james-murdoch-british-library?INTCMP=ILCNETTXT3487.

Simon, M. (2012) 'Alexandria 2.0: one millionaire's quest to build the biggest library on Earth', *Wired*, 20 August 2012. Retrieved from: www.wired.com/threatlevel/2012/08/brewster-kahle/all/.

Suber, P. (2012) *Open Access*. Cambridge Mass.: MIT Press.

Tanner, S. (2013) 'The value of Welsh Newspapers Online', *When the data hits the fan! The blog of Simon Tanner*, 28 March 2013. Retrieved from: http://simon-tanner.blogspot.co.uk/2013/03/the-value-of-welsh-newspapers-online.html.

Terras, M. (2011) 'The rise of digitization: an overview', in *Digitization Perspectives*. Oxford: Chandos Publishing (Educational futures: rethinking theory and practice, 46).

Toobin, J. (2007) 'Google's moon shot: the quest for the universal library', *The New Yorker*, 5 February 2007. Retrieved from: www.newyorker.com/reporting/2007/02/05/070205fa_fact_toobin?currentPage=all.

US News (2012a) 'National liberal arts college rankings, education: colleges'. Retrieved from: http://colleges.usnews.rankingsandreviews.com/best-colleges/rankings/national-liberal-arts-colleges.

US News (2012b) 'National university rankings, education: colleges'. Retrieved from: http://colleges.usnews.rankingsandreviews.com/best-colleges/rankings/national-universities.

7 Conclusion

Where we're going, we'll still need Ranganathan

Introduction

The much-maligned term "impact" is becoming more pervasive in the public sector, informing many of the activities that organisations now undertake:

> In times of crisis and financial uncertainty, such a measure is useful for demonstrating the transformative and essential work that is being undertaken. Such a measure also provides an opportunity to examine the collective benefits and value of digital resources at a national level, leveraging the wealth of digitized content to demonstrate the impact and benefits of this transformative digitization work and providing arguments for the contribution made to the UK's knowledge economy by the academics, teachers and users who create and exploit them.
>
> (Tanner and Deegan, 2012)

It is essential, given the pressure on funding across the cultural heritage sector, that libraries are able to express their value in terms that can be understood by funders. There remains, though, a sector-wide problem in developing methodological frameworks for studying the impact of digital resources. A recent OCLC Research report (2015) indicated that a lack of established metrics for impact limits the opportunity to collect, analyse and compare statistics across the library and archival sectors. Some researchers have tried to address this problem, bemoaning the lack of deeper analysis of digital resources based upon evidence from a number of sources (Tanner, 2012). Despite their efforts, our understanding of large-scale digitisation as a technological phenomenon still lags some way behind its widespread adoption. There is no clear conceptual framework for how contemporary researchers will use burgeoning digital collections or for how their role will look in widening participation. Our considera-tion of impact has also, to date, been largely unsuccessful in identifying what issues face non-users of our resources. In my own work, it was existing users of digitised newspapers that drew attention to the huge inequalities that existed in opportunities to access digitised technologies. User studies can call on an increasing range of methods with which to interrogate the uses and impacts of digital technologies on existing communities, but questions remain over how best to reach non-users. I hope to achieve a balanced consideration of both sides and to leverage insights into how and why users have adopted large-scale digitisation in order to better understand the existing audience. By understanding the audience for digitised collections, we can better develop a sense of where the major successes lie and what challenges remain ahead of us. I will therefore conclude by examining the major themes of this book through a deep consideration of the interplay between digital technologies, libraries as institutions, and users of digital resources. I also hope to address the barriers to non-users in the methodologically innovative demographic analysis of access to digitised collections of Chapter 6.

This final chapter will situate the book's central themes in the gap between theoretical and empirical research into large-scale digitisation. It will summarise the major findings as they relate to user behaviour, institutional change and the wider social impact of digitised collections. It will also provide a series of recommendations for implementing the changes to digitised collections that have been suggested. In addition, it will address ways to build a deeper understanding of the real-world impact of mass digitisation. Tanner's (2012) definition of impact, as the measurable outcomes which demonstrate a change in the life or life opportunities of the affected community, provides a useful aspirational definition in its sentiment. However, I have argued that there is also a need to go beyond our intended communities to assess the extent of impact for the diffuse user base of the digital age. Memory institutions do not exist in a vacuum where their collections are relevant only to their existing audiences. There is a risk that, by focusing on the successes of large-scale digitisation for those it was intended to benefit, we ignore the wider context in which libraries operate. We need to consider more deeply how efforts to serve a specific model of large-scale digitisation impact on and interact with wider social issues, including the digital divide, access to cultural heritage and the supposed democratisation of information. I therefore begin here by asking a specific narrow question, which this conclusion will expand upon: what has changed as a result of the creation of large-scale digitised newspaper collections? There have been examples of change for users, certainly, and the ability to access historical sources at scale beyond the physical confines of the library building is perhaps the most revolutionary. Online access frees researchers from the need to travel to view archival materials, once digitised, and has the potential to widen access and participation considerably. Users can interrogate larger quantities of material than ever before, more efficiently, and through methods which were impossible before digitisation. Yet I have also argued that the promise of large-scale digitisation has not been fully realised. The disruptive influence of digital technologies, so often referred to in technocentric terms, is really influenced by a variety of contextual factors which ensure that change is negotiated rather than assured. These contextual factors include the limiting impact of stringent copyright conditions and widespread paywalling of content for users. Indeed, the challenges of funding and licensing materials for large-scale digitisation ensure barriers to access for many users, which cannot be addressed merely by referring to the theoretical abilities of a technology.

By comparing online use of digitised newspapers to information behaviour in material archives, we can see that the overall pattern of usage has not, for the majority of users, shifted dramatically. The foundational tasks of research, or scholarly primitives (Unsworth, 2000), have remained constant. Archival research has long taken place within institutions that contain more information than can be processed by humans, and thus information discovery in physical archives already relied on filtering and retrieval devices. Filtering is one aspect of user behaviour that can be recreated online, allowing users to efficiently search millions of pages of historical artefacts free from geographical and time constraints. In allowing the geographic dispersal of library resources, digitised newspapers supplement the research process rather than disrupt it. Rather than wholesale changes in user behaviour, we have seen changes which focus on benefits in location, working conditions and availability of material. In comparison to the technocentric narrative of disruption that is tied so closely to digital media, these impacts are somewhat more modest. I have argued that it is precisely the contextual factors that the hyperbolic technological discourse has ignored that ensures that this is the case. We have not, for instance, adequately addressed the fundamental impact of interface design upon user experience. It is difficult for users to fundamentally change their working practices, when the majority of tools created by the library sector provide little in the way of advanced functions. Users are compelled to begin every research question faced by a blank search box on their screen. As Bolter and Grusin (2000) theorise for other technologies, digitised newspapers have not yet asserted their own identity: instead they provide skeuomorphic renditions of source materials and rely upon web norms in the design of user interactions. The result is an inadequate translation of material artefacts that struggles with codifying two conflicting modes of understanding through a single interface. This is caused in no small part by the need to support novel uses more thoroughly, the need to develop suitable interfaces for utilising digitised materials in novel ways and the lack of interoperability between digitised resources. In time, if we begin to treat large-scale digitised materials as a new intellectual medium, we can expect the change to be more extensive and more widespread. At this moment, though, there is a sense that we are only at the start of a lengthy learning process that libraries must go through to maximise impact for users. This is particularly evident when we consider access to large-scale digitised collections. While users have certainly benefited from widened access, this benefit is felt selectively and largely in line with existing social inequalities.

Access to digitised library collections

In Chapter 6, I presented a case study which queried the extent of the perceived democratisation of access to library resources via the internet. I presented a method for mapping access to digitised newspapers at a demographic level, by understanding access to paywalled resources to be fundamentally linked to the individual's institutional affiliation rather than their location at the moment of access. The standard web analytics measurement is based on the individual's IP address at the moment of access, but this becomes less relevant as a demographic indicator when we consider the networked infrastructure through which they connect. Castells notes the inadequacy of metrics for access:

> The fundamental digital divide is not measured by the number of connections to the Internet, but by the consequences of both connection and lack of connection. Because the Internet, as shown in this book, is not just a technology. It is the technological tool and organizational form that distributes information power, knowledge generation, and networking capacity in all reams of activity.
>
> (Castells, 2002)

The chapter presented subscription data for British Library Nineteenth Century Newspapers and the Times Digital Archive, linked to demographic data for the HE sector and English public library authorities. It showed that subscription-based digitised collections contribute to reinforcing existing divides between information-rich and information-poor communities. This is not to say that large-scale digitisation has not improved access overall but that the improvements have been felt most strongly by those who already benefited most from other opportunities to access similar resources. The digital divide is multifaceted: it is a global, democratic but also social divide between different groups in society. Existing research into this "second-level" (Hassani, 2006) digital divide suggests that those from higher economic backgrounds generally benefit most from technological developments. Similarly, I have argued that paywalled digitised collections risk creating a "digitised divide" between those with access and those without, based on demographic lines which reflect and reinforce existing inequalities.

Universities are particularly well-served by digitised resources, thanks to the admirable efforts of bodies such as JISC and the fact that many collections are created with the academic community in mind. But it is evident that there is a divide in access between HE institutions that correlates strongly with the status of a university. Similarly, English public library authorities were far more likely to provide access if they were based in less deprived regions or served a relatively large population. These findings support Hargittai's (2008) claim that social position plays a vital role in defining an individual's use of digital media. Unequal access to resources has long been an issue for researchers, but the rhetoric of universal access has ignored how inequality can be replicated online as a facet of wider structural inequalities. As digitised content proliferates, the expectation that scholars will use it also increases, and the idea of democratised access can become a damaging myth for those left behind. Technological inequality never entirely disappears, but instead is shifted towards a new domain. As I have argued, libraries in England serve a diverse audience drawn from all socio-economic levels. There is an enthusiasm among the public for using digitised collections in their own research and a clear case to be made that these collections can enrich the nation's cultural life. It is therefore disappointing to see that the public are less well-served in access to large-scale digitised collections than the academic sector and that the divide between communities of access is defined so strongly by the socio-economic status.

It is concerning that the inequalities brought to light so closely mirror existing divides: the problem is structural and encompasses the political and cultural spheres. Underfunded public library services cannot afford to provide access to a wide range of digital resources, and the lack of countrywide digital library infrastructures denies us a consistent offering at national level. Localism, in provision of digital services, has led to a huge gulf in regional spending power for library services, leaving smaller areas and their residents behind. Earlier I pointed to the visionary approach of the DPLA for inspiration: it suggests the possibility of a unified national digital library which would allow the public to access digitised collections online for free. In the UK, a similarly thorough and consistent offering at national level would go a long way to addressing my concerns over access. Centralised provision of a digital library service would have the combined effect of standardising digital opportunity, while allowing public libraries to focus their efforts on high quality locally tailored services and support through digital skills training. While the removal of facets of public library services could prove unpopular due to the risk of further undermining their position, the digital offering of public libraries in the United Kingdom is already fragmented. At national level, there are major inequalities in outcomes which are dependent on an individual's location, while the global impact of the UK's flagship LSDC is limited by placing them behind paywalls. The erosion of services is already occurring – this is therefore not a call to cut overall budgets but instead to explore the development of a world class, centrally managed digital library which would benefit all UK residents.

The definition of what constitutes access is, in itself, problematic. Meyer, for instance, has referred to Google Books enabling access to digitised books

(2011). But Google's definition of access largely relates to the ability to undertake searches within a massive database and is therefore too limited to represent a model of access that supports users to have meaningful interactions with digitised collections. Search represents the first step in a successful access model, rather than a desirable end in itself. Mere discoverability makes digital resources the equivalent of a well-stocked shop window: online resources mimic the department store, where users are free to browse the goods, to spray the fragrance samplers or to taste a small lump of cheese. At some point though, they must pay to take their interaction with the product beyond the superficial. The idea of "search as access" can be seen in the work of some memory institutions, and it limits the potential for meaningful impact for digitised collections. By contrast, we can look to the NLA for a global success in newspaper digitisation. As Holley notes, Trove's newspaper collection has been successful for a number of reasons:

> The usability and functionality of the service; being able to migrate users successfully from the previous eight separate services to Trove; and raising awareness of the existence and usefulness of Trove in the community.
>
> (2010)

The NLA has significantly improved access to its newspaper collections by rationalising disparate services into a single point of access for Australian digitised collections, thus helping users to discover vast amounts of material with minimal inconvenience. Just as importantly, the NLA tries to provide universal access and the freedom for users to interact with materials. By facilitating technologically innovative activities, its actions refer to the service-driven librarianship championed by Ranganathan, including his desire to provide access to all and provide for different types of information behaviour. Trove's success makes it clear that it is possible to create large-scale digitised collections that successfully build a thriving and engaged community. It is also clear that the wider context of digitisation is largely responsible for defining the impact of digital collections, which themselves exist as a function of the balance between available funding and the library's ability to support its own aims and objectives through building resources. Trove therefore emphasises the unique contribution that libraries can make:

> Libraries are different to Google for these reasons: they commit to providing long-term preservation, curation and access to their content; they have no commercial motives in the provision of information (deemed by various library acts); they aim for universal access to everyone in society; and they are "free for all".
>
> (Holley, 2010)

Holley's description of the uniqueness of libraries outlines the contribution that they *can* make to information provision in the digital age. But there are steps that they can take to come closer to the noble aims that permeate the literature, as well as library strategic plans. The first of these is to recognise the role that their resources play in defining usage.

In Chapter 1, I explored hyperbolic claims that digitisation could have profoundly negative effects on human behaviour. Digital remediations of physical texts are presented by critics as inadequate reproductions rather than unique artefacts (Birkets, 1994; Carr, 2005; Wolf, 2008; Lanier, 2011). Their representation of digital media is based on idealising deep reading as the most intellectually valid way to engage with textual materials, a flawed premise which ignores the multifaceted information behaviour of researchers. Yet I have argued that there is some truth to the theory that digital media change our understanding of the text in ways which will have an impact on user behaviour. This shift is often represented by the idea of loss, where digital scholarship is thought of in terms of a conceptual transitioning from scholars as "readers" to "users" (Brake, 2012). However, digitisation only manifests itself as an overall loss to users if we assume that digital media hold no meaningful benefits in comparison to original artefacts, which is certainly not the case. The almost universally positive reaction of researchers to large-scale digitisation of newspapers underlines this point: the improvements in access, breadth of material, time and financial savings, and increased opportunities for innovative research are some of the many aspects of digitisation that downplay the loss of material context which has vexed so many critics. In cases where the material artefact is lost or destroyed, such as Baker's (2001) infamous double fold complaint, Conway's (2013) argument that digitised texts are new artefacts imbued with their own unique characteristics offers a far more positive lens for assessing their impact, because it recognises the importance of the medium in defining meaning for the user. He emphasises that digitised content is part of a hybrid information ecosystem, where users continue to find value in both material and digital resources and, indeed, users still view libraries as primarily physical spaces.

This is not to say that translating newspapers to digital form has no effect. Mussell (2012) has argued for the transformative effects of decoupling the content of newspapers from the physical form and for the increased profile of the nineteenth century press in scholarly research and teaching. If we consider newspapers at a material level, it is clear that the locus of research has been affected by large-scale digitisation. The web interface has become increasingly central to the user experience, and thus the usage of digitised collections more closely resembles the web-centric "user" of technology than the "reader" of texts. I reject the idea that this shift demonstrates a diminished intellectual engagement with the material; instead, this engagement takes place at a layer of abstraction from the original artefact. It is this abstraction that the critics of digitisation refer to in mourning the transition from physical to digital media. In assuming that the impact is disruptive, and inevitably negative, they fail to account for the widespread desire among users for digitised content. Behavioural norms in physical archives explain the transition more readily than accounts which centre on disruptive models of technological adoption. Reading is not always a priority for users of digitised collections, certainly. Many describe their behaviour with words such as "searching", "cutting and pasting" or "navigating" multiple websites in the same session. The terminology may be unique to the digital, but the behaviour is not. Users of the physical archive have similarly faced up to the need to adopt browsing and filtering techniques to find what they need among potentially tens of millions of pages of archival materials. I have argued that there are corollaries for the behaviour of users of large-scale digitised collections in the sociology of the city. The internet shares a particular type of freedom with cities, in enabling a large variety of available interactions, but this comes at the cost of information overload. It is through this lens that we must view usage of digitised collections: they are fundamentally vehicles for assisting users in coping with information overload. Users of LSDC are therefore deeply engaged information agnostics – people who use a wide variety of websites with little demonstrable loyalty but with deep levels of engagement that allow them to interrogate web interfaces in ways which meet their information needs. But unlike technocentric theories of disruption, which treat people as passive recipients of new technological forms (Giddens, 2009), the decision of online users is a conscious reaction to the need to process large quantities of information. Simmel has referred to cities as providing a state of constant novelty, arguing that this demands an intellectual response on the part of inhabitants:

> It creates in the sensory foundations of mental life, and in the degree of awareness necessitated by our organization as creatures dependent on differences, a deep contrast with the slower, more habitual, more smoothly flowing rhythm of the sensory mental phase of small town and rural existence. Thereby the essentially intellectualistic character of the mental life of the metropolis becomes intelligible as over against that of the small town which rests more on feelings and emotional relationships.
>
> (2002)

The intellectual life of LSDC similarly necessitates a conscious process of adoption on the part of users. User behaviour is a negotiated relationship between the individual user, the interface, the material and the social framework within which it is provided. The mass audience is engaged with the interface, as I argued in Chapter 5, but the individual is seeking ways to navigate this relationship in order to extract the information necessary for their particular research question.

Ranganathan's (1931) definition of the reader is relevant here: he uses the term to refer to a user of a library's collections, rather than an individual in the specific act of reading. His combination of the terms "user" and "reader" is useful because it switches the definition of the reader to mean an individual with the need for library services and because it situates the library as serving the needs of this nominal reader. LIS theorists throughout the twenty-first century have posited service as a key value of librarianship, thus implicitly contextualising library developments from the perspective of the user. In understanding that a key role for libraries is to facilitate users' intellectual freedom and development (Gorman, 2000), we can see that a technocentric focus on large-scale digitisation effectively ignores its key beneficiaries. Ranganathan argues that the role of libraries is to serve readers regardless of the reason for their information needs or the ways in which they choose to engage with library collections. He neatly cuts through the value-laden debate around online user behaviour to recognise that the library's role is not to judge the reader's choices but to understand them in order to provide a better service. This reinforces the idea of the library as a service and as a flexible provider of information, which aims to meet the needs of the user rather than limit and define how its collections should be used. By this logic, the behaviour I have drawn attention to in this book is positive because it demonstrates a potential future for digitised materials as a medium, with an intellectual life that is distinct from those which have come before. Large-scale digitised collections can provide relevant information regardless of original format, allow new interactions for researchers and demonstrate that digital remediations have the potential to be more than surrogates. Reader behaviour must inevitably change to fit the shifting demands of different media formats, but it should be viewed as part of a wider process of diffusion in which the individual user is an active participant in defining the social life of new technologies. If we are to recognise the continued relevance of Ranganathan's five laws of library science to the contemporary information professions, then we should celebrate the opportunities that large-scale digitisation offers and support both innovative and traditional research behaviours.

Recommendations

With the above in mind, this section will provide a series of general recommendations for the planning and development of large-scale digitised collections and a list of features that would allow a digitised collection to provide the service-based model of digital librarianship that I have advocated. These are designed to support the creation of flexible collections which are well-placed to cope with future changes and which can facilitate varied uses, including emergent research practices. The focus is therefore upon openness, flexible licensing and continued assessment of impact and user requirements. First, as others have previously noted (Meyer *et al.*, 2009; Tanner, 2012), it is essential that impact analysis and user analysis become integral parts of any digital project. Data gathering for impact analysis is often done after the event, which can leave a gap between the launch of a collection and the commencement of data collection. Furthermore, Stroeker and Vogels (2012) report that just a third of digital collections collect usage statistics, and anecdotally I have found obtaining metrics for my own work extremely challenging. Funders should therefore make user analysis a key criterion when funding digital projects and ensure that funding is provided to continue these activities through the resource lifecycle. This work should be done in conjunction with endeavours to define the expected audience and purpose of digitised collections before they are created, to assist in defining indicators of success and to provide the data sources necessary to evaluate them. This first point addresses the need to more closely consider existing user communities, but steps should also be taken to widen participation beyond the intended audience. Where possible, any digital collection which receives public funding should aspire to the highest level of openness. This should begin with open licensing for public domain materials, in line with the recommendations of the European Commission, which has indicated a number of challenges in this respect:

> Nine member states … reported obstacles in ensuring that public domain material remains in the public domain after digitisation, mainly in connection with photos and photographers' rights. The complex issue of a new layer of rights triggered by the digitisation itself in some cases is mentioned as a potential source of legal uncertainty.
>
> (European Commission, 2014)

There is a need for regulatory clarity in this regard, but it has already been pre-empted by the actions of organisations such as the NLW, which has taken steps to ensure that its materials remain in the public domain after digitisation. This suggests that the problem is partly regulatory and partly a matter of will on the part of organisations. In conjunction with this point, access should not be tied to a physical location where possible. Enforcing physical limitations on public domain material is a retrograde step that favours commercial rights holders; at a minimum, online access to digitised resources should be free to all cardholders of a library involved in digitisation. Although it would not meet the highest standards of openness, it would address the reality of commercial partnerships. Commercial partners could still monetise the resource beyond these registered library members and thus maintain a more equal balance between user needs and the rights of providers to get a return on their investment.

The inadequacy of interfaces for LSDC should also be addressed. It is important to build flexibility into front-end functionality and facilitate multiple user behaviours including close reading, distant reading and serendipitous discovery. We can achieve this by attempting to create "generous interfaces" (Whitelaw, 2015) which support users with several routes into the data. Serendipity is one of the big challenges for digitised collections over the coming years. Duff and Johnson argue convincingly that what we consider to be serendipitous is actually a deliberate strategy:

> Although historians often speak about the role of serendipity in their discovery of relevant materials, there is strong evidence to suggest that this process is influenced less by serendipity and more by the deliberate tactics of the expert researcher. In other words – what appears to be accidental discovery is accidentally found on purpose.
>
> (2002)

But the way in which information is presented supports this kind of discovery: for a reader to discover similar books in the same physical area of a library, librarians have to purchase, classify, categorise, process and place stock correctly. Similarly, online users are dependent on the interface for serendipitous discovery. Their ability to leverage it for serendipitous discovery relies on it providing support for this in the first place. Some projects have already taken steps to address serendipitous discovery online. One model for serendipitous discovery has been created by the Serendipomatic tool (http://serendipomatic.org/) which applies an algorithm to any supplied segment of text to return relevant results from the DPLA. It harnesses algorithms to recreate the suggestive links that can be made by experienced researchers in the physical archive. I expect to see an increasing focus on link creation in coming years, fuelled by the linked open data movement and providing imaginative ways for users to uncover relationships between disparate datasets.

This book has outlined a framework for understanding how large-scale digitised collections can be useful in meeting the needs of users. We can define the parameters for success partly on how libraries describe their own aims and objectives. Holley (2010) argues for the differences between libraries and the web-based information giants such as Google, with libraries largely defined as altruistic organisations which aim to expand access and reach new communities with their collections. This is backed up by the public mission statements of many major research libraries, which can be summed up as aiming to increase access to collections and to support a wide range of research tasks. It is this mission-driven aspect of library service that I have been working to establish for digitised collections, and the following list represents the idea of success in terms of the features that would allow this mission to be achieved. A successful large-scale digitised newspaper collection is one that recognises the source material, while simultaneously recognising that digital remediation provides us with an intellectually divergent resource that is suited to new models of engagement. It serves a variety of purposes: it allows an international audience of researchers, academic and non-academic, to access digitised materials from around the world, for free; it provides access to full text, metadata and scanned images under licences which encourage reuse; it provides an interface which supports multiple approaches to the material; and it builds user-focused design into its planning and implementation. If the library sector achieves these aims, then large-scale digitisation will have an even more expansive impact than I have argued for in this book, facilitating further opportunities for academia, society and culture. This successful digitised collection is likely to share some of the following characteristics:

- It provides high quality scans with standards-compliant metadata to support interoperability with other digital resources. Image and metadata licences will be open and will allow for reuse.
- It offers a high quality search interface, after Whitelaw's (2015) model for generous interfaces, and thereby supports multiple approaches to the material.
- It either provides features to support distant reading or offers an open API and access to full text files to allow users to develop their own digital research tools.
- It includes a high quality content viewing tool, which allows users to move between article- and page-level with minimal effort.
- It ensures high levels of discoverability via search engines, library websites and social media. If it must be paywalled, the resource will provide clear instructions on how to log in and will adopt the WAYF or Shibboleth authentication models, widely used to provide access to academic journals.
- It includes accession dates for content and allows users to filter content based on its accession date.
- It utilises stable, unique identifiers for all content, and it provides clear instructions for how to cite items in the collection.
- It adopts a user-focused design model which relies on impact assessment and dialogue with its users to ensure that an iterative process of improvement is used to maintain the relevance of the resource over time.

As a sector, we are currently some way from achieving these aims. Users of large-scale digitised collections find difficulties in using search functionality to return accurate results due to poor quality metadata and OCR scanning. They also face the enforcement of a particular type of search and browsing behaviour, created by inflexible interfaces, which force all users into a narrow range of interactions. Inconsistent citation practices are caused by unstable URLs, a lack of guidance on citing scholarly digital resources (Breeding, 2009) and an inability to link deeply to individual items in collections online. These are all surmountable obstacles, but each needs to be addressed to ensure that we can talk about the impact of large-scale digitisation in much broader terms than we can currently. At the heart of this need is the question of access, which I believe is the largest challenge that libraries will face in the digital age.

The stakes for digitised collections

This book is, by my own admission, only nominally about digitised newspapers. They form the focal point of a wider consideration of why there is such a disconnect between the hyperbole surrounding digital media and the way in which existing frameworks of information dissemination and regulation play a huge role in limiting their true impact. The digital age, if we live in such an era, is characterised by the tension between the possibilities for universal access to online resources on the one hand and the desire of corporations to control access on the other. Aguilar-Millan *et al.* published an ambitious flight of fancy which explored the "post-scarcity world" of 2050 in light of technical advancements which they argue will decrease costs to providers until almost everything becomes free to the end user. On large-scale digitisation, they have the following to say:

> The ability to digitize, or "convert atoms to bits", is increasingly removing scarcity from the business equation. Traditional scarcity theory posits that, when one item is used, there is one less item available (thus increasing scarcity); in the digital world, however, when one item is used (copied, connected to another) there is at least one more item (thus decreasing scarcity). The logic is completely reversed but explains exactly how digitization is driving an age of free goods and removing scarcity.
>
> (2010)

In this post-scarcity world, the concept of charging consumers to access infinitely reproducible sequences of code no longer applies. Yet, in reality, the tension between free information and commercial interest has merely been transposed to the digital domain. The stakes for libraries are huge: in an era where they compete with unfeasibly rich multinational companies such as Google for the attention of users, libraries can provide value by allowing free access to their collections and by supporting users in accessing them. Widening access is at the heart of any future for library services online. We are only 35 years from the post-scarcity world imagined by Aguilar-Millan *et al.*, yet the long-term prospects for such a world seem increasingly unlikely for one simple reason – closed platforms. In summary, I would like to propose three grand challenges for libraries in the digital age: by addressing these challenges, libraries can ensure that their undoubted value is clearly expressed in terms of the primary difference between the library sector and commercial providers of information.

Libraries, as they are conceived, are forces for public good, and vehicles for ensuring wide access to the treasures of the public domain. To achieve the maximum possible impact for the digitised collections which they are creating to support this service-driven aim, libraries need to address the challenges of providing open access collections, creating open interfaces and engaging in open dialogue with other stakeholders.

Open access

The value of freely available – and open – aggregated data is widely recognised by a variety of regulatory bodies and cultural organisations. The UK Research Excellence Framework has mandated that publicly funded scholarly outputs should be made freely available through open access in institutional repositories, and new models for scholarly publishing are emerging. The Open Library of the Humanities (https://openlibhums. org), which officially launched in 2015, is one such model. It provides a platform for publishing open access scholarship with no author-facing article processing charges, leveraging a library subscription model to finance a high quality web platform which plays host to a number of journals. This model holds promise for academic publication, but the large-scale digitisation of UK collections has taken a different route, with libraries partnering with commercial organisations to provide materials at the scale demanded by users. While steps have been taken by some organisations to provide open access digitised materials, the constrained finances of the heritage sector mean that this is not always possible. In the case of the BL, the stark choice has been between paywalled digitised collections and no digitised collections. The need to rely on commercial investment and the resultant need for a return on investment make it inevitable that some LSDC will not be made freely available online. In these cases, there is a need to find the balance between ensuring the social and scholarly value of digitised resources and allowing commercial companies to make a positive contribution which is rewarded by allowing sustainable business models to emerge. This pragmatic position is driven by necessity, but it demands that we address the current imbalance in access.

We have seen that closed resources are less valuable to scholars, with the aggregated newspaper collection of BNCN garnering fewer links than a solitary open access digitised newspaper (Eccles, Thelwall and Meyer, 2012). We have also seen that, despite widespread access to British Library Nineteenth Century Newspapers, the picture for users of UK public libraries is more complex. Overly restrictive digitised collections are already transferring existing inequalities into a new domain, with access to large-scale digitised collections being more likely for those who are already members of traditionally information-rich demographic groups. Additionally, the need to defend intellectual property for commercial digitisation limits the potential for users to reuse and remix materials and to make links between collections and other materials. It is worth remembering that impact can be both negative and positive, and paywalled collections fulfil a complex role in simultaneously expanding access to cultural heritage and constraining its wider impact in fundamental ways.

Hughes notes that the value of digitised materials changes depending on the audience:

> A digital text may be valuable to a scholar because it enables the use of text mining tools to undertake historic research, or it may be valuable to family historians as it mentions an ancestor, or to scholars of material culture through its description of objects. It may gain value if linked to other digital content through "virtual reunification", where collections held in disparate archives around the world can be combined in digital facsimiles. Value is subjective, changes over time and has different meanings that are contingent on external factors.
>
> (Hughes, 2012)

She points out that, for libraries, one value of large-scale digitisation is enabling access to a global audience via the internet. The changing role of libraries towards creating new media forms through digitisation means that the sector now has an active role in defining the extent of value to the communities which we intend to reach. For this global audience, large-scale digitised collections can be made more valuable and can support a wider variety of behaviours, if we move towards viewing them as a strategic way of supporting new user communities and new research. While commercial digitisation is a necessary and positive influence on the growing digital library organism, the open approach to digitisation advocated by the NLW and the DPLA suggests a model for supporting the emergence of an intellectual identity for digital cultural heritage – an identity distinct from the prevailing print paradigm. Green argues that public libraries exist as a public good:

> Public libraries were established and still flourish as a means of ensuring that all members of society, irrespective of their circumstances, could have access to all published knowledge. Traditionally their method of achieving this goal was to offer a place where any citizen could read and usually borrow any printed publication. The 21st century equivalent is surely to offer citizens free access, where possible online, to publications in digital form. It follows that, in the case of those publications already in print, libraries – in particular, I would suggest, national libraries, that have a duty to preserve and give access to their countries' published output – should do their best to arrange for their online public accessibility.
>
> (2009)

The impact of large-scale digitisation is still in the process of being defined and understood but our sector can push back against some of the more insidious by-products of commercial digitisation by re-appraising resource creation with this understanding. This means adopting the most flexible approach allowed by funding to ensure that potential reuse scenarios are not excluded by restrictive licensing. Digital library collections provide the opportunity for reaching new audiences and for aligning the sector with the idea of service to our user communities. Open access collections will allow libraries to reach new audiences, on their own terms, and will help them to respond to new developments in scholarly practice and user behaviour.

Open interfaces

Open access collections can address the need to support widening participation, but there is a second aspect to ensuring the impact of large-scale digitisation. The interface of the large-scale digitised collection is responsible for shaping the network-centric model of user behaviour that has been observed. The web, as currently conceived, privileges search over other forms of interaction; indeed, the need to cope with the information glut faced by the modern researcher lends itself to filtering behaviour. Because researchers are so reliant upon these filters, there is a continued need for search facilities in digitised collections. But the intellectual space within which the search paradigm exists is based on the idea of information as an abstract entity, with human characteristics and its own identity. It assumes that digital information must be experienced, at least initially, as word-level information to be sifted, sorted and returned to the user in order of relevance. Digital technologies theoretically flatten the information structure of digitised media, driven by the need to parse any interaction through some form of computing technology. This sits in opposition to the manner in which the interface of the digital collection has come to signify a variety of concurrent research tasks:

> In digital information spaces, there will continue to be repositories of information, but the emphasis shifts to the flows between them and between them and their users. These repositories may contain metadata – catalogues and other data which assist in the discovery, use and exploitation of resources – or resources themselves. In this environment, the activities of discovery, locate, request, and deliver, currently carried out in multiple incompatible circuits need to be brought into a common framework of communicating applications.
>
> (Dempsey, 1999)

The implications of Dempsey's observation should be considered in conjunction with Levy's (1997) argument that the digital interface is the locus for several research activities and not merely for information seeking. Mass digitised resources such as Google Books resemble virtual bookstores rather than libraries: their purpose is not to provide access to the millions of books contained within, but to allow users to more easily purchase books via an unimaginably large sales catalogue, replete with samples. They are bookstores on an unprecedented scale and with public domain freebies to enrich their offering. The difficulty is that user expectations for digital resources are created in these virtual shopfronts. They expect the white search box and arrive at large-scale library collections with this knowledge of web norms already formed. But libraries are intellectually distinct from these offerings. Green's (2009) argument that digitisation should act as a public good represents a model of digital resource provision which must serve a variety of user requirements. A number of national libraries have committed to addressing this need by digitising their collections in an open manner. The NLW, for instance, has committed to making its digitised resources as open as possible: this includes their refusal to claim copyright over scanned images and the release of metadata under an open licence. Cohen (2010) has pointed out that digital humanities research, which relies on large-scale datasets, can work with messy data, but this quantification of abstract digitised corpora is not the only future for research. For those involved in considering the material forms of media, such as book historians, the requirements for digitised materials are very different. Digital research exists on a spectrum, from those researchers intimately engaged with material forms to those who rely on computational methods to provide new insights into historical texts. In the middle are the group I have argued constitute the majority: those who use digitised collections to quickly discover and access the information they require to answer their own specific research questions. There is no one-size-fits-all solution for designing interfaces for all of these audiences.

There is a need, then, for libraries to address access to their materials at a more fundamental level. Creating LSDC which serve the diverse needs of their user communities requires rethinking how artefacts are digitised, how they are licensed and the range of options which are available to researchers. Whitelaw has described this in terms of generous interfaces, providing a seductive view of what they would represent:

> A more generous interface would do more to represent the scale and richness of its collection. It would open the doors, tear down the drab lobby; instead of demanding a query it would offer multiple ways in, and support exploration as well as the focused enquiry where search excels. In revealing the complexity of digital collections, a generous interface would also enrich interpretation by revealing relationships and structures with a collection.

(2015)

I have argued that user behaviour in digital collections is a conscious reaction to the problem of information overload, but this behaviour is still defined by the boundaries of what the interface allows. Whitelaw outlines the aspects of generous interfaces, citing the need for rich, navigable representations of digital collections which invite exploration, support browsing and allow users to engage with materials at scale and in detail. Search is certainly an aspect of this, but there is a further need to enhance digital collections in order to ensure that research is supported rather than defined by libraries. The ability to deliver more suitable interfaces is contingent on a variety of technological, cultural and regulatory aspects of large-scale digitisation. Creating more generous interfaces for digitised heritage collections is reliant on reconsidering how digitisation is undertaken at a fundamental level: it requires new approaches to the licensing of digitised images, metadata and full text to allow for reuse, and a deeper understanding of current and future directions in research.

Open dialogue

As a graduate trainee librarian, I was told by my line manager that the library is not a place for shrinking violets. Her words bear particular importance in the digital age. The contemporary library is one where librarians must proactively assert their relevance to users. These users are source-agnostic: they can be more bothered about accessing information online than they are about the organisation which provides it. As a result, there is a disconnect between the relevance of modern libraries, which is not in question, and the public perception of this relevance, which certainly is. The value of digital collections is difficult to express to external stakeholders without falling back on financial return or metrics for usage. Hughes (2012) argues that funders often fail to appreciate the qualitative value of digital resources because of the time it takes for the scholarship they enable to become visible. The same goes for users but in a different way: they can fail to understand the value of the modern library in enabling access to digital resources, even as they use these resources. The sector is full of anecdotal accounts of professors who inform their subject librarian that they never use the library anymore because they can access their journals online. Library digital resources have been reasonably successful in integrating themselves seamlessly into the workflows of users, to the point that the source of these efforts can become invisible. The digital scholarly environment is like an iceberg: users see the result of library's efforts poking above the water, represented by the range of resources they can access, the way that their library catalogue will automatically resolve links from Google Scholar, and the myriad resources which the average scholar can access freely using their single sign-on. But under the surface of this efficient and increasingly seamless online environment are a series of unseen dependencies; infrastructural, human, financial and technological structures which enable users to use resources provided by their institutional library without even realising they are doing so. Like the proverbial iceberg, the contemporary role of libraries in supporting a rich online research environment goes largely unnoticed.

Yet libraries, as I have argued, are also dependent on dialogue with users to ensure that the resources they create are suitable for supporting a diverse range of user requirements. This approach to digitisation demands that the user is central to the decision-making process. It is evident from my discussions with scholars and the wider community that users have a great deal to offer libraries in the evaluation and development of large-scale digitised collections. Users increasingly display high levels of technical knowledge and a growing familiarity with web resources. While we should recognise that respondents to web-based impact evaluations are the most engaged, and probably most highly skilled, users, they provide an important community of expertise. Their high familiarity with digitised resources also shapes the environment in which libraries operate. Individual digitised collections, while extremely important, only ever operate as one resource in a wide digital ecosystem. Like the web in general, users inevitably spend more time on other collections. Their understanding of digitised resources is therefore shaped elsewhere, and any given resource will inevitably be judged against the best examples in the domain. This increases the importance of sharing best practice on an international basis to ensure a strong digital offering, which recognises that the library is no longer the user's first resort. Libraries have already taken steps to engage with users of digital resources in a proactive manner. The BL has created a dedicated team of digital curators, whose job it is to work with digital scholars to shape the library's collections in the coming years. A collaborative model, where libraries engage in two-way dialogue with their users (McGregor and Farquhar, 2013), or harness their expertise and enthusiasm to enrich collections via crowd-sourcing and discussion (Holley, 2010), allows libraries to react to emerging researcher needs. The three grand challenges are therefore intricately linked: an open dialogue needs maintaining with users, but in order to act upon it the sector must look to its practices to ensure that they are able to adapt effectively. Access is the theme that ties these related strands together: digital technologies present us with the opportunity to reimagine what access to digitised heritage could mean in the digital age. However, in order to achieve this, we must continually re-align our practices to ensure that they work in synergy with the scholarly, social and cultural objectives that underpin the identity of libraries.

Summary: library digitisation as a public service

The role of the library has been heavily theorised, but the most convincing accounts of the sector's continued relevance in the face of digital technologies have focused on the ways in which large-scale digitisation can support the public good (Green, 2009; Niggemann, De Decker and Levy, 2011; European Commission, 2014). The library in the digital age is information provider, curator and producer all tied into one. Its users are increasingly diverse, with high expectations of the opportunities that large-scale digitisation can bring. But library efforts to support digital humanities research often fail to take advantage of the possibilities offered by digital media and thus struggle to assist in the intellectual development of digitised cultural heritage as a resource with an identity distinct from its print forbears. McLuhan noted that "we look at the present through a rear-view mirror. We march backwards into the future" (1967). Despite the impact of digitisation on user behaviour, institutional practices and our theoretical understanding of the nature of information, it is clear that previous technological paradigms exert a long shadow over large-scale digitisation practices, in a way that give a lie to the more extreme predictions. The bibliographic code of the print form still dominates how we understand the digital, defining how digitised resources are used and limiting the intellectual life of the new digital artefacts that Conway (2013) argues are the result of digitisation.

In Chapter 4, I drew attention to Torkington's (2011) inflammatory keynote speech to the National and State Librarians of Australasia, which addresses the relevance for libraries in the digital age. His call for us to improve access to digital collections is simultaneously idealistic and pragmatic. It is idealistic in the sense that it proposes a rich future for libraries based upon the possibilities provided by opening up their collections, and pragmatic in that it recognises that the privileged position of libraries as trusted repositories is under threat from the actions of large tech corporations. The creation of digitised knowledge can be a public good but not without addressing the barriers to access that have been outlined here. While we wrestle with questions of what the future of digital resources will resemble, we should nevertheless focus upon providing materials to users in the locations, formats and licences that are most useful to them. By doing so, we can foreground the user as the key beneficiary of library activities. We can also ensure that library digital collections will have the widest possible impact, thus benefitting the public profile of the library sector and demonstrating its direct relevance in addressing the challenges posed by the internet and widespread digitisation of cultural materials.

Libraries inevitably have a role to play in reinventing digitised media. The editorial process, which Mussell (2012) argues is at the heart of the digitisation process, is part of the library's mission, but it can only be done with close regard to the needs of researchers, from both scholarly backgrounds and the wider community of genealogists, family historians and intellectually curious members of the public, who form the audience for large-scale digitised newspapers. Digitised newspapers provide an interesting case study for the wider issues discussed in this book, precisely because they encompass so many of the promises – and frustrations – of the digitised library. Our understanding of new technologies is developed in addressing the ways in which innovation interacts with social, cultural and institutional pressures to create new forms of meaning. We must enable users to contribute to the negotiation of media forms that is occurring and to harness the media-specific benefits of online digitised collections in their research. Librarians and users can successfully collaborate to make sense of the contested impact of the digital world; indeed, this provides a powerful model for progression in the digital age.

Bibliography

Aguilar-Millan, S., Feeney, A., Oberg, A. and Rudd, E. (2010) 'The post-scarcity world of 2050–2075', *The Futurist*, pp. 34–40.

Baker, N. (2001) *Double Fold: Libraries and the Assault on Paper*. New York: Random House.

Birkets, S. (1994) *The Gutenberg Elegies: The Fate of Reading in an Electronic Age*. New York: Ballentine Books.

Bolter, J. D. and Grusin, R. (2000) *Remediation: Understanding New Media*. Cambridge, Mass.: MIT Press.

Brake, L. (2012) 'Half full and half empty', *Journal of Victorian Culture*, **17**(2), pp. 222–229. doi: http://dx.doi.org/10.1080/13555502.2012.683151.

Breeding, M. (2009) 'Maximizing the impact of digital collections', *Computers in Libraries*, **29**(4), pp. 22–24.

Carr, R. (2005) *The Oxford-Google mass digitisation programme: contribution to the Opening Plenary Panel Session of the CNI Spring 2005 Task Force Meeting*. Retrieved from: www.bodley.ox.ac.uk/librarian/rpc/CNIGoogle/CNIGoogle.htm.

Castells, M. (2002) *The Internet Galaxy: Reflections on the Internet, Business, and Society*. Oxford: Oxford University Press.

Cohen, D. (2010) 'Initial thoughts on the Google Books Ngram Viewer and data-sets', *Dan Cohen's Digital Humanities Blog*, 19 December 2010. Retrieved from: www.dancohen.org/2010/12/19/initial-thoughts-on-the-google-books-ngram-viewer-and-datasets/.

Conway, P. (2013) 'Preserving imperfection: assessing the incidence of digital imaging error in HathiTrust', *Digital Technology and Culture*, **42**(1), pp. 17–30.

Dempsey, L. (1999) 'Library places and digital information spaces: reflections on emerging network services', *Alexandria*, **11**(1), pp. 51–58.

Duff, W. M. and Johnson, C. A. (2002) 'Accidentally found on purpose: information-seeking behavior of historians in archives', *The Library Quarterly*, **72**(4), pp. 472–496.

Eccles, K., Thelwall, M. and Meyer, E. T. (2012) 'Measuring the web impact of digitised scholarly resources', *Journal of Documentation*, **68**(4).

European Commission (2014) *Cultural heritage: digitisation, online accessibility and digital preservation – report on the implementation of Commission Recommendation 2011/711/EU*. European Commission. Retrieved from: http://ec.europa.eu/information_society/newsroom/image/recommendation-2011-2013_progress%20report-final-clean-shared%20with%20eac-ga%20approved-22-09-2014-final_6953.pdf.

Giddens, A. (2009) *Sociology* (6th edn). Cambridge: Polity Press.

Gorman, M. (2000) *Our Enduring Values: Librarianship in the 21st Century.* Chicago and London: American Library Association.

Green, A. (2009) 'Big digitisation: where next?', Digital Resources for the Humanities and Arts conference, Belfast. Retrieved from: www.llgc.org.uk/fileadmin/fileadmin/docs_gwefan/amdanom_ni/dogfennaeth_gorfforaethol/darlithoedd_ac_erthyglau/dog_gorff_dar_erth_bdwn_09S.pdf.

Hargittai, E. (2008) 'The digital reproduction of inequality', in Grusky, D. (Ed.) *Social Stratification.* Boulder, CO: Westview Press.

Hassani, S. N. (2006) 'Locating digital divides at home, work, and everywhere else', *Poetics*, **34**(4–5). doi:10.1016/j.poetic.2006.05.007.

Holley, R. (2010) 'Trove: innovation in access to information in Australia', *Ariadne*, 30 July 2010. Retrieved from: www.ariadne.ac.uk/issue64/holley/.

Hughes, L. M. (Ed.) (2012) *Evaluating and Measuring the Value, Use and Impact of Digital Collections.* London: Facet Publishing.

Lanier, J. (2011) *You Are Not a Gadget.* London: Penguin.

Levy, D. M. (1997) ' "I read the news today, oh boy": reading and attention in digital libraries', in *Proceedings of the Second ACM International Conference on Digital Libraries.* New York, pp. 202–211. Retrieved from: http://renu.pbworks.com/f/p202-levy.pdf.

McGregor, N. and Farquhar, A. (2013) 'The Digital Scholarship Training Programme at British Library', in *Digital Humanities, 18 July 2013*, University of Nebraska-Lincoln. Retrieved from: http://dh2013.unl.edu/abstracts/ab-264.html

McLuhan, M. (1967) *The Medium Is the Message.* Harmondsworth: Penguin.

Meyer, E. T., Eccles, K., Thelwall, M. and Madsen, C. (2009) *Usage and impact study of JISC-funded phase 1 digitisation projects & the Toolkit for the Impact of Digitised Scholarly Resources (TIDSR).* Oxford: Oxford Internet Institute, University of Oxford. Retrieved from: http://microsites.oii.ox.ac.uk/tidsr/sites/microsites.oii.ox.ac.uk.tidsr/files/TIDSR_FinalReport_20July2009.pdf.

Meyer, E. T. (2011) 'Splashes and ripples: synthesizing the evidence on the impact of digital resources'. London: JISC, 2011. Retrieved from: http://ssrn.com/abstract=1846535.

Mussell, J. (2012) *The Nineteenth-Century Press in the Digital Age.* Basingstoke: Palgrave MacMillan.

Niggemann, E., De Decker, J. and Levy, M. (2011) *The new Renaissance: report of the 'Comité des Sages' reflection group on bringing Europe's cultural heritage online.* Brussels. Retrieved from: www.eurosfaire.prd.fr/7pc/doc/1302102400_kk7911109enc_002.pdf.

OCLC Research (2015) *Making Archival and Special Collections More Accessible.* Dublin, Ohio: OCLC Research.

Ranganathan, S. R. (1931) *The Five Laws of Library Science.* Bombay: Asia Publishing House.

Simmel, G. (2002) 'The metropolis and mental life (1903)', in *The Blackwell City Reader.* Oxford and Malden, Mass.: Wiley-Blackwell, pp. 11–19.

Stroeker, N. and Vogels, R. (2012) 'Survey report on digitisation in European cultural heritage institutions 2012'. ENUMERATE Thematic Network. Retrieved from: www.enumerate.eu/fileadmin/ENUMERATE/documents/ENUMERATE-Digitisation-Survey-2012.pdf.

Tanner, S. and Deegan, M. (2010) 'Inspiring research, inspiring scholarship: the value and benefits of digitised resources for learning, teaching, research and enjoyment'. London: King's College London. Retrieved from: www.kdcs.kcl.ac. uk/fileadmin/documents/Inspiring_Research_Inspiring_Scholarship_2011_ SimonTanner.pdf.

Tanner, S. (2012) 'Measuring the impact of digital resources: the balanced value impact model'. London: King's College London. Retrieved from: www.kdcs.kcl. ac.uk/fileadmin/documents/pubs/BalancedValueImpactModel_SimonTanner_ October2012.pdf.

Torkington, N. (2011) 'Libraries: where it all went wrong'. 23 November 2011. Retrieved from: http://nathan.torkington.com/blog/2011/11/23/libraries-where-it-all-went-wrong/.

Unsworth, J. (2000) 'Scholarly primitives: what methods do humanities researchers have in common, and how might our tools reflect this?', in *Humanities Computing: Formal Methods, Experimental Practice*, King's College London. Retrieved from: http://people.virginia.edu/~jmu2m//Kings.5-00/primitives.html

Whitelaw, M. (2015) 'Generous interfaces for digital cultural collections', *Digital Humanities Quarterly*, **9**(1). Retrieved from: www.digitalhumanities.org/dhq/vol/9/1/000205/000205.html.

Wolf, M. (2008) *Proust and the Squid: The Story and Science of the Reading Brain*. Cambridge: Icon Books Ltd.

Index